Too many Christians believe th[...] dirty. Some are, and that is pr[...] people to take a leap of faith a[...] Bunni Pounds stepped out in fa[...] sharing her story with the rest of the nation. Her plan is to get believers to pray, vote, and engage—all of which are more important than ever before in our history.

—The Honorable Scott Walker
Former Governor of Wisconsin; President,
Young America's Foundation

Bunni Pounds is one of my newest heroes in this nation. Not only has she been salt and light in the political field for sixteen years and taken on the IRS to protect every Christian ministry, but she understands the importance of the body of Christ. She knows the church is the only answer for every ill in our land and wants to see every Christian reach their potential in God. *Jesus and Politics* will inspire you to walk with Jesus and impact America.

—Dr. Robert Jeffress
Senior Pastor, First Baptist Dallas; Bible Teacher,
Pathway to Victory

I endorsed Bunni in her eight-person primary because I saw a woman who was unafraid, solidly conservative, and passionately in love with Jesus. As someone who has worked here for over a decade now, it is hard in Washington, DC. Anyone who has ever been elected will tell you that the election is just the beginning. We need God in our lives as elected officials, and Bunni is stirring up Christians all over this nation to pray for their elected officials and nation, to vote in every election, and to engage in civic involvement. *Jesus and Politics* will transform your life if you let it. If every Christian in America prayed, voted, and engaged, we would have a different world.

—The Honorable Mark Meadows
Former Member of Congress (R-NC); Former Chair, House
Freedom Caucus; Former Chief of Staff
to President Donald J. Trump

Bunni Pounds inspires through her personal story from the front lines of American politics. She consistently calls us to humble ourselves and pray and to every day turn from our selfish ways, take up our cross, and follow Jesus. The motto of the United States of America is "In God We Trust." Bunni encourages us through her captivating and charming mission to turn to God both individually and as a nation.

—Rep. Cathy McMorris Rodgers (R-WA)
Former Chair, House Republican Conference; Chair, House
Energy and Commerce Committee

When I served in the US Congress, Bunni Pounds was one of my most important and trusted aides, not to mention dearest friends. I can attest that she is a woman of integrity in every realm and has a deep burning passion for God, her family, and our great nation. Very few people I have ever met fight for faith, family, and freedom like this woman does. I simply know of no one better to help grow a movement of Christians who can positively impact the governance of America for generations to come.

—THE HONORABLE JEB HENSARLING
FORMER MEMBER OF CONGRESS (R-TX); FORMER CHAIRMAN,
HOUSE REPUBLICAN CONFERENCE AND
HOUSE FINANCIAL SERVICES COMMITTEE

The simple truth is that Bunni Pounds is a leader. Her story will rejuvenate your spirit and rekindle hope for our country!

—STATE REP. MATT SCHAEFER (R-TX)
NATIONAL ADVISORY BOARD MEMBER, CHRISTIANS ENGAGED

Bunni Pounds is unstoppable, mainly because she is following Jesus but also because that is how He made her. She will have a great impact on this country, and her story is a must read. So many people of faith run from politics. Don't. Bunni's story should help every believer understand that representing Christ in every area of our life, including government, is both a stewardship responsibility and an incredible opportunity to impact the lives of others and our nation.

—KELLY SHACKELFORD
PRESIDENT/CEO, FIRST LIBERTY INSTITUTE; NATIONAL ADVISORY
BOARD MEMBER, CHRISTIANS ENGAGED

Our culture has lost its way, and the rapidity of the transformational destruction of many of our cherished institutions has been shocking. We assumed our leaders would do the right thing, but most did not. We are now beginning to wake up and reengage. In *Jesus and Politics*, Bunni Pounds, who has been actively involved in the civil arena for decades, empowers this generation to live out their faith and transform a culture that has lost its way.

—DAVID BARTON
FOUNDER, WALLBUILDERS

When I heard about how the IRS had denied the tax exemption status for Christians Engaged, I was floored, so I reached out to Bunni. What I found was a woman who was bringing her skills and political background to the table to help the church impact America for the long term. Bunni is not just a former political consultant and candidate; she is an intercessor and a voice for this generation who wants to inspire everyone to walk with Jesus. *Jesus and Politics* is the book we all need now to help us walk more with Jesus in a hostile culture. I believe it is going to impact hearts for years to come.

—DAVE KUBAL
PRESIDENT AND CEO, INTERCESSORS FOR AMERICA; NATIONAL ADVISORY BOARD MEMBER, CHRISTIANS ENGAGED

Bunni Pounds is a well-known Christian leader and former political consultant who advocated for families and life throughout her political career. She is 100 percent correct that walking with God as a woman fully surrendered to Jesus is the key to standing firm for our beliefs with both dignity and grace.

—PENNY NANCE
PRESIDENT, CONCERNED WOMEN FOR AMERICA

Bunni Pounds has let God transform her life in the place of prayer. This woman is an intercessor, disciple maker, and preacher of the gospel. I have been honored to be a part of her life and watch how God has used her obedience during her race for Congress and now even more as she wakes up the church around this nation through Christians Engaged, a cutting-edge ministry that is bringing the body of Christ together like few others. If you want your heart to burn and to be awakened, read Bunni's story and let the power of walking with God transform your life.

—COREY RUSSELL
INTERCESSOR, AUTHOR, AND SPEAKER

Very few people understand the ministry world and the political world like Bunni Pounds. Bunni knows the Word of God and has walked with Christians from all denominations for years. Not only that, she also thoroughly understands how government works at every level. Our family has had the opportunity to walk with Bunni through the years, and we've seen the consistent fruit of her life and ministry. Christians need to walk in government as real Christians—Bunni shows us how in *Jesus and Politics*.

—THE HONORABLE MATT KRAUSE
FORMER MEMBER OF THE TEXAS HOUSE OF REPRESENTATIVES (R-TX); OF COUNSEL, FIRST LIBERTY INSTITUTE; DISTINGUISHED SENIOR FELLOW, TEXAS PUBLIC POLICY FOUNDATION

As a pastor, I must be honest that I have struggled with the convergence of the kingdom of God and American politics, but I think we can all agree that every Christian should be praying (we do that a lot in the UPPER-ROOM church culture), every believer should love their neighbors by electing righteous people (thank God for the Founding Fathers, who gave us that freedom), and every believer should engage outside the walls of our churches (we call that the "in and out lifestyle"). Bunni Pounds' book,

Jesus and Politics, lays out for all of us how we can be intercessors, disciplers, prophetic voices, and good stewards of our relationships wherever we go. I highly encourage you to read *Jesus and Politics.*

—Pastor Michael Miller
Founder and Senior Leader, Upperroom Dallas and
Upperroom Global

Boldness, truth, grace, and the presence of the Holy Spirit are evident in everything Bunni Pounds does. In a time when pastors and churches are scared to speak, Bunni and the team she has built speak the truth in love. We don't have time to waste! Every Christian needs to be involved in the cause of liberty. Christians Engaged is a simple blueprint to do that every day of our lives—pray, vote, and engage. Together we can impact America!

—Rev. Rafael Cruz
International Minister; Father of US Senator Ted Cruz;
National Advisory Board Member, Christians Engaged

The joy and fire of God that follow Bunni Pounds wherever she goes is an honor to endorse. Whether she is on the streets leading a Time to Revive team in evangelism or sitting with an elected official, she is the same person. This book is the story of a life lived out in obedience to Jesus, and it will inspire Christians to live fully for God for decades to come. I love how God is using Bunni and Christians Engaged all around this nation to awaken the church for its well-being but more importantly to inspire us all to live our lives as offerings poured out to His feet in radical obedience. The gospel of Jesus Christ is the only answer for our nation, and Bunni understands that to her core.

—Kyle Lance Martin
Founder, Time to Revive; National Advisory Board Member,
Christians Engaged

What our nation needs right now are people who are not only engaged in the culture but also watchmen and watchwomen who are in love with Jesus. Our mission to reach the world and protect the children has to go beyond political activism—we have to know Him, raise our families to know Him, and spend time in His presence. In her book *Jesus and Politics,* Bunni shows us how to walk in intimacy with Jesus even as we engage in cultural activism. It is a much-needed modern-day manual for Christians. I would stand and lock arms with Bunni Pounds any day of the week. Grab her book today!

—Elizabeth Johnston
Mother of Ten, Author, Podcaster, Blogger

Since the time she was a homeschooling mom and an adult student here at Dallas Baptist University, Bunni Pounds has lived with a humble heart and let God move her into places of influence that she could never have imagined. *Jesus and Politics* is that powerful story and an example for us all as we walk our paths. It is the mission of DBU to produce servant leaders, and Bunni Pounds is living out her life as a servant leader. Servant leadership should be demonstrated in every career path as we intentionally follow Jesus daily and live according to His Word.

—Dr. Gary Cook
Chancellor, Dallas Baptist University

I have known and walked with Bunni Pounds for years in the political movements, and there is no one better I know to lead an army of Christians and activate them to pray, vote, and engage. Her story and the truths she lays out on how to walk with Jesus in these spaces are priceless. Every dollar you spend on this book will be an investment into your discipleship and your personal impact for America.

—The Honorable Scott Turner
Associate Pastor, Prestonwood Baptist Church; Former Member, Texas House of Representatives (R-TX); Former Executive Director, White House Opportunity and Revitalization Council; National Advisory Board Member, Christians Engaged

Bunni Pounds shares her life story as an instructional example of a political calling by a true believer. How do you reconcile a deep personal faith with the worldliness of politics? It takes an understanding of the Scripture and a recognition that politics is a mission field. Every Christian should be engaged, and this book explains why and how. Bunni brings her experience to bear to encourage and inspire us.

—Kevin D. Freeman, CFA
Host, *Economic War Room With Kevin Freeman* (BlazeTV); National Advisory Board Member, Christians Engaged

Jesus and Politics is a book about politics, powerful relationships, a lifestyle of prayer, and most importantly the power of the Holy Spirit. As American Christians we have a responsibility to stand up for truth, but we must watch our souls and walk with Jesus as we do it. Bunni's story is a creative narrative of her journey that will teach us along the way how to be better citizens and children of God.

—The Honorable Marilyn Musgrave
Former Member of Congress (R-CO); Vice President of Government Affairs, Susan B. Anthony Pro-Life America

Bunni Pounds, who just so happened to listen to the *Point of View* radio program when she was young, is now leading a movement of Christians to pray, vote, and engage. She is also teaching citizens how to understand and apply a biblical worldview on the issues. This book helps you understand politics, government, and political campaigns. But mostly this book is about Jesus and how to be a good citizen in the twenty-first century.

—KERBY ANDERSON
HOST, *POINT OF VIEW* RADIO TALK SHOW

Prayer. Politics. How do those go together? In God's heart for justice, they both go together; but we have a responsibility in the body of Christ to do works of justice on God's terms. Bunni Pounds shows us through her sixteen years in the governmental trenches how to walk out the truth of the gospel with the heart of Jesus.

—STUART GREAVES
EXECUTIVE DIRECTOR, INTERNATIONAL HOUSE OF PRAYER, KANSAS
CITY; AUTHOR, *FALSE JUSTICE*

Can Christians serve in the political arena without becoming tainted themselves? Can we enter into this hate-filled, volatile arena without becoming hateful ourselves? Can we be thoroughly engaged with the affairs of this while still maintaining intimacy with God? In this book filled with candid conversations and eye-opening anecdotes, Bunni Pounds takes on these complex questions, showing us that, yes, all this can be done and, even more importantly, it must be done.

—DR. MICHAEL L. BROWN
HOST, *LINE OF FIRE* RADIO BROADCAST;
AUTHOR, *THE POLITICAL SEDUCTION OF THE CHURCH*

Bunni Pounds is a bundle of energy who loves to dig into the Word of God and knows how to motivate us to be light in the midst of darkness. Like never before, we need to know the Word of God and give the truth of God to hurting people. This unique book helps us learn how to navigate the political world while being grounded by the spiritual world to make the greatest impact possible.

—JUNE HUNT
FOUNDER AND CHIEF SERVANT OFFICER,
HOPE FOR THE HEART AND THE HOPE CENTER

The message of Jesus is often maligned when well-meaning Christians mix politics and faith too carelessly. That's why I was thrilled to learn that Bunni Pounds had written this thoughtful book. She has experience in the political arena and plenty of raw courage too. But her close relationship with the Lord tempers her words and actions. With a firm but delicate hand she calls us to influence our culture for Christ without ruining our witness. Read this book carefully, repent if you need to, and be the salt and light that our culture needs!

—J. Lee Grady
Former Editor, *Charisma* Magazine; Director,
The Mordecai Project

Throughout the pages of this book, Bunni Pounds uniquely intertwines her deep and genuine faith, her personal life experiences, and her substantive knowledge to give the reader provoking thoughts and insights to consider and process. Like Zephaniah, who addressed the reform of Josiah in 622 BC, Bunni understands that for any lasting reforms or change, there must be the exposure of the inward issues of the heart. She understands that we must first pray and then engage if we want to see God's redemptive purposes and plans for our nation and our generation. Regardless of your personal or political preferences, I believe you will find this book insightful, intriguing, and informative.

—Doug Stringer
Founder and President, Somebody Cares International

News flash: Washington, DC, will not save America! John Adams warned us that "our Constitution was made only for a moral and religious people. It is wholly inadequate to the government of any other." In spite of this, too many Christians have allowed the lies, intimidation, or even just the busyness of life to keep us from being the salt and light God calls us to be. And our nation—and the world—is suffering because of it.

Christians Engaged was created not only to encourage every believer to pray, vote, and engage but also to empower people of faith with the tools and knowledge necessary to be an effective influence while maintaining a witness that honors God.

The moment I met Bunni, shortly after her race for Congress, I knew we were supposed to work together. It has been exciting to watch what started out as a campaign working relationship grow into a ministry that is impacting our nation. My wife, Rosel, and I are honored to work with Bunni and know her as a true friend. We recommend you read this book, as she empowers us all to know God more and to disciple a nation. If we walk with God every day, together we can impact America.

—Rep. Michael Cloud (R-TX)
Member, House Appropriations Committee; National Advisory
Board Member, Christians Engaged

Jesus and Politics uses Bunni's personal experiences to illustrate the critical necessity of Christians walking out their faith in *every* area of life, including how we treat our neighbor and form our society. All of us should be Christians who know Jesus intimately and know how to navigate our civic duties. Be inspired by Bunni's story in this book, and then let's get to work to protect liberty together.

—THE HONORABLE RICK GREEN
FORMER TEXAS HOUSE OF REPRESENTATIVES (R-TX); AMERICA'S
CONSTITUTION COACH; FOUNDER, PATRIOT ACADEMY AND
BIBLICAL CITIZENSHIP

My friend Bunni Pounds fought the IRS to protect people of faith—and she won! That is the kind of courage our country needs to combat the tyranny of weaponized government, and I am honored to have been a small part of it. Her book is a timely call to mobilize and inspire an army of Christians to ensure we enjoy the God-given liberty to pursue happiness and advance the kingdom.

—REP. CHIP ROY (R-TX)
MEMBER, HOUSE JUDICIARY, RULES, AND BUDGET COMMITTEES

This book is for any believer who feels called to government or politics but also every believer who wants to walk with God more. Bunni's experience at multiple levels of politics and government, and her example of listening for the Lord's voice and following Him, will encourage all of us to make our lives count and to focus on the things that really matter.

—STATE SENATOR BRYAN HUGHES (R-TX)

We read in Scripture that during the time of King Saul, there were no blacksmiths in the land of Israel (1 Sam. 13:19–22). Only Saul and his son Jonathan had swords and spears. The Philistines would not allow the Israelites to have weapons nor allow any practicing blacksmiths in the land—keeping the people of God in slavery.

We need spiritual blacksmiths in our land today—not only in our local churches but in our nation as a whole to reshape its culture. We need influencers like Bunni Pounds, who can reform the ranks of government, business, education, and the media. Bunni is a gifted crafter, and God is using her to reshape men and women for His service. The battle is too great for Sauls and Jonathans to handle alone. Her book *Jesus and Politics* is truly an eye-opener to how God has molded her into a strategic and effective leader in these United States. I urge you to help Bunni redeem free America.

—DENNIS G. LINDSAY, DMIN
PRESIDENT AND CEO, CHRIST FOR THE NATIONS

Jesus

AND

Politics

BUNNI POUNDS

JESUS AND POLITICS by Bunni Pounds
Published by FrontLine, an imprint of Charisma Media
600 Rinehart Road, Lake Mary, Florida 32746

Unless otherwise noted, all Scripture quotations are taken from the New King James Version®. Copyright © 1982 by Thomas Nelson. Used by permission. All rights reserved.

Scripture quotations marked MEV are from the Modern English Version. Copyright © 2014 by Military Bible Association. Used by permission. All rights reserved.

While the author has made every effort to provide accurate, up-to-date source information at the time of publication, statistics and other data are constantly updated. Neither the publisher nor the author assumes any responsibility for errors or for changes that occur after publication. Further, the publisher and author do not have any control over and do not assume any responsibility for third-party websites or their content.

For more resources like this, visit charismahouse.com and the author's website at BunniPounds.com or ChristiansEngaged.org.

Cataloging-in-Publication Data is on file with the Library of Congress.
International Standard Book Number: 978-1-63641-347-1
E-book ISBN: 978-1-63641-348-8

23 24 25 26 27 — 9 8 7 6 5 4 3 2 1
Printed in the United States of America

Most Charisma Media products are available at special quantity discounts for bulk purchase for sales promotions, premiums, fund-raising, and educational needs. For details, call us at (407) 333-0600 or visit our website at www.charismamedia.com.

This book reflects the author's present recollections of experiences over time. Some names and characteristics have been changed, some events have been compressed, and some dialogue has been re-created.

To my best friend, husband, best father in the world, and love of my life—Tim Pounds—who, in obedience to the Lord, told me he loved me and wanted to marry me just before I left for Latin America.

Tim, there is no one else whom I would rather do constant 180-degree turns with than you. Thank you for supporting me day in and day out on this adventure of being a missionary to America in politics. The journey with you has been priceless. I love you with all my heart. Let's walk with Jesus together every day of our lives.

CONTENTS

ACKNOWLEDGMENTS

To MY BEST friend and the Lord of my life, Jesus—thank You for capturing my heart through Your Word, worship, and prayer and allowing me to walk with You every day.

Thanks to my beautiful family: Tim, the love of my life; Israel, our creative worshipper; Ben, our loving shepherd; and the two most incredible women I could have ever dreamed for our boys, Teodora and Giulia. I feel way too young to be Grammi Bunni, but nothing gives me greater joy than loving my grandbabies.

Thank you to my mom, Sandra, who taught me to be diligent in everything I do, is the best administrator I know, and has always been my biggest cheerleader in life through every 180-degree turn; and to my stepdad, Brent, who has received me as a daughter and would do anything he could to bless our family.

To my dad, Jack, who gave me his unquenchable thirst for truth and the Word of God and instilled in me an adventurous spirit to follow Jesus wherever He leads—thank you for teaching me about the finished work of the cross, the work of the Holy Spirit, and my identity in God. I know you are still cheering me on from the great cloud of witnesses (Heb. 12:1).

Thanks to my sister, Sunni, for being my best friend and the one I run to when I am stressed out, and to her husband, Eddie, for always caring for her and our family at every turn. To my niece, Ava—you are beautiful, smart, and kind and have my unquenchable yearning for truth. You are the daughter I never had.

To the mentors and disciple makers who believed in the call of God on my life from the beginning through today—Mark and Sandy Jobe, Steve and Diane Solomon, Danny and Cynthia Norris, David and Janet Halvorson, Mike and Helen Lambert, Cornel and Dorina Bistrian, Ronald and Pauline Wolthuis, Corey and Dana Russell, Kyle and Laura

Martin, Rafael Cruz, and James and Betty Robison—you were the ones who brought me around your kitchen tables, took me on ministry trips, empowered me to lead, prayed with me, spoke the word of the Lord over me, gave me opportunity in your pulpits, tag team preached with me, and supported me however you could. Yours are the shoulders I stand on.

To Jeb Hensarling, my political mentor who gave me a chance to run his campaign from the beginning—you taught me how to do things right and run an organization with stability while I did the work of the ministry.

To my Bunni Pounds & Associates team—we built a great company together that empowered conservatives to impact America. Thank you, Glonda Mooney, Mike Mooney, Ian Stageman, Ashley Biard, Susan Neri, Bethany Stephens, Leslie Recine, Colette Parker, Tina Aviles, and the best intern ever—Emma McIlheran.

To my Bunni Pounds for Congress campaign team—Kevin Brannon, David O'Connell, Jordan Powell, Glen Bolger, Aaron Liebowitz, Julie Hooks Dwyer, Ashley, Bethany, Colette, and Susan—we left it all on the field.

Thanks to Trayce Bradford and Ian Stageman for believing in the idea of Christians Engaged and coming alongside me to get it started; to Michael and Rosel Cloud for being flexible at every stage while I got this ministry off the ground; to Scott Jones and David Halvorson for being leaders I can trust and lean on; and to Ben and Julie Quine because we found each other at the exact right time.

To the Christians Engaged staff, advisory board, governing board, supporters, and volunteers—thank you for believing in me to run this ministry for the glory of God. Let's get every American Christian we know to take the pledge to pray, vote, and engage.

To Nicole Williamson, my first editor, who took this work and made sense of it—thank you for believing in me as a writer so many years ago. Also thank you to Shelly Grandpre for reviewing this work and guarding my life as my assistant and dear friend, and to Ben and Julie Quine, Margaret Smith, and Kevin Brannon for reviewing this manuscript to get it ready to pitch to a publisher.

To Carol Stertzer, Dr. Michael L. Brown, J. Lee Grady, and Doug

Stringer—thank you for helping me make this incredible connection to Charisma House and believing in this story. To everyone who let me use their house to get away and write—thank you John and Liz Murray, Gina Parker, and Jeb and Melissa Hensarling.

To the team at Charisma House—Steve and Joy Strang, Ken Peckett, Debbie Marrie, Adrienne Gaines, Margarita Henry, and everyone else who worked on this project—you have been a joy to work with. Thank you for taking a risk with a woman with a political résumé who wants to be used by God. Let's go impact America together, one heart at a time.

Finally, thank you to Vice President Mike Pence for always believing in me, James Robison for your incredibly affirming foreword, and Michele Bachmann for your beautiful afterword and for believing in Christians Engaged. I am deeply humbled.

FOREWORD

BY JAMES ROBISON

MORAL DECAY IS all around us. It's no wonder that many people fight hopelessness as they look at the media, education, politics, and even our churches. As I shared in *Indivisible*, the book I wrote with Jay W. Richards in 2012, "If we're going to escape decline, we have to make a hard turn—and fast."[1] We could put that statement in all caps today.

Though I was conceived by rape, my story is one of hope because when my mother took me to a doctor to be aborted, he miraculously refused to do it. After that, my mother prayed, and God led her to give birth to that unplanned-for baby. God had plans for my life and allowed this broken young man to eventually help rescue others. When I was eighteen, God supernaturally and clearly called me to preach. I have been in evangelism for over sixty years, communicating the gospel and love of God to millions. My wife, Betty, and I were high school sweethearts. We have been married for over sixty years. We want to leave a legacy—the opportunities freedom affords—not only for our children, grandchildren, and great-grandchildren but for all people.

When I see what Bunni Pounds is doing for freedom in America, hope rises in my heart. This young woman has created a discipleship ministry that activates the church for the well-being of everyone Jesus gave His life to redeem. She has taken simple weaknesses within the body of Christ that God highlighted to her—prayer, voting, and engagement—and given us a path forward to strengthen our hands. She empowers us to be disciples of Jesus through prayer, meditation on the Word, and worship—and to then go outside the walls of our churches to impact our cities, counties, states, and nation.

HOW OUR LIVES HAVE INTERSECTED

As a depressed pastor many years ago, Bunni's father was impacted by my ministry. God used me on a simple television screen to present life and hope to his heart and to reassure him that God wasn't done with him yet. Their family moved to Texas, and Bunni grew up with our daughter Robin in youth group.

Bunni then worked here at LIFE Outreach International while she attended Christ For The Nations Institute. She worked in our prayer center for two years in the afternoons and evenings and then for a season as the night supervisor of that department.

After thinking she was going to serve in global missions, she ended up running businesses with her husband, Tim, and then God called her as a "missionary to America" within the political and government realm. I am deeply honored to have been a small part of her life, even meeting with and ministering to her former boss, Congressman Jeb Hensarling, before he ascended into House leadership.

I watched as she ran for Congress in 2018, and though she came up slightly short, I knew God wasn't done with this dynamic woman. After she started Christians Engaged, she became a contributor to *The Stream*, the online publication I founded, and she has been widely received as someone who motivates and empowers others through her knowledge and passion. What I know about Bunni is this: she is a visionary, is authentic with everyone she meets, loves people deeply, and has spent her life studying and interacting with Jesus through His Word.

WHY READ THIS BOOK?

After sixteen years of walking with Jesus within government, Bunni created from scratch a national organization that calls for the very thing Jesus left us here on this earth to do: make a kingdom impact on America and the world. Through Christians Engaged, Bunni equips believers to be engaged in what matters to all of us who love *faith*, *family*, and *freedom*.

Through this book, she teaches us with simple stories and examples how together as ordinary people we can help lead Americans to restore freedom's foundation. God can use our lives for His glory. Being involved for the cause of liberty through civics, politics, and government is not evil; it is necessary for our nation. We can restore God's truths and the unshakable principles that must be put back in place, leading us to sound policies essential for freedom's survival.

We cannot check out on the responsibility to choose strong, principled leaders. You don't hand the future of freedom and the well-being of our families and every person God gave His Son to redeem to those committed to Satan's lies and his desire to take over God's planet and the people He loves so much. We don't hide the light, and we don't allow the positive effect of salt in our lives to be diminished.

Proverbs 29:2 says, "When the righteous are in authority, the people rejoice; but when a wicked man rules, the people groan." Bunni has lived this verse on the front lines as she has attempted to get godly people elected for decades and then walked with them as a friend and confidante after they entered the halls of power. Through her humble example, she demonstrates how to walk in this space while keeping pride, anger, fear, bitterness, and corrupting influences out of our lives.

JOHN 17 UNITY

One of my main messages for years is another truth that Bunni understands to her core, and it is this: The only power here on earth that the gates of hell, death, division, and dissension can't stand against is the body of Christ, the church. When the family of God comes together in supernatural unity, nothing can stand against us.

Bunni loves all flavors of the body of Christ and understands that when we come together to pray and work, answering the prayer of Jesus in John 17, we are unstoppable. She has laid down a lucrative career in consulting because she believes, as I do, that the church is the answer to every issue and problem in our nation.

The body of Christ must awaken and work together under the head—Jesus, our Lord and great Shepherd. He will lead us into the shelter of freedom essential for all families. We are representatives of God and His kingdom purposes, and we can be effective overseers protecting the future of freedom in our nation if we will stand up together and become a shining city on a hill (Matt. 5:14).

United in the furnace of our national battles, Bunni's team is showing us an example lived out. They don't care what denomination people are from, if they are male or female, or what race or socioeconomic class they represent. They are seeking to inspire every Christian in this nation to make God's kingdom impact on America.

PRESERVING THE FUTURE OF FREEDOM

I believe Bunni Pounds has established an organization essential to help restore and preserve the future of freedom. Like Esther in the Bible, God put Bunni here for "such a time as this." She can help us make a transforming impact on all Americans and show us how to inspire national leaders in all areas of life, including the local and national political arenas. Do not hand the future of freedom to the father of lies, the deceiver, the divider, and the murderer—Satan—who seeks to put himself in God's place. It is only God's family that can defeat him.

I believe Bunni lost her race for Congress because God had bigger plans for her—to make a difference within the body of Christ, to wake us up, and to get us all moving in the same direction so we can help save freedom in the United States of America.

I know as you read her story, you will be encouraged to live the rest of your life for Jesus and our heavenly Father, making a kingdom impact for the glory of God and the future of freedom.

—JAMES ROBISON
FOUNDER AND PRESIDENT, LIFE OUTREACH INTERNATIONAL
PUBLISHER, *THE STREAM*

DEAR FRIENDS,

This book is about government, politics, and campaigns, but mostly it is about *Jesus*. It is about living the Christian life extravagantly, even in a hostile environment.

If you have picked up this book, you most likely have an interest in news, culture, politics, or government. Thank you for being interested in our nation and desiring to know more about how you can serve it. America is the "land of the free and the home of the brave." I have served in the trenches of political movements for almost two decades as a political consultant, former congressional candidate, and follower of Jesus. I love this land and its people so deeply. While many people enjoy football, sports, movies, or video games, my passion is politics.

Through this book I want to loudly affirm that God is not done using Christians in the political space. All parts of our culture, especially politics, need followers of Jesus to be involved within the system. I want to inspire you to get involved somewhere. The founders of our nation gave us a gift in our Constitution, but our liberty requires our participation. America needs *you*—your participation, your involvement, and, most importantly, your heart. America needs your prayers, your vote, and your ongoing engagement.

While this book will not give you every reason or practical way to get involved in politics and government as a Christian, I do hope you learn much through the reading of my story. You will learn how our nonprofit ministry, Christians Engaged, was created to give you the resources needed to get involved in government. We provide daily, practical education for your life to help you build habits of prayer, voting, and engagement for the well-being of America. Connect with us at ChristiansEngaged.org.

God has led me into unexpected places in my political career. From being the only person in the 2018 primary season endorsed by the vice president of the United States, to having a word from God for a congressman on an airplane that soon shifted him into a new leadership position, to having a dream about an elected official outside my own party that led to an encounter that impacted both of our lives, I have been amazed by what God has done in and through my life.

Through the simple telling of my story, my deep hope is that you will discover, as I have, that God wants to walk with you intimately every day. You are the passion of His heart. I pray that wherever you are in this season of your life—maybe a student, business owner, schoolteacher, elected official, legislative staffer, or parent—you will be inspired to simply walk with Jesus wherever He leads you. May you learn through that daily interaction with Him how much He is at work, moving in every circumstance of your life. Seek to hear Jesus' voice, know His Word, and be obedient to Him daily—this is how we change the world. My story might involve walking with members of Congress, but we can all impact someone's life somewhere. Our nation is changed one heart and life at a time, and God loves to use weak vessels just like us.

Lastly, my calling is to share Jesus with everyone I encounter. He captured my heart when I was a thirteen-year-old girl, and I have never been the same since. The only way we can survive in this dark world is to lean into His love. I am a missionary to America. Jesus is the *only* answer for our broken lives, families, and nation. Above everything else, I hope you find Jesus in this book. If God can use an ordinary girl like me with a political résumé for His glory, then He can use anyone.

Know this—I love you!

—Bunni Pounds

For to you it has been granted on behalf of Christ, not only to believe in Him, but also to suffer for His sake.

—PHILIPPIANS 1:29

Location doesn't matter to God. He is not as concerned as we are about where we live. He is more interested that we walk with Him in this adventure called life. Momentary suffering only brings us closer to Christlikeness.

Chapter 1

THE DARKEST PLACE
ON THE PLANET

JUST BEFORE THE 2018 Texas primary runoff, I told a friend, "I don't think you have lived until you have had almost a million dollars in negative advertising thrown at you." I was raw and vulnerable in that moment.

Almost five years later, I can still say that while I will never experience the pain Coptic Christians in Egypt feel as they are murdered for their faith or the depths of rejection former Muslims encounter after coming to faith in Jesus, I do understand suffering through years of working in a mudslinging political profession as a consultant and later as a congressional candidate myself. Yet I will never regret these decades of laboring for America that have shaped who I am today.

At the beginning of 2018, I spent my days driving around East Texas, going nonstop through seven counties, speaking and campaigning, all while using my cell phone to raise money every day. I was on a mission with destiny, and I knew it.

My former employer, US congressman Jeb Hensarling, had announced his retirement from representing the Fifth District of Texas in Washington, DC. I was now running for his seat. This shift in my life had come out of nowhere. I had never considered running for anything, let alone for Congress. I was completely fulfilled working behind the scenes as a political consultant for thirty-two candidates and elected officials.

Then, in a flash, I had gone from desperately trying to find another candidate to run for my former boss's congressional spot to now sacrificing

1

my own life, career, consulting firm, and even my own house to run in an eight-candidate primary. This was crazy!

I was running for Congress myself!

Some days during that season I felt incredibly brave. On other days I felt a little stupid, yet I knew I was on a mission. After having served as Congressman Hensarling's campaign manager for over a decade, I knew everyone in that district, including all the volunteers and donors. I had deep relationships inside DC's Capital Beltway and around Texas. I understood federal public policy. I had small business know-how after having run three companies (a pest control company and two restaurants) with my husband, Tim. But most importantly, I cared deeply for the people of the district.

I found an album by Chris McClarney titled *Everything and Nothing Else* and played it nonstop whenever I was alone. On that live worship album, Chris sings a song based on Exodus 33:15 called "Came to My Rescue." In it, he cries out to God that he doesn't want to go anywhere if God's presence doesn't go with him—that he just wants to be where God is.

This was my daily prayer during that turbulent season: "God, I just want to be where You are."

In those intense months of my life, I continually told the Lord, "I am willing to go anywhere You lead me, Jesus, even to Washington, DC," though I said the latter with a bit of reluctance. "God, I am willing to go to the darkest place on the planet." At that point, I had worked in politics for ten years. I was walking into this congressional race with eyes wide open, knowing full well what I had signed up for, knowing the extreme darkness of Washington, DC. If there was any doubt left in my mind about the reality of what I was stepping into, Congressman Hensarling briefed me fully on the intense stress the job brought to his body, soul, marriage, and children—even to his spirit.

I knew that there was no way I could operate in my own strength and do this work successfully. Having to study policy papers, listen to people's detailed problems with the federal government, and deal with the media was intense. Because the circumstances of the race forced me to raise more money than I had ever done for any of my clients—and in the shortest amount of time—I needed to walk with Jesus through it. I had no other option but to walk in His peace and joy, or I would not survive.

Let me just say, you have not lived until you have been on the front lines of a battle far from the place where your own abilities can make something happen. I was now living there in an adventure of complete dependence on God.

THE ADVENTURE OF POLITICS

I have always been an adventurer—not the kind who would jump out of airplanes (that was just too dangerous for me) but the kind who ate hot sauce on my popcorn and relentlessly beat my newlywed husband at chess. Or the kind who took my boys to a Switchfoot concert on a school night and stood with them at the very front until midnight. The boys thought I was the coolest mom ever, but their teachers...well, not so much, as my boys slept through class the next day. I was the kind of adventurer who, at twenty years old, called my mom to let her know I would be staying in Guatemala for an extra two months of mission work, without any money committed to support me.

Politics and government have always been to me a great adventure— a rugged terrain that few people know how to navigate. Adventurer that I am, I followed the call of God on a quest to impact the America I love on this mountain, despite the debates, campaigning, backstabbing, and mudslinging involved. Like Colorado's Pikes Peak that stands so lofty and beautiful, the mountain of government continues to beckon me to climb its high altitudes, even though it has also led me to some of the lowest valleys in my life. Many times, I have felt out of breath and exhausted by it, yet I have stayed the course for almost two decades. I have never wanted to leave it, though I've journeyed from one work assignment to another, trying to find the perfect fit for a current season.

There is a deep sense of camaraderie around political campaigns. It's kind of an inside world that pulls people together, sort of like a sports team or a mission trip. However, one mistake on a campaign can make or break someone's future career. The pressure, the long hours, and the loyalties all have fascinated me as both a leader and an overachiever. I call it leadership in a pressure cooker, because any mistake will not only affect you but also impact an entire campaign or a member of Congress.

Establishing policies and laws and making Americans' lives better are important to me. But the competition and adventure of the political field have been the attraction for me from the beginning.

Through all the mundane and demoralizing experiences, the rewards have been few and far between. Yet those rare moments have strengthened my belief in God's calling on my life and my passion for this mission field—one that few Christians seem willing to take the time to understand.

Above everything else, I have learned to walk with Jesus in politics. Not perfectly but consistently. He has watched over my heart and has continually pulled me back toward Him anytime my soul began to fill with the dirt of this profession.

CENTERS OF POWER

Through the years, my story of going from homeschooling my sons to being a congressional staffer, running one of the largest GOP consulting firms in Texas, and becoming a congressional candidate myself has inspired young activists. I have pushed them to keep moving forward, to get involved wherever they can—to go make a difference. I have laughingly commented that I was willing to go to the darkest place on the planet—Washington, DC—and that maybe they should be willing to go too. Even though I joke about our nation's capital being a dark place, I believe there is a kernel of truth to it.

Washington, DC, is a consuming place where the gods of this world—gods of power and prestige—take center stage. The founders of our nation vigorously debated the idea of a strong centralized federal government. Those against it were wary of the power it would bring. I don't think they could have ever envisioned what we are seeing today inside the Capital Beltway.

We have a two-party system where Congress members and their staff are consuming generalized talking points. They continually mix these talking points with their own charged words and then throw them at each other on the twenty-four-hour news sources, on social media, and on the floors of the House of Representatives and the Senate.

It is a world where these same members don't even know each other's thoughts on the issues, let alone their constituents' opinions. They fly into this epicenter of activity on a Monday and fly out after the last votes on Thursday evenings.

This is the place where the federal bureaucrats sitting in every executive branch department—from the Department of Education to Homeland Security to the Treasury—actually run the show yet with hardly any oversight by busy legislators. The media stirs up fear, worry, jealousy, and lies while corporate interests and highly paid lobbyists work their relationships on the Hill to get what they want. It is a cesspool that tries to stop good federal public-policy decisions from happening, while also subtly trying to destroy the people who work there.

Over the years my heart has been increasingly burdened for the people, specifically for those serving in the federal government. These citizens work in an institution that has taken on a life of its own. Many strong leaders have worked to reform and improve the lives of ordinary Americans from this hard and dysfunctional place. They have toiled, and then they have left.

When we think about the government, we tend to focus on the United States Capitol, but that is just one aspect of this war-torn picture. The battle is repeated in all our state capitals. National politics consumes and tears apart our counties, our cities, and the school boards in our local communities too.

Working with members of Congress for over sixteen years, I have seen the underbelly of our nation's capital. I have also walked beside some incredibly beautiful people who choose to get up every morning and try to impact their world through politics. There are Christians who have been called to DC and who truly walk with God, know His Word, and hear from His Spirit, even in the middle of the lion's den. They are, however, few and far between. There should be many more.

Though many people claim the name of Christ and use their religious credentials to get elected, few actually walk with God in a way that impacts their decision-making, let alone influences their colleagues.

Government—whether on the federal, state, or local level—involves institutions, systems, and bureaucracies, but understand this: government is ultimately people. Every day, people who go to work in those places do so to make sure our government works...or doesn't work. "When the righteous are in authority, the people rejoice; but when a wicked man rules, the people groan" (Prov. 29:2).

There is a direct correlation between the righteousness of those in authority and the peace enjoyed by the citizenry. Righteous men and women are those who carry the name of Christ and are washed by the blood of the Lamb. Because of this identity, they exhibit a certain level of morality and a conscience that is quick to repent. Even those who are not Christians but operate with a moral compass are better than those who are controlled by wickedness, deception, and lies.

When righteous people are in places of authority, we have more freedom. When righteous people are in the key decision-making rooms, there is discernment and clarity. But when the wicked rule, we can feel it in our souls and spirits and, I would even say, in our bodies.

As people of faith our goal is not to establish a theocracy but to elect more people who walk with Jesus and put them in places of authority. If we do that, then everyone will experience more liberty and peace as these people of faith impact our cities, states, and federal government with good policies.

We need people with godly convictions to serve their communities, to try and make life better for others through local government. Collectively these simple servants are the ones who have the potential to impact millions of people's lives. These servants include city managers, who help plan communities; county commissioners, who navigate huge county budgets; and state legislators and their staff members, who not only push for good legislation but also push back against bad legislation.

Federal judges, administrative and executive personnel, and congressional members and their teams all work in Washington, DC. These are just a few of the thousands of positions inside the federal government. This doesn't even include campaign managers, political consultants, public relations and media firms within the political field, as well as the fundraisers—the people who raise millions of dollars for politicians and political causes.

Governments and political systems are only as good as the people who sign up to work in them. Unfortunately, many Christians in America have run far away from these places of influence, just as they have from many other areas that shape our culture.

This should not be.

To see real change in America, it will take people of faith answering the call into government and all places within our culture. It will take citizens who want to learn and interact more with their elected officials as they start to take these steps of faith. We must find our faith and fortitude in the pages of the Bible and then let that internal life flow into these spheres of influence to see hearts change one at a time. We need revival, and it starts with one person's obedience—one step at a time.

Suffer for "His Sake"

Years ago, when I attended an independent Bible school, Christ For The Nations Institute (CFNI) in Dallas, I was a typical young, starving student consumed with trying to survive while desperately trying to seek God. I was still living at home with my mom, commuting to classes, working every day at a part-time job with LIFE Outreach International (led by James Robison), and scraping to pay my tuition one week at a time.

I was living on Subway and Taco Bell, trying to keep myself cool after the AC in my red Nissan went out in the middle of a blistering hot Texas summer. It was all I could do to keep my bills paid. I wanted to be faithful to what I felt the Lord told me to do, which was to abandon my plan to attend the University of North Texas and reach for a destiny that, at the time, felt so ethereal. It was what we in the church world refer to as "the call of God."

"How could I ever be a world changer?" I thought.

I had followed God's plan and entered CFNI, and I will never forget the day when my adventurous spirit took root in a word that God gave me for my life. One day after the school's worship service had concluded, I sat in the balcony of the semidark auditorium. My professor had assigned our class the task of reading the Book of Philippians twenty times. Thankfully Philippians has only four chapters, but even for a nineteen-year-old girl who loved to read, that assignment seemed overwhelming. After many times through the book, I was bored with the words and ready to go on to the next task. Nevertheless, I pressed onward in faith, hoping this exercise would produce some fruit in my life.

There in the dim light of that auditorium, I was about to read Philippians again—for the fifteenth time—when I heard a scripture declared just as loud as if it were in an audible human voice: "For to you it has been granted on behalf of Christ, not only to believe in Him, but also to suffer for His sake" (Phil. 1:29). Its power hit my heart. I didn't have to pick up the Bible and read it because I knew the passage already. Somehow all that Bible reading had, indeed, made its mark.

It was like God was shouting that one scripture loudly over my life, trying to get my attention. I remember that moment like it was yesterday.

But what did it mean?

Specifically, what did it mean for me, a young Bible school student just embarking on life?

"God, what are You trying to say to me?" I wondered.

I can't tell you how I knew, but I understood that this scripture was going to be one of my life verses. It was a divine directive to my heart that I would not just believe in Jesus but also, somewhere in my life story, suffer for His sake.

Though I was fully aware that my belief and devotion to Jesus were miracles in themselves, this word took my heart in a whole new direction. I had been living in miraculous faith as a young person—giving myself in radical obedience to God and a life of service to Him ever since my deep experience with Him as a thirteen-year-old. But at that moment in the CFNI auditorium, I knew God was calling me to an even deeper place of surrender.

"Where are You taking me, God? When I leave this place, how are You wanting to use my life?" My thoughts instantly went to whom I was around all the time. Working at LIFE Outreach, I was surrounded every day with pictures of pain—needy people in hurting parts of the world.

In the early 1990s, during the Rwandan war, the ministry was involved in feeding starving children in Africa, sending missionaries into battleground areas, and showing the love of Christ in tangible ways. I worked as a phone counselor, took donations, logged prayer requests, and tried to provide good customer service for our mission. I didn't have any real authority or high-profile position, but I tried to stay faithful to the task in front of me and be sensitive to the person I was speaking with on the phone.

As I sat in the auditorium balcony, my thoughts instantly went first to Rwanda and other war-torn areas and then to the 10/40 window, an area between ten degrees north and forty degrees north latitude from Africa to Asia, where a high concentration of unreached people groups—those who have never heard the gospel—reside. (I had just been learning about this at school.)

"God, are you sending me to Rwanda? Am I going to die a martyr in a Muslim nation in the 10/40 window?"

Then it came: the flood of tears. They were flowing down my face.

A rush of emotion washed over me as I felt the call of God on my young life in a new and deep way. I was in a Bible school that focused on missions, so it was not unusual to think that God would call me to an unreached people group or even to a hostile area for the sake of the gospel. Whatever it would look like, this was my moment of calling, and I knew it.

Would I accept whatever God called me to do?

Was I willing to go anywhere for the sake of His name?

Whom would I love deeply enough to "waste" my life on them, or would I be willing to give it all up for Jesus?

I wept and wept. I couldn't stop.

How deep was Jesus' love for me!

How shallow was my commitment to go disciple the nations in comparison to that love.

Would I be willing to go through any door He opened?

Would I be willing to follow Him not just throughout my young life but for decades?

As I knelt beside a hard wooden bench, through buckets of tears, my answer was a resounding yes.

"Yes, I will go, God."

GOVERNMENT AFFECTS US

Now, after years in this political field, I am frequently asked questions like these:

- Bunni, how do you handle politics? Isn't it such a mean sport?

- Why would anyone want to get involved in something so dirty and muddy?

- Why would anyone want to serve as a staffer, be a government administrator, or run for office? That seems so difficult and hard.

Anything of value that we do in our lives will cost us something. I ask the following questions in response:

- What kind of difference do we want to make in this world as believers?

- As we see how messed up our culture is, do we really believe we are the *light*?

- Do we understand that government affects our lives and families whether we are paying attention or not?

Can we relive the year 2020 for just a few minutes? How many of us didn't know the name of our governor, county judge, or mayor before that fateful year? The truth is, whether we knew their names or not, whether we prayed, voted, or engaged with them or not, they had the power to shut down our places of businesses, close down our churches, and even keep us in our homes for months at a time without our consent. Government impacts every individual, family, business, and church. You cannot get away from it.

The question then comes to us: Will we interact with our government? Will we get involved with politics at all?

MAPPING OUT LIFE IN DC

Whom will I marry? Where should I live? What should I do for a living? These questions are important, but there is an even bigger question we should ask ourselves: Whom am I walking with day in and day out?

Choosing the people you spend time with is vital. A few key friends of mine and I respect each other, work seamlessly together, and push each other for greatness. I could go anywhere in the world with these friends and be happy. Whether in Saudi Arabia, Brazil, Romania, or South Dakota, I would be in a good, solid place if they were with me.

Whom we are with is more important than where we are going. When I decided to put my life on the line to go to DC, I realized my security couldn't be in where I lived or whether my family was nearby; it had to be in whom I was going with. If God was calling me to a new city for part of the year, He would walk with me through the newness and the hardness of that place. He had promised never to leave me or forsake me (Heb. 13:5).

When I decided to run for Congress, I couldn't grasp this huge shift in my life. I had never considered running for anything before, let alone going to Washington, DC. I had walked alongside an incumbent congressman for ten years and had helped federal, state, and county-level elected officials—so why in the world would I want to do this? I knew I had to flip something in my vision. I had to see myself there in DC and get my head wrapped around this new reality.

Some members of Congress live in their offices on air mattresses, shower in the members' gym, and don't have a private space to retreat to outside their offices. I knew that wasn't for me, so I went on a research adventure. Searching online for apartments near the United States Capitol, I found a simple one-bedroom apartment that looked nice and wasn't too horrible of a price for DC. It was a few blocks from the Capitol and the Rayburn House Office Building where my former boss's office had been for some time, which was good, because I also knew that I didn't want to pay for a car in the city (where I hated to drive anyway). I would be the congresswoman who walked around town when I didn't have staff to transport me.

Prayer is important to me, so I was glad to see that the Justice House of Prayer was nearby—as well as a Trader Joe's, which is absolutely essential.

While mapping everything out to see what my life might look like in this overwhelming city, I ordered a cup from the Justice House of Prayer DC online store that read "History Belongs to the Intercessors." Then I went to task creating a sample budget for my family based on the current congressional salaries.

I was starting to be able to visualize it. On top of the policy papers, I scribbled notes about committees I thought I might want to serve on. I then began a list of pros and cons. I considered whether or not I would be the first woman to join the Freedom Caucus, if elected. I could see more clearly what kind of member of Congress I would be by the way I was planning my daily life there.

WAS POLITICS MY SUFFERING?

Thinking deeply about my calling, my plunge into politics, and my victories and defeats, I realized again that what really matters is not where we are going but whom we are with.

After years of reading my boss's Facebook and Twitter feeds, along with our campaign emails, I thought I was prepared for a congressional run. I had read the high praises of favor as well as the scourge of criticism. I had gotten involved in Austin politics working for state senators and state representatives where the conservative movement was divided right down the middle. Political people consumed each other for sport, maligning others for the purpose of elevating themselves. I had navigated the divides relatively well in the political consulting world, but now it was my turn—my life, my family, and my reputation on the chopping block.

Was I still willing to say yes? Was I willing to go anywhere for Jesus and for service to others? Was I willing to follow Jesus to this city that looked like continual chaos, where everything seemed upside down and the opposite of common sense? Was I willing to trust that God could use me there? If He opened the door for me to go to this dark city, Jesus was going with me. He would not leave me alone.

For the thousands of government workers in DC who needed me to walk into their sphere and for the roughly 750,000 potential constituents in Texas who needed me to serve them well, I was willing to put myself on the firing line. I was willing to open myself up to having a million dollars spent against me—nearly half of that in negative advertising by a super PAC during the primary runoff. I was willing to be called a Washington insider (because I walked with Congress members), a Never Trumper (because I voted for Sen. Ted Cruz in the 2016 presidential primary), a carpetbagger (because I moved three miles back into my district after I had been redistricted out), and a swamp creature (because I raised money and consulted for congresspeople).

My husband would get so angry and frustrated at the negative publicity that I stopped sending him the daily emails highlighting the marketing against me.

It didn't hit me how much I had suffered until the six-month race was almost over.

Was this the deep calling that God had on my life all along: suffering in politics?

One night during the race, after a close friend had rejected our campaign, not wanting to endorse me, and lies were being hurled in full force, I heard Jesus' voice: "For to you it has been granted on behalf of Christ, not only to believe in Him, but also to suffer for His sake" (Phil. 1:29). It was the same word I had received from Him back in the Christ For The Nations auditorium. For over two decades I had tried to make sense of this word about suffering. After feeling called to missions as a young person and then marrying my best friend, having babies, and running three small businesses, my journey looked different than what I expected. I had always wondered, "Where is the suffering in my life?" Surely Jesus wasn't talking about first-world problems in America at a time when Christians were losing their lives around the world.

And now I was still questioning. How would I fulfill this deep calling— to "suffer for His sake"? Had I been overly zealous in Bible school to think that God would give me some deep calling to fulfill, something that would involve suffering? Where did my love for government and politics fit into this high calling of God for my life? Had I really taken all my potential, my depth of understanding of God's Word, and my love for people into the right career path?

BE LIGHTS

During my race for Congress, I had a divine encounter that put me before the then vice president of the United States, Mike Pence. He spoke some words that would become my guiding light not just for that race but even for my work today: "Bunni, Karen and I will be praying for you every day; we need your light in Washington, DC."

In a new and powerful way, I realized that God had called me into the world of politics and government to let His light shine through me. Whether or not I ever got to DC as a member of Congress wasn't important. Up to that point—after fourteen years in political work—my light had shone enough so that the vice president and the second lady had noticed it.

In this career field full of daily potential pitfalls, deception, out-of-control egos, and land mines for families, God has continued to prove faithful. If more Christians saw politics as a calling and a mission field and embarked on an adventure to be lights within the government, imagine what God could do for our country. The political mission field is often overlooked by the modern American church, yet the government impacts millions of lives each day. How many citizens could one Christian impact as a town mayor, a county judge, a sheriff, a congressperson, the secretary of state, or even the president of the United States?

Think about the effect of Christians who walk into their government offices or campaign headquarters every day looking for whom they can serve, pray for, educate, or impact. This is how we change the world through government.

> You are the light of the world. A city that is set on a hill cannot
> be hidden. Nor do they light a lamp and put it under a basket,
> but on a lampstand, and it gives light to all who are in the house.

Let your light so shine before men, that they may see your good
works and glorify your Father in heaven.

—Matthew 5:14–16

CAMARADERIE WITH SEAN DUFFY

Leaders who make the largest impact on other people's lives sometimes
don't even realize they are doing it. Friends make a huge difference in
each other's lives. We can't underestimate the power of a simple conversation, shared laughter, or sense of camaraderie.

In 2015 Congressman Hensarling hinted that he might not be in office
forever. I decided to start my own political consulting and fundraising
firm not only because I needed a safeguard but also because I had genuinely connected with a legislator from Wisconsin named Sean Duffy. I
wanted to help Sean in an ongoing way, and I had to figure out how to
do that.

When Congressman Hensarling had become the newly minted
chairman of the US House of Representatives' Financial Services
Committee—on which Sean served—I facilitated a fundraiser on my
boss's behalf. Jeb wanted to help raise funds for the four GOP members
on his committee who seemed to be having the hardest time going into
the next election cycle. This included Sean. Jeb's decision to bring them
all to Dallas for a benefit meant that his campaign manager and fundraiser—me—would be doing most of the work.

On the day of the benefit, I picked up Congressman Duffy from the
airport and took him to the event. When I drove him back to the airport
at five o'clock the next morning, I made sure I had coffee ready for him
just like he liked it. The congressman said that and my winning smile
won him over.

Sean Duffy is a down-to-earth, faithful Catholic and a caring husband
and father of nine children. He met his wife, Rachel Campos-Duffy, in
1998 on the set of MTV's *Road Rules: All Stars*, both of them partici-
pating as alumni of *The Real World*, one of the first reality TV shows in
the nation. They both have thrived in media, eventually getting their own
separate contracts with the Fox News channel.

Before winning his congressional seat, Sean served as the district attorney in Ashland County, Wisconsin. I later found out from other staffers on the Hill that he had been a champion logroller earlier in life.[1] During his time in Congress, he hosted an annual fundraiser for his leadership PAC, where he taught the skill of logrolling.

During the three years that I had my political consulting firm—before I made the decision to blow up my life running for Congress—I did two fundraisers for Sean in Dallas. I even went to San Antonio to facilitate some meetings and another event for him there. We had a blast and enjoyed working together. He talked me up to other potential clients when I launched my firm, and I was very thankful. He was my firm's first client after Jeb Hensarling.

When I decided to run for Congress, Sean Duffy was the first sitting member of Congress to write me a check for the primary and again during the runoff—knowing he was going on the record for me. Those acts of kindness and his words of encouragement meant so much to me during that season.

In December 2018, shortly after losing the runoff election, I went to Jeb Hensarling's retirement party in DC. As I exited the stage after thoroughly roasting my former boss, I saw Congressman Duffy next to the open bar that Jeb had provided. (It was a once-in-a-lifetime moment that Jeb, a fiscal conservative, would give anything away for free—and that evening hundreds of people were enjoying his generosity.) Sean hugged me and commented on my speech. Then, my friend of four years told me, "Bunni, I am so upset you lost your race. You don't understand—I needed you here fighting with me in DC."

In that moment, it really hit me square in the face how important camaraderie and friendships were for the members of Congress in DC. The people they were surrounded with in that place mattered to them, and when one person won or lost after years of friendship, it affected them.

Then it became even more personal to me—the loss I had experienced a few months prior affected not just me but others too.

I might not have been able to join Congressman Duffy in the hallowed halls of the US Capitol, but I wasn't going to let discouragement and self-pity keep me from continuing to shine the light of my life in politics. I hadn't realized that I was having this kind of effect on people in my chosen field, but now that I did, I wanted to minister to them even more. My heart turned even more toward the people in places of influence whom God loves so much.

Hard Places

God loves to lead us into hard places and push us toward the darkest places on the planet. If the goal of our lives is to ultimately be crafted into the image of Jesus—become more Christlike—then hard places are great training grounds.

> And not only that, but we also glory in tribulations, knowing that tribulation produces perseverance; and perseverance, character; and character, hope. Now hope does not disappoint, because the love of God has been poured out in our hearts by the Holy Spirit who was given to us.
>
> —Romans 5:3–5

Hard circumstances force us to seek God. In these dark places, He shows us that we need Him. Here is where we find character.

God wants to shine through our lives—in our weakness—through our dependence on Him. He teaches us how to live on the front lines of our destinies, operating not just through our talents and skills but through His abilities that go beyond what we can do alone.

God wanted to see if I was willing to go on an adventure with Him to Washington, DC.

He wanted me to be willing to let my light shine brightly wherever He took me.

Jesus wants to go on a daily journey with all of us, leading us into full dependence on Him. This is the greatest adventure we could have in this life. If we want to truly live our destinies, we must be willing to go anywhere with Him—whether to unreached people groups or to Washington, DC.

I do not speak because I have need, for I have learned in whatever state I am to be content. I know both how to face humble circumstances and how to have abundance. Everywhere and in all things I have learned the secret, both to be full and to be hungry, both to abound and to suffer need. I can do all things because of Christ who strengthens me.

—Philippians 4:11–13, mev

If our identity is wrapped up in whom we know and how important we think we are, we will miss the sweetness of His presence when we are all alone with nothing else but our own breath to keep us company. Jesus is our ultimate reward.

Chapter 2

THE HIGHEST OF HIGHS AND THE LOWEST OF LOWS

POLITICS CAN TAKE a person from an extremely high place to an extremely low one—and fast. It can be a roller coaster of careers, legislation, and emotions.

Within a month a shift can happen that impacts a whole state and multiple players. The people holding the power can change from one election cycle to another. A politician can be up one year and down the next. A community of people can love a candidate one moment and hate the same candidate the next moment. I have seen elected officials look like they can do no wrong and be beloved by millions of people—only to make one mistake and be put on the back side of history. Memories are long in politics, and one shift can impact a politician for a lifetime.

One thing I have learned about politics is that the wind can change in an instant. You might think you are winning a race as a campaign consultant. But then the candidate makes a stupid comment, is outdone on a fundraising goal, or, even worse, has a moral failing and crashes and burns. It can sometimes be a brutal career.

My family has come to expect me to plan our vacations and family events around the election cycle. I can't make plans on a whim like normal people. For years as a campaign manager, I would wait until after the election to go on mission trips to Romania—in December, the middle of winter. I had to skip July Fourth gatherings with family because I had parades to staff.

For me, the worst part of politics is that relationships and friendships are constantly shifting. They can be tight for a time based on an alliance but later become hostile because of whom we pick to campaign for in a race. I discovered quickly that political "friends" are not real friends. In the political world real friendships happen only when people commit to staying friends over the years—maintaining the relationship even after they choose to support different candidates in a race.

For believers in Jesus who are engaged in politics or business, it is important to make sure we do not find our identities in our latest roles or job titles. Our successes or failures in politics can often define our careers, but our self-worth cannot be measured by the success of the politicians we are "in with" at the time. Our identities cannot be found in whether we are at the top of our game or have fallen behind.

If we are political activists working hard to effect change in our states, our marks of success cannot rest in having the personal numbers of state senators or getting our state representatives to take our calls on important votes. We must be grounded in Jesus and who *He* says we are.

One moment we may think we are on top of the mountain, and the next moment we might feel like we've fallen off a cliff, having lost a vote on an issue we care about or a race with a candidate we believe in. In those moments, it may look like we are not important anymore, but that is not true. The truth is found in who we are deep inside—far from the drama of politics. We must remember that the winds of politics cannot define us. Only Jesus can define us! Even with personal callings to engage in this work, we cannot let it destroy us.

Jesus is our good Shepherd who will cause us to "lie down in green pastures" (Ps. 23:2). He will deliver us from evil and "prepare a table before [us] in the presence of [our] enemies" (v. 5; see also verse 4).

An Economics Nerd and a Friend from Indiana

In 2007 Representative Hensarling decided to invite his best friend in Congress—a mostly unknown congressman from Indiana named Mike Pence—and his wife to Dallas. He wanted Mike and Karen to meet a few potential donors in Big D, the city some people describe as the ATM of the Republican Party.

Jeb, an economics nerd with a heart of gold, had served as a staffer himself as a young man. He had run the Texas state office of US senator Phil Gramm, was the executive director of the National Republican Senatorial Committee during the senator's tenure as chairman, and then was the campaign manager for Gramm's run for president. Congressman Hensarling knew how the system worked, yet he still believed he could make it better.

One financial backer compared Jeb to a class nerd. Whereas the class clown has the outgoing personality and consumes all the oxygen in the room, seeking all the attention, the nerd is the one who waits patiently for the clown to mess up and then offers to help. The nerd knows exactly what to do all along but has to wait for the clown to quiet down so he can then fix the situation. Jeb is a fixer. Jeb is extremely smart, but his talents go way beyond being the one with all the answers.

During his congressional career Jeb was a master communicator. He had the ability to articulate extremely hard subject matter into the language of the common individual. This humble, five-foot-seven-inch man was thoroughly respected among his colleagues. He was always polite to his staff yet laser focused each day to get something done. He was a master political strategist, and it was apparent every day at work.

Jeb left his two children at home in Texas each week, to be raised alone by his wife, Melissa, because he had a goal to accomplish something of lasting value. Every week, he flew to Washington with an ambition grounded in a deep conviction. Jeb's heart was set on leaving his children and future grandchildren a freer America than what he had inherited. He made this statement over and over again through the years: "The thought of my children growing up in an America with less freedom, less opportunity, and a lower standard of living is a long-term pain I cannot and will not bear."

Ready to move into my own calling in government with gusto, I was excited that, only six months into my new job, I was going to meet a second member of Congress—this one from Indiana. Mike Pence led a weekly congressional Bible study that my boss attended. Congressman

Pence also carried a prayer journal filled with the requests of his colleagues. He prayed for them diligently. Many called Mike Pence a "happy
warrior" in the US Capitol.

I had never done a fundraiser for another member of Congress besides
my boss, so I didn't really know what to expect. After serving as an intern
in Jeb's office, I had been hired full-time six months prior by Jeb's chief of
staff, Dee Buchanan. Dee trained me on a quick one-day trip and left me
instructions to call or email him if I needed anything. He also left me a
hastily compiled ten-page standard operating procedure manual, telling
me to add my own input to it going forward, which I did with conviction.
The manual soon reached over sixty pages.

Thankfully, Congressman Hensarling was extremely gracious to me as
a campaign newcomer. Staffing for a member of Congress was very different from owning a small business. I was no longer in charge, but I was
still working with a budget, projects, expectations, and goals. I was determined to run this Friends of Jeb Hensarling campaign committee with
excellence—just as I had run my businesses.

We invited about fifty people to a donor luncheon for Congressman
and Mrs. Pence, and Jeb and I made calls regarding the event. For the
venue we chose a small upscale restaurant in the Uptown part of Dallas,
close to Southern Methodist University and other key landmarks. We had
a set menu of chicken, potatoes, vegetables, and a dessert and arranged to
have coffee available for any potential donors who wanted to linger.

However, only around half of the invited guests showed up. It was
low attendance, but it was also a Saturday afternoon when people were
extremely busy—and a day of scattered showers. I was flustered and nervous, feeling like I wasn't properly trained for this.

By the end of the day I had collected over $12,000 in checks—not much
for a member of Congress then or now, but it was a start to new relationships for Congressman Pence. Jeb seemed satisfied, figuring it was a
developmental beginning in a new location for his friend.

When I took the name tags, giving forms, and everything else I had
brought to the venue back to my car, it was sprinkling outside and a
rainbow had formed. Stepping back into the private party room, I looked
at the two congressmen and Karen sitting there like old friends, sipping

coffee and relaxing together. Melissa had left by this time, and the Pences' flight had been delayed a few hours. They were content to hang out with Jeb, catching up on news of the children and some fun family tidbits. I imagined that this was the way they often interacted at the Capitol Hill Club across from their offices in DC.

I had intended to say my goodbyes, make my exit, and leave them to discuss things that needed to be talked about in secret—like ways to change the world. But as I approached, Congressman Pence called out, "Bunni, how did you get with this guy?" His question made me stop and delayed my escape back to my home in Garland. Tim and our two young boys would just have to wait a few more minutes.

"I don't know, sir. It really is a miracle," I replied. "I testified in front of the platform committee on an educational issue at my first state convention four years ago, and I was hooked. I came home and told my husband that I wanted to take a government class. That led to a constitutional law class, and then after three and a half years of night school, I finally graduated. I think Congressman Hensarling picked me to be his campaign manager because I was a proven project manager, but we have never really had that conversation since he hired me."

I looked over to my boss at that moment and smiled. "I am just extremely grateful, sir."

"He is a little crazy," chided Congressman Pence. "I hope you can handle him."

"I am sure I will be fine."

Then I said something unexpected. "Sir, I am a missionary to America. I thought I was supposed to be a missionary to another country, but God called me into politics and government. I am not sure where this train is going, but I am honored to be here and to serve."

"It is interesting that you say that, Bunni," Congressman Pence replied. "I am a missionary to America too." Then he patted the chair next to him, diagonally from where Karen sat and directly across from my boss. I accepted the invitation and sat down. "Have you ever heard my history?"

Leaning my chin on my hand, I relaxed as if I was with an old friend and said, "I have not."

"I started out as a negative campaigner doing everything I could to win," he continued, "until I realized that might not be the best way forward. I got my vision back after a huge loss in a run for Congress. I tried again. The third time was the charm. I finally won, but more important, I won the right way."

Congressman Pence went on to tell me more of his experiences as my new boss looked on. Karen smiled at me from time to time, adding a few anecdotes about their faith into the story. Then the congressman asked me for more of my story.

It was a privilege that day to spend thirty minutes with those two precious people. I was glad to avoid the rain, as well as to let Congressman Hensarling hear some of my heart in a friendly fellowship with him and his colleague.

The Pences' flight delay allowed for a beautiful spiritual connection. It was something I couldn't have made happen on my own. Walking out of that restaurant, I thought of what an incredible honor it had been to simply hang out with another member of Congress—one from a state where my family had roots. My grandparents still resided in the Hoosier State, my dad had pastored there during my early years of life, and my sister had been born there. I would have been born in Indiana too had my dad not been attending university in neighboring Michigan at the time.

What an incredible privilege to be asked by a member of Congress to share a part of my story. Better yet it was an honor to hear him articulate a real and living faith that gave him purpose and drive to live like Jesus in the nation's capital every day. It was a moment I would not soon forget.

I was thankful to have met Mike and Karen Pence that day. As I walked out the door, I had no idea how that small conversation would shape my destiny ten years later.

The Beginning of the Primary

The 2018 Texas primary took off with a bang as a total of eight of us in the district rushed forward, giving everything we had to win. Thankfully, I had political knowledge on the current issues and the district that I served, as well as experience in the field as a campaign manager and fundraiser. I was ready to compete.

I waited two long weeks before Jeb announced his endorsement of me. He made me work for it. He wanted me to call one hundred potential donors and grassroots activists in the district to see whether they would support me if I ran. After this thorough vetting, I received his endorsement and the help of my best friend in politics, Kevin Brannon. Kevin had been the congressman's general consultant, was godfather to Jeb's son, Travis, and was now my political consultant for this important race.

I raised $200,000 in December 2017, securing my last $20,000 on New Year's Eve. My last-day strategy was to call all my Jewish friends whom I had met through my pro-Israel activism. They were the only ones who would answer the phone on a Sunday before the New Year. Graciously, they helped me reach my goal, together with some of our lifelong friends who gave the last $1,000 I needed at 11:55 p.m. Raising that much money in the first month established me as one of the front-runners in the race. My team celebrated as we put out our press release to the media about this accomplishment.

Using our contracted pollster, our campaign took our first poll a few weeks into this process, focusing on favorable name recognition (referring to whether voters know a candidate's name and think well of him or her). I got the news I expected. However, seeing it in black and white was hard. Although I had worked for the incumbent congressman for over a decade and had volunteered in the district before that, I was an unknown to the primary voters. I had organized twenty fundraisers a year, made relationships with all the donors, and led all the volunteer efforts for the campaign, yet only 3 percent of the GOP primary voters we polled knew who I was well enough to give me a favorable rating.

To make matters worse, Jason Wright, a Ted Cruz staffer who came into the race from a neighboring district, had a 3 percent favorable name ID as well. Here was a man who had few relationships in the congressional district, yet he was equal to me in name recognition. It was devastating, even knowing that neither one of us had ever held office in that district.

Our race was focused on approximately 26,000 households in a district of more than 750,000 citizens who had a habit of voting consistently in a Republican primary. To think that the few I knew within that sea of names would make a difference was naive, but my passion to succeed went far beyond wanting to *be someone*. I had a calling to serve the people of the Fifth Congressional District.

To win, I would need to chart a fresh path against the sitting state representative Lance Gooden, who represented two of the seven counties, and former state representative Kenneth Sheets, who had represented a part of the district in Dallas County. In our December poll, Gooden had a 28 percent favorable name recognition, while Sheets had around 12 percent. My only hope for victory was to out-fundraise them both by leaps and bounds. I had to get my name out to enough voters before the primary to land a second-place finish and a trip to the runoff.

This was going to be a hard mountain to climb—and a great adventure.

THE MAIN OPPONENT—LANCE GOODEN

Tall, lanky, and personable, Lance Gooden had served in Austin for two previous terms, from 2011 through 2015. Beating his former boss, state representative Betty Brown (a stalwart conservative), Gooden won with 50.5 percent of the vote in the heated 2010 race. I had known Betty for years, and it had always bothered me that this young staffer had taken on the person who jump-started his legislative career.

After Gooden's first victory, his next opponent was Dr. Stuart Spitzer. Spitzer, a medical doctor, was supported by most of the conservative issue-based organizations in the state and a multitude of grassroots activists who didn't like Lance's "go along to get along" attitude with the house speaker and moderate Republican leadership.

In 2012, Lance kept Dr. Spitzer at bay by defeating him with a healthy seven-point margin (53.5 percent to 46.5 percent). In 2014, Dr. Spitzer came back with a vengeance and a greater movement of support than before. In a strong conservative year when the Tea Party movement was at its peak, the good doctor narrowly beat Gooden by 342 votes (51 percent to 49 percent) in one of the closest races in the state.

On the waves of the Tea Party movement, a little-known retiree named Bob Hall took out an incumbent state senator, Bob Deuell, in an overlapping district by only three hundred votes. Now senator Bob Hall calls it the Gideon victory. That same year, homebuilder Don Huffines beat powerful incumbent GOP senator John Carona, and a woman named Konni Burton defeated a Democrat incumbent named Wendy Davis—who famously staged a filibuster on the state senate floor in her pink tennis shoes to support Planned Parenthood.

Lance Gooden came back for a third head-to-head matchup with Dr. Spitzer in 2016, this time staging a comeback and beating his opponent, making the doctor a one-term representative. Gooden won by just under a thousand votes (14,500 to 13,502, 51.8 percent to 48.2 percent). Every year back then, the races for this state representative district had been close and had drawn the attention of political junkies around the state.

State Representative Gooden married a beautiful Greek woman, Alexa (a former Austin lobbyist), while making his comeback in 2016 and was in a strong place personally and professionally. He renewed his friendship with the moderate Republican speaker, Joe Straus, and picked up an influential donor whom he had helped in a fight against the Tarrant County Water District. By helping to keep the water company from putting a pipeline through a ranch in Henderson County, Lance made a very powerful friend.

Pastor Marty Reid Enters the Scene

In 2017, Dr. Spitzer was already planning another race against Gooden. But this time a storm was brewing on the horizon: a pastor named Marty Reid was getting more politically involved.

Pastor Reid was good friends with Dr. Spitzer. He was a spiritual leader who was not afraid to talk about voting and political engagement to his small charismatic church. He hosted many of the Tea Party meetings in the area and loved history and politics. Pastor Reid started considering a potential run against Gooden for state representative. Looking at Representative Gooden's voting record, he did not like what he saw. Gooden was leaning more moderate in his approach to the district than what Pastor Reid thought was representative of Kaufman and Henderson Counties.

As he weighed his options, several people encouraged Pastor Reid to reach out to me. At that time I was one of the top political consultants in the area. And this politically active pastor already knew of me through my work with Congressman Hensarling and a ministry conference I hosted in the Dallas-Fort Worth area.

My firm was now being defined as the social conservative Tea Party political consulting firm in the state because I was willing to take on "rebel" clients like Sen. Bob Hall and Sen. Konni Burton, both of whom had won against the establishment. Senator Hall, a graduate of The Citadel, a former navy engineer, and a retiree, was the conservative hero in the overlapping state senate district. He had ended the political career of a twelve-year incumbent who'd left over a million dollars in his bank account, thinking this Tea Party grassroots campaign with only $45,000 didn't have a chance. This movement was making waves for Gooden.

After a quick phone meeting with Marty Reid, I knew I wanted to be involved in this district fight; I wanted to help this pastor. We came up with a plan for me to fully run his campaign as both his fundraising consultant *and* his campaign manager. We got voter files, picked a software company for block-walking purposes, scheduled a few fundraisers in Kaufman and Henderson Counties, and set up a website and social media accounts for a big campaign launch. As a long-term strategic planner, I had the race planned out from start to finish.

Pastor Reid called his friend, Dr. Spitzer, and let him know he was going to be running in the primary with him. The key word here is *with*—not against—as both incredible men reached the same conclusion: having another person in the race might be to the conservative movement's advantage. Potentially pushing Representative Gooden into a runoff where one conservative candidate might have a chance to come out on top sounded like a good plan—one that we hadn't yet tried. To avoid a runoff, a candidate has to receive more than 50 percent of the vote. With more strong candidates in the race, the chance of avoiding a runoff is unlikely. And the benefit of a runoff is that turnout is about 30 percent fewer participants than in the main contest, usually giving the candidate with the most passionate supporters the advantage.

Everything was set for our campaign launch that fall. Knowing I had limited time due to all my other commitments, I had to make sure we swiftly got a team together that could pull off a victory. I was excited about working on this competitive race. I saw huge potential in Pastor Reid, and though it would be an uphill battle against an incumbent representative *and* a friendly challenger who had also previously served in the district, I saw this race as a learning opportunity.

We began hearing early through the grapevine that Representative Gooden was a little worried about having two strong conservative candidates in the race against him. Our strategy to run two candidates against the moderate was being well received by potential donors who were interested in funding both.

RETIREMENT ANNOUNCEMENT

Then came a shift in our plans: Rep. Jeb Hensarling announced his retirement from Congress.

I was one of the few people on the planet who knew it was coming, yet it still hit me like a ton of bricks. Years before, while driving back to Dallas from East Texas, Jeb had hinted at the possibility, telling me he would not be around forever in his current role and likely wouldn't stay past his tenure as chair of the Financial Services Committee. He then asked me if I had ever thought about helping the conservative movement in a greater capacity by taking on additional clients.

At first, I was completely opposed to the idea of starting my own firm. I loved being focused only on Congressman Hensarling's campaign. I had successfully grown his campaign funding year after year and helped him fulfill his goals in Congress, while also pushing back on opponents. There was nothing else I wanted in my political career at that time. I knew my job so well that I had time to do ministry, like building a house-church movement with my husband, Tim, on the side. If I started my own consulting firm, I knew it would take over my life and cut out much of my ministry focus.

Congressman Hensarling had risen to the fourth spot in House leadership as the GOP conference chairman and then chair of Financial Services, and he had no ambition to be Speaker of the House or have any other role. He wanted to get home and be with his family by the time his daughter, Claire, turned sixteen. She had been born the day after he won his first primary in 2002, and he had missed living at home full-time during her entire childhood. Now it was time for Jeb to spend time with Claire; his son, Travis; and his wife, Melissa, who had given up a career in criminal justice to stay home during his sixteen-year career in Washington, DC.

It was the end of October and much later than I had expected it to happen. As Financial Services chairman, Jeb had been trying to get a fix to the Dodd-Frank Wall Street Reform and Consumer Protection Act through the House. He knew that the moment he announced his retirement he would be a lame-duck member of Congress and most likely wouldn't get anything accomplished. Now the day was here.

I put together the email announcement after our chief of staff, Andrew Duke, sent it to me. After formatting the email in our distribution system, my eyes filled with tears as I hit the send button. The email correspondence was out. The world would now know.

Suddenly I not only had to run Pastor Marty Reid's state representative campaign and fundraising for my other thirty clients, but I also had to find a candidate to replace my political mentor and hero. I was overwhelmed.

I had developed a list of elected officials and other key people in the district who I thought should run when this day came. So, I went to work, calling Texas state senator Bryan Hughes of Mineola first—never imagining for a minute that the candidate for Congress to replace my boss in just a few weeks' time would be me.

PREPARING FOR A PRIVATE MEETING

Fast-forward to the race. The primary on March 6, 2018, was less than three weeks away.

I had raised over $400,000 and hired a full team, beginning with a general consultant (my long-time friend in politics Kevin Brannon) and a campaign manager (David O'Connell, who had run over eleven competitive races around the nation). From my firm I brought onto the campaign a full-time fundraiser, a part-time fundraiser, a field director, and a scheduler. My campaign was now moving at full force.

Our media team had dropped over twenty pieces of mail into the mailboxes of the GOP primary voters. We were also using digital ad buys to educate the district's voters on social media. My message was simple: I was the small-business owner and executive leader who understood public policy—and the real conservative warrior they needed in Congress. We emphasized my history as a homeschooling mom, Bible teacher, author, and entrepreneur who owned three companies.

As my consultants and Congressman Hensarling said, mine was a great American story: a mom who had a passion for engaging in government and making a difference in her world. I was convinced I was telling my story well—at least well enough to compel people to support me through their endorsements, contributions, or volunteering. We were making great headway in the few months we had from December 1 to March 6.

Then Jeb called and told me I had an upcoming private meeting with the vice president. I was stunned.

"Does the VP know how well I am doing and how hard I am working?" I wondered. "Does he understand how hard this road ahead is going to be for me—to get into a two-person runoff and then to try to win this seat?"

Kevin called and went on and on about what a big deal this was to get a private meeting with Vice President Pence. Though I knew this was a huge development politically, I kept thinking back to that first meeting with Mike and Karen in 2007. I considered them my brother and sister in Christ. That day had been so special as we had spent precious time talking about our relationships with Jesus and our calling as missionaries in politics.

I thought about the time Mike Pence came to Dallas in 2013, while he was governor of Indiana. Jeb and I hosted another gathering of friends at a fancy house in Preston Hollow, an upscale area of Dallas, to build more future donor relationships for the governor. It had been a little easier to gather people that time than when he was a relatively unknown member of Congress.

When Governor Pence arrived, he greeted me gently and asked where he needed to go and whom he needed to talk to first. Then he sincerely asked how my husband and two boys were doing. We talked about my boys' school, our house-church ministry, and God's goodness in the middle of our crazy busy lives.

Later that night before we all left, I briefly shared with him a scripture I had been praying over him and Karen all that week. I asked whether I could quickly pray that word over him and his family right there. I encouraged Governor Pence in his calling to love God deeply and to serve the precious people of Indiana with integrity. We took pictures with a few of our team members and Congressman Hensarling, and then he hugged me goodbye.

Each time I talked with Mike Pence—whether as congressman, as governor, or later as vice president—he treated me never as a staffer but always as a friend. I could only imagine that he treated every person with whom he interacted in that same fashion. It made me feel like more than just a political operative; I felt like a sister in Christ.

In 2016, when presidential candidate Donald J. Trump announced that he was picking Governor Mike Pence of Indiana to be his running mate, I fell on my knees in my living room. "There is a God, and He really cares about the affairs of men," I thought. The Hensarling team had hoped that one day Mike Pence would be recognized on the national stage for the leader that he was. When that day came, I couldn't believe it! Tears ran down my face as I thought about the power of a man of God such as Mike Pence walking the halls of the White House.

Fast-forward to two years later, when I realized that in just a few days I would be standing before the vice president of the United States as a congressional candidate for the US House of Representatives. It made me want to weep.

"God, what are you up to?" I prayed.

I had to get ready for my private meeting with the vice president. I had to get a new pantsuit and schedule someone to fix my hair. Kevin worked with my team to make sure they got me all fixed up and ready for this once-in-a-lifetime meeting. This was a big deal.

I was like Esther going before the king.

THE NIGHT THAT CHANGED EVERYTHING

It was February 17, 2018, at the Omni Hotel in downtown Dallas—a date and place I will never forget.

My good friend Missy Shorey, who was the Dallas County Republican Party chairwoman, had taken her job as the local party leader to a whole new level. For over a year, she had made the case to the Trump campaign that the Dallas County donor base was funding wins for Republicans all over the nation but that we needed their help. She pushed the powers that be for a headline speaker for our annual gala to help fund the local party. She landed their top pick after President Donald J. Trump was unable to come: Vice President Pence. By the providence of God, this had been scheduled several months prior, long before I ever considered running for Congress.

When I arrived, I was led in by a security officer and an advance staffer for the vice president. Walking through the hotel, I tried not to act nervous. They led me into a room made of partitions next to the banquet hall. Secret Service agents were outside the room. It was vacant with the exception of two flags standing upright against one wall. Later it would be the place where all the donors who had paid $2,500 or more to attend would get their pictures taken with the vice president and the second lady between those two flags.

Jeb met me there in the empty space and quickly went to work—not as the congressman but, in a strange role reversal, as my staffer. He hurriedly asked a member of the vice president's team for a table and two chairs. "We can't get pictures in front of the flags like everyone else," he told me. "People must know that this is a private meeting with the vice president that only you have received." He worked diligently to put together a makeshift office with a six-foot-long white table, two hotel banquet chairs, and a few pieces of blank paper. "These are your campaign plans that you will be discussing," he said matter-of-factly.

I laughed, seeing in that moment my perfectionist boss and political mentor doing the job of advance staffer for me. He had taught me everything I needed to know about running a political organization, and now believing that I would be his successor, he was going to get this meeting right one way or another.

As soon as Jeb had set up the room to his satisfaction, in walked Vice President Pence. He greeted his friend and longtime colleague with a hug and then reached over to extend a hand to me.

"Bunni, I am super excited about your campaign and everything you are doing. I was thrilled when Jeb told me a few months back you were running for his seat in Congress. Karen and I are just thrilled."

He looked me straight in the eyes with genuine respect and excitement. I thought, "Who am I that the vice president of the United States would pay attention to my campaign?"

The vice president continued, "Tell me everything that is happening. How are we going to win?"

Jeb then made a point to push us both toward his makeshift office. He grabbed my phone off the table and muttered, "We will never get the pictures from that White House camera; I am taking these." (He was right. After multiple attempts to get the pictures from the official White House camera the next week, the ones that ended up on our mailings and digital ads were the pictures Jeb took on my phone. The man was a better photographer than I would have expected from someone who had been serving in Congress for sixteen years and rarely took pictures himself.)

The vice president and I sat at the white table chatting for seven or eight minutes. He listened intently to my story about the search for the right person to run for the congressional seat, my motives for running myself, and my hopes and dreams for America.

My boss of ten years and political mentor had a big grin on his face while taking pictures like a proud father. He was making sure to get every shot that I would possibly need. Then the vice president stopped talking for a minute and turned to the congressman. "Where else do you want me, Jeb?" he asked.

Jeb motioned us over to the flags, where we took additional pictures, though not in the normal staged way that most people would get photos that evening. The vice president was completely relaxed and happy to have a few minutes with his longtime friend and his friend's younger protégé.

This private meeting was supposed to be only five minutes. It was only when his staff finally got him to leave that I realized our meeting had lasted twelve minutes. He ran late to a private reception that he was headlining for the National Republican Congressional Committee before the other big dinner. Just before the vice president left, he said, "Bunni, Karen and I will be praying for you every day; we need your light in Washington, DC." I took that as a word from the Lord over my life and for my political career.

Twelve long minutes with the vice president of the United States that would change my life forever. Twelve minutes where I was thankful again for the doors God had opened for my career in a supernatural way. Twelve minutes where I had hope that my journey to be a missionary to America in a greater way was just beginning.

I have a picture of Jeb and me at our dinner table that night, both of us smiling as we considered the future. His joy came from finally being able to go home to his family after all these years. For me it was the adventure I was living. I had a lot of hope that when the gavel struck for the next session, I would be serving in Congress. I would make Jeb proud. While the meeting with the vice president was over, my God story of running for Congress was just beginning.

BETTER THAN THE VICE PRESIDENT

In politics, as with anything in life, when we experience momentum and purpose, it is easy to get wrapped up in the thrill of it all.

To say I was high on life as I came away from that memorable meeting would be an understatement. My sense of destiny was deep, and in my heart I knew the importance of my purpose during that season of my life.

The next morning I headed to church as I did every Sunday. I could have easily stayed home and relaxed on Sundays since our house church met on Friday nights, but I needed to worship even more and loved meeting new people around the district. That particular Sunday I had been invited to Storehouse Church in Dallas to speak for a few minutes and to allow the church to pray for me and the race.

When I was running for office, I could barely breathe. I was running to and fro, my schedule maxed out with meetings, speaking engagements, and donor calls. I was thankful for the years of extreme time management experience while I built my consulting firm so quickly. I was thankful that God had never left me unprepared, even in the small things.

As the music played that Sunday morning, I breathed deeply and worshipped Jesus like I hadn't in a long time. I worshipped like I did as a young Bible school student or as a worship leader at my piano in our house church. I was real with God, and He was real with me.

I knew I was about to be called on to speak, but I couldn't stop the tears that were welling up in my eyes. Then I had a thought: "This is so much better than being with the vice president." That moment, before the presence of God, was so much better than even one of the best nights of my career. There I was not all fixed up and trying to prove myself in front of a person of power. I was completely free in front of the King of kings. Jesus, the One who had captured my heart, was much more important than the vice president. Jesus was the One who had rescued me from religion, freed me from sin, and given me purpose. He was the One who had called me to not just serve Him but walk with Him daily in love. He was the One who cared for my soul and was empowering me to run for Congress.

There I was with Jesus.

Previously I had questioned my own heart and motives in this race. "Am I running for Congress to try to *be* someone or to make myself great in the eyes of people?" I wondered. Would I have the strength even as a strong believer in the Word of God to withstand the temptations of a dark city and corrupting systems? Would I make it there? Could I be a Christian that defied the odds?

But now, as I worshipped God in that moment, I realized that if He was going to send me to the darkest place on the planet, I would be okay because Jesus had my heart. I was with Him.

Jesus was more real to me than anything. More real than being in the presence of my greatest political hero at the time, Mike Pence. If Ronald Reagan, my favorite president, had been standing in front of me in that moment, I knew I would pick Jesus over him too.

It may sound strange to think we would pick a human over God, but let's be real: How many times do we choose the world's identity for us over what God desires for us? How many times do we pick our careers over prioritizing our time with the Lord? How many times do we let entertainment, media, and business icons tell us who we are and what to believe instead of the Word of God?

The loudest voices shaping my identity in politics were from friendly people who meant well but told me that I could *be* someone and *do* something important if I just sacrificed more, served more, worked harder, and got around the right people. Now I was reminded again that Jesus is my King.

He would shape my identity if I allowed Him to. He was the most important One to me, even during the highest of highs of my political career.

FULL ENDORSEMENT

The pictures worked. The quick shots Jeb had taken on my phone, along with another $100,000 that I raised, made the difference. It was enough for a marketing blitz to get the pictures and talking points of my private meeting with Vice President Pence out to the voters in the district.

On March 6—after the polls closed—our little team celebrated at Pastor Marty's church. I had come in second place to state representative Lance Gooden and made it to the runoff election for Congress.

The initial primary had been an up-and-down political roller coaster for all of us. After Jeb announced his retirement, as I desperately searched for a candidate to run in his place, I heard through the grapevine that State Representative Gooden was considering a run for Jeb's congressional seat. Lance was facing a potentially tough reelection for his state position since I was running Pastor Reid against him and he also faced Dr. Spitzer. Seeing an opening, he decided to take a risk on Congress. It would be hard for anyone who didn't already serve in an elected position within the district to get his or her name out there in time for the primary. Knowing this, Lance quickly made his plans for a launch. After my decision to run, he jumped in squarely behind me in a race that would take both of us on the ride of our lives.

In the span of three months, I had beaten former Texas representative Kenneth Sheets, Jason Wright (one of Sen. Ted Cruz's staffers, from Tyler, Texas), Sam Deen (a small-business owner and veteran who made an incredible showing in Van Zandt County), and three other opponents. Now I was ready to fight in round two against the man whom I had wanted to get out of office all along.

Later I would find out that of the forty-six Republican candidates running for the six open congressional seats in Texas, I was the only woman who had made it to the runoff ballot. The open seats were districts vacated by incumbents, giving a fresh opportunity to those wanting to make a difference. To have that kind of response from a district that I had served for so long was an honor.

In my mind, my story with the vice president was over. Mike Pence had been so gracious to let me have that private meeting with him, and I expected nothing more. But then a month later, on a rare occasion when I was making fundraising calls at my home desk rather than from the passenger side of my car as my campaign manager drove me around, he surprised me again.

I had just finished a call with a donor and put my phone down on my big mahogany desk when, all of a sudden, my phone began blowing up with Twitter notifications and texts from friends. "What just happened?" I wondered.

Four weeks into the runoff—to my shock—my fellow missionary to America tweeted, "Proud to stand with Bunni Pounds for Congress in TX-5! Bunni is a strong conservative and will be a great supporter of the #MAGA agenda! Vote @bunnipounds on May 22."[1]

I was the only person in the entire United States during the 2018 primary season endorsed by Vice President Pence. President Trump didn't even know who I was.

The story of this sudden endorsement ended up on one of the front pages of the *New York Times*. Speculations were thrown around that the vice president's best friend had asked for a favor. I knew the truth, though: this miracle had everything to do with a deep conversation that had taken place years ago in Dallas.

The truth hit me—one conversation changed my life. Walking with Jesus was an adventure!

THE LOWEST OF LOWS

In the true nature of politics, the high of getting endorsements from the vice president and others during the runoff and then being in the *New York Times* and the *Dallas Morning News* quickly came to an end.

The clock was running out on my race. I always said to my team that each campaign had the same twenty-four hours. If we used our twenty-four hours in a wiser way than Lance's team, we would be hard to beat.

We heard through the grapevine that a poll from an outside source showed me neck and neck with Representative Gooden. I felt the momentum shifting. But to go from 3 percent favorable name recognition to winning would be a miracle. The harsh reality was that we had only two and a half months to overtake a sitting state representative, and I had a strange feeling that it wasn't going to happen.

In a year when public educators were watching our state legislators closely, Lance Gooden had been very smart and jumped into the congressional race. In my mind, he was escaping his fate of ending up in a runoff with either Dr. Stuart Spitzer or Pastor Marty Reid and ultimately losing to one of them.

Having committed to the congressional race, it looked to me that he did everything he could to recruit two new candidates to replace him in the race for state representative. He wisely pitted them against each other *and* the conservative candidate in hopes that the race would end up in a runoff. Driving up attendance in a low-turnout race in the two counties where he was known would not hurt him. As soon as it looked like two more-moderate candidates were in, Pastor Marty dropped out to consolidate the conservative movement around Stuart and to make sure the good doctor made it to the runoff. In Pastor Marty's mind, he had fulfilled his duty in getting the moderate incumbent out of the state house and moved on to help his friend.

Lance's master plan worked, and it became clear to us that the state representative race was the real focal point in the district. With public educators coming out in force to support whomever they saw as the best defender of public education, this former homeschooling mom was not the right candidate in that moment.

One of the state representative candidates, Keith Bell, a successful businessman and a deacon at his Baptist church, put in $437,500 of his own money to beat Dr. Spitzer during that race.[2] Keith, a good man that I always got along with, touted his experience on the Forney Independent School District school board and his support of public education against the man endorsed by the Texas Home School Coalition. I was also endorsed by the homeschool coalition, so Stuart and I were tied together in many minds.

With the local independent school districts being the top employers in those counties, the educators' jobs were the most important issue on the ballot. During the entire race, we never advertised for school choice or about our views on public education, yet the people of Kaufman and Henderson Counties were not rushing to the polls to support me. They were, however, coming out in droves to support Keith Bell for state representative against Dr. Spitzer to keep public education strong.

Lance and Keith seemed to be working together to get their voters to the polls. Lance, a strong defender of public education who had worked in the past to kill a charter school in Terrell, was being blessed by this movement. Though Stuart and I were not working as closely together, most people who were paying attention knew we were aligned in friendship, organizational endorsements, and political philosophy.

For me, the big problem lay in the fact that no other races were happening in the rest of the five counties, except a district attorney race in Van Zandt County and another state representative race in Anderson County, where my client Thomas McNutt was running against Cody Harris. The political energy in the counties where I had won in the first round was literally nonexistent.

Our team was looking at the number of people coming out for early voting. We wouldn't know until election night whom they were casting their ballots for, but we knew we were in a tough fight based on which counties were showing up to vote. Kaufman and Henderson Counties, my opponent's base, were coming out 2 to 1 over my strongest counties. I was in trouble!

WORSHIP IN THE MIDDLE OF LOSS

The Friday before Election Day, as tired as I was, I knew I needed to spend some time worshipping the Lord. The house church that we pastored loved to join Oaks Church every now and then for Nights of Worship when our friend Clayton Brooks was leading. I had clung to his songs throughout the campaign. Since Tim was worn out and our boys were away (one was in Romania and the other at Bible school), I went with our friend Colette, who'd also become my scheduler during the campaign, and her husband, Tim. It was good to be with friends who really loved me, whether I was to ever be a congresswoman from the Fifth District of Texas or not, as I felt starkly alone and uncovered, like I was about to be exposed to the world.

In my heart that night I knew I was losing, and I suddenly realized that the next Tuesday I would have to be at the polls all day greeting people and asking them for their votes, all while knowing that I would not be successful. The painful disappointment, shame, loss, and embarrassment—and ultimately my own failure—hit me like a ton of bricks. I had never failed before.

As Clayton sang his beautiful worship songs that night, I allowed myself to feel—really feel—the pain of the race since the runoff had begun.

Because I was so behind when we started the runoff, my team knew we had to contrast my inspirational story and conservative record with Lance's more moderate legislative record in Austin. In a 2017 Rice University analysis of Texas State legislators, Lance was listed as the fifth most liberal Republican in the Texas House.[3] We knew we had to play that up and paint him as someone who would not represent the district well.

Every piece of mail in the runoff that we sent to the voters contrasted my biography with his record. A super PAC from Club for Growth was funding over $300,000 in the runoff against Lance. Its efforts were separate from our campaign, but they also highlighted his moderate record as well as potential conflicts of interest with donors and his insurance consulting work.

Lance and his team countered it all by calling me a liar. A long-time donor and friend of Lance's created a super PAC called Our Conservative Texas Future. It ran ads with scary music calling me a Washington insider, a Never Trumper, and a swamp creature. They used the worst pictures of me in the ads, trying to convince people that I was a bad person who should never be elected to Congress. It's the way the game is played. I had been a part of the political world for a long time, but it's different when it's *your* face on the negative ads and *your* career being smeared all over the district.

Since there were eight of us in the race during the primary, it had mostly been a friendly exercise of carving out our niches, marketing our stories, getting our first endorsements, and nailing down our conservative talking points. But during the runoff it got ugly. It was an all-out war between my team and Lance's team, and it was one of the most highly watched races in the state of Texas.

Our team went over the top to make sure everything we advertised was cited with sources so people could see Lance's record in black and white. I didn't enjoy signing off on those ads, but the people had to know what he really stood for.

I became calloused to the attacks. I kept my head down and did my work, talking with voters and raising money. I brushed the offenses off time and again by telling myself and others, "This is how the game is played, unfortunately." But the attacks were affecting Tim so much that I stopped showing him everything. He had a restaurant to run and a life to live, and like any normal American husband, he wanted to beat the tar out of anyone who attacked his wife.

Now it was almost over, and I was losing.

I felt like a failure. And then it hit me: I had the endorsement of the vice president of the United States. I was failing him. I was failing my former boss, and I was failing the beautiful people of the Fifth Congressional District, whom I loved so much. I had gotten into this race to make sure they were well represented, but somehow we hadn't made a strong enough case.

Like watching a bad movie, I replayed all the moments of the intense season. One that stood out was a TV ad that pictured Lance and his beautiful wife, Alexa, holding their new baby, Liam. They all looked perfect as they walked in a beautiful area of East Texas. At the end of the ad, Lance turned to the camera and called me a liar. Another was a video of a pink bunny dancing in the streets of DC throwing money in the air. The voiceover said, "Bunni Pounds is just dancing around the truth, saying she is a real conservative. But she is *not.*"

Slowly, tears started to fill my eyes and then came rushing down my face. I hit the floor of that church while everyone else worshipped happily. They must have looked at me like a crazy woman, but I didn't care anymore. I was undone and tired of being put together all the time.

"Why?" I cried out to God. "Why did I have to go through this? Why did I risk my consulting firm? Why did Tim and I sell our home of twenty years, where we raised our kids and had our house church for over a decade?" (Because of redistricting, we moved three miles down the road to get back into the Fifth Congressional District, where I had worked and lived for decades.) "Why have we gone through all the pain of moving and selling our home only for me to be called a carpetbagger and then lose this race?"

I thought about all the rumors that had been going around in East Texas and the smears my family had to endure. The Gooden campaign even used a secret Facebook group to quickly share information about us. Some of the people who worked for the campaign were ugly, unkind, and unnecessarily hurtful, and even some political friends had turned against me, creating hashtags on social media to get under my skin.

There on the floor of the church during that worship service, I ugly cried, with mascara running down my face. I didn't care; I was letting it out. I was feeling it all. Recovering from this intense journey was going to take time, and the first step to starting again was acknowledging where I was. It was hard.

After Clayton and his worship team sang the last note, I finally got up off the floor. It was then I heard the Lord say something to me that changed my life. Jesus said so sweetly to my heart, "You don't have to be the congresswoman from the Fifth District of Texas. You have Me."

I knew again that my identity was not found in a job title, a position, my popularity, or the fact that I could raise a million dollars. The security of my heart was not set on thousands of people who believed in me or those who hated me. My identity was found in Jesus. He was enough.

My thoughts then went even deeper: "I get to walk out of this church tonight and walk with Jesus. I get to wake up on Tuesday morning knowing I am losing a race for Congress but walk with Jesus. I get to walk with Jesus next week, next month, next year, and next decade."

And then I prayed a scripture, "One thing I have desired of the LORD, that will I seek: that I may dwell in the house of the LORD all the days of my life, to behold the beauty of the LORD, and to inquire in His temple" (Ps. 27:4).

In the stillness of His voice, I knew He was enough for me—in my highest of highs as well as in my lowest of lows.

Jesus would always be enough.

For God did not send His Son into the world to condemn the world, but that the world through Him might be saved.

—JOHN 3:17, MEV

If God's power and love are reserved only for the clean, pure, and healthy, what good is that? Jesus, by example, showed us how to live intentionally in the world to impact people's lives. He walked with the tax collectors, the teachers of the Law, and the whores all at the same time.

Chapter 3

POLITICS IS NOT
INHERENTLY EVIL

A<small>S A TWENTY-NINE-YEAR-OLD</small> mom going to college at night, I consumed textbooks cover to cover. I read two big volumes of American history from colonial America to the Civil War and then to the early 2000s. I paid for those books myself, so I read every word of them.

In my American government textbook, I read that politicians decide who gets what, when, and how.

Politics is not that complicated, yet it is something many believers in Jesus run from in fear. We have politics in our businesses, in our schools, and even in our churches. Politics is just the "art or science of government," according to Webster's.[1] Anywhere someone is governing something, there is politics. If you are a parent, you have political action manifesting in the back seat of your car when your kids are lobbying you about where they want to eat after church.

Though they get a bad name in American politics, lobbyists exist to educate legislators on what they think the legislators need to know and do for their cause. Corporations, interest groups, and even local municipalities (to my chagrin) have lobbyists in some form or another. Legislators are busy people dealing with hundreds of issues at one time. Lobbyists, whether they are volunteer citizen activists or highly paid professionals, are there to convince the legislators that their cause should be top priority. Most of the time, lobbyists are highly paid consultants with knowledge of both the governmental process and a specific issue.

EARLY MARRIED LIFE

At twenty years old, after serving for several months on the mission field in Latin America, I decided not to join Youth With A Mission as I had intended because—out of the blue—my best friend, Tim, proposed.

Our friendship had grown deep as we were discipled by the same loving spiritual fathers and mothers, and we loved doing life together in Dallas-Fort Worth. After hearing from God that he was supposed to marry me, Tim popped the question abruptly in the International House of Pancakes parking lot. (I will share the full story later.) We started our married life together soon afterward.

Tim had a pest control company, and after we married, I went to work for him. I wanted to serve him by balancing his checkbook and running his office. I also wanted to keep from having to commute through Dallas traffic, anticipating that we might soon have kids.

From 1996 to 2001, Tim and I grew our Bluebonnet Pest Control business to nine trucks and fifteen employees. We enjoyed building a business together, having babies, and then raising our energetic boys, Israel and Benjamin.

In those early years, we cut our teeth on business while parenting. After doubling the business year after year, Tim and I finally decided to sell. I helped negotiate the sale to Centex Home Services. We made a good profit and were able to take some time off to recover from all the hard work. After skiing all over Colorado for five weeks, we tried to figure out what we wanted to do when we "grew up." One of our former pest control clients owned two small semi-fast-food establishments called Roly Poly, and through a series of conversations, we eventually bought the sandwich shops from him and launched into the restaurant business full-time.

We had fun learning a new line of work. In essence, we sold sandwiches with meats and cheese rolled up in large tortillas. We learned restaurant Spanish from our guys in the kitchen, navigated the permits, and tried to figure out our profit margins.

My restaurant was at Preston Center, right in the middle of the wealthiest part of Dallas. It was open from nine in the morning to four in the afternoon each day. This allowed me to take the boys to school and then pick them up in the afternoon, leaving my assistant manager to close up shop at the end of the day. We eventually sold that store once I started back to college, as it wasn't as profitable as we had hoped.

Tim, on the other hand, spent the next sixteen years running a Roly Poly restaurant next to Southern Methodist University, a block south of the George W. Bush Presidential Library. Apart from doing ministry in our home each Friday night, Tim invested in hundreds of people's lives while at the register tending our customers and during his frequent visits to the Starbucks next door.

INSPIRED BY LAURA INGRAHAM

While working at Roly Poly and running my energetic boys back and forth to school, I started listening to a woman named Laura Ingraham on talk radio. She was smart, funny, and educated at Dartmouth College before earning a law degree from the University of Virginia School of Law. She had clerked for Justice Clarence Thomas, and I found her absolutely fascinating. As I listened to her every afternoon on my way home with the kids in the back seat, I started to realize that America was in trouble. Our nation was not all right.

I began watching Fox News regularly during the 2000 election with the recounts and hanging chads in Florida. The Constitution had to be followed exactly, and the Supreme Court had the final word. I marveled at our Founding Fathers' brilliance and foresight regarding future constitutional crises like this one, as well as their desire for the well-being of our republic. I fell in love with the Constitution—an incredible document that I became increasingly thankful for.

Laura Ingraham's radio program educated me even with her funny "separated at birth" bits, which highlighted current national political figures and how they looked like other people in the culture. I was enthralled at why she thought these people were important, at least enough to make fun of.

In all seriousness, though, Laura's passion specifically for the pro-life issue awakened something in me that had been dormant for a while.

During my first semester as a CFNI student, I was a part of the moral issues student ministry. We had taken several trips to an abortion clinic in Dallas to pray and talk to women who were considering abortion. It set a fire in my heart to see unborn babies saved.

Laura's faith, passion, and conviction as a talk-show host inspired me to want to make a difference as well. I began studying Bible passages about people who made an impact on nations, from Daniel to Esther to Nehemiah. I realized that I had been narrowly focused on the fivefold ministry gifts of apostles, prophets, evangelists, pastors, and teachers inside the church walls.

"Were apostles, prophets, evangelists, pastors, and teachers only full-time employees of a church?" I wondered. Then I saw that these gifts were given to the church by Jesus Himself:

> And He Himself gave some to be apostles, some prophets, some evangelists, and some pastors and teachers, for the equipping of the saints for the work of ministry, for the edifying of the body of Christ.
>
> —EPHESIANS 4:11–12

Did that mean that the work of the ministry was, in reality, outside the church walls?

This paradigm shift in my heart and mind was setting me free from my narrow thinking of what ministry was and what it should look like. Much of that philosophy had been subconsciously imparted to me at Bible school and in my religious upbringing. Rarely, if ever, did anyone who was not in full-time ministry (getting paid from a religious institution) instruct the students from the pulpit. Many soon came to realize, however, that this narrow focus on what defined ministry was a mistake.

My father, who was a pastor or in some capacity of ministry for over twenty-five years, had instilled in me that God had a call on my life. From the time I was nine years old, he told me that I would be teaching the Bible at some point in my life. In his mind, that meant I would be in vocational ministry.

But then I read Jesus' words in Matthew, instructing us to be salt and light in the world. Our Savior called us to make a difference, to disciple nations, and to promote His love, character, and values in this life. How were we supposed to do that if we never interacted with people who were not Christians?

Again, I contemplated Matthew 5:13–16:

> You are the salt of the earth; but if the salt loses its flavor, how shall it be seasoned? It is then good for nothing but to be thrown out and trampled underfoot by men. You are the light of the world. A city that is set on a hill cannot be hidden. Nor do they light a lamp and put it under a basket, but on a lampstand, and it gives light to all who are in the house. Let your light so shine before men, that they may see your good works and glorify your Father in heaven.

KAREN HUGHES, COUNSELOR TO THE PRESIDENT

After the 2000 election, as I continued to follow the news of the Bush White House, I bought my first real political book: *Ten Minutes from Normal* by Karen Hughes. Karen had worked at the Texas Republican Party helping George W. Bush when he was governor of the state. When he ran for president, she helped run the communications and media team for the campaign. When he was elected, she moved her family to Washington, DC, so she could be his senior counselor. She shocked the world two years later when she moved back to Texas so her son could finish high school there. Even from her home in Austin, she continued to advise the president and served him in multiple capacities.

Karen was an inspiring model of an everyday woman who worked extremely hard to get where she was. She ultimately made the decision to put her family first in the middle of one of the most influential jobs in Washington, DC. Her story of walking with powerful people, even during seasons of crisis like the aftermath of September 11, 2001, began forming a desire in my heart to make a difference for my nation.

"I could do what Karen did," I thought. "Maybe not in the White House but somewhere."

I loved business. I was good at it. Even as Tim and I wrote large checks to foreign missions, I was thankful for our impact but still was unsatisfied.

"There has got to be something for me here in America," I prayed. "God, I am raising my boys to love You and to impact the world; I am serving my husband and our family. But is there something here in this nation for me?"

A Church's Obedience

Shortly after praying about what I could do for my nation, I got a call from a family friend, Pastor David Halvorson, an associate pastor at a small church in Fort Worth.

Tim and I had met each other at a home group associated with that church in 1992. While working as the lead children's minister there one summer, I had written a curriculum on God's army, designing it to teach kids to be bold and courageous in their walks with God. When the team of pastors started another church in Dallas (just after our son Benjamin was born), they asked if I would lead worship at the new church plant, and I agreed. I led worship there for over two years and solidified many lifelong friendships.

Even though Tim and I had been gone from that church for a few years by that time, Pastor David wanted to let me know that they were having a seminar at the Fort Worth church that Saturday to teach everyone about the political processes. A Texas primary was coming up, and his local church was not afraid to get involved with political parties. The church's pastors were in leadership in the Republican Party and wanted others to understand the convention system, the importance of platforms and party rules, and all the nuances involved in a system that is completely foreign to most people.

I was all in. I was going to go to that seminar.

A few weeks before this I had commented to a friend about how our five-year-old and seven-year-old boys were playing together all the time and leaving me alone. "I can finally read a book all the way through," I told her. "Now that they are enjoying each other more than me, I am getting bored. I am either going to have to have another baby soon or go back to college." Although I said this tongue in cheek, there was some truth to that declaration.

Over the course of that half-day seminar, our little group of twenty believers learned why it was important for the church to get involved in politics. The two pastors and their wives taught us about the precinct conventions (held after the primary elections) and why the platforms, which spelled out each party's beliefs, were important for Christians to understand and follow. They also taught us how to get a resolution to the platform committee. They even showed us how to fill out the paperwork at the precinct convention if no one else showed up for the meeting.

I was excited at the prospect of being a delegate to the senatorial convention in my area and then potentially going to the Texas State Republican Convention. The vice chairman of the party in Texas that year was David Barton, a historian on the Founding Fathers. He had spoken for over a week at my Bible school years ago, and I had huge respect for him. If he thought it was important to get involved, maybe I should consider it.

As these pastors shared stories from their experiences working with the Christian Coalition, and Peggy Borchert, wife of one of the pastors, shared her passion for education issues, I was hooked. I felt a sense of purpose in the whole prospect of getting involved and letting my voice be heard on the issues I cared about. This was my path into the political fray—taking a trip to San Antonio for the Republican State Convention.

THE ISSUES THAT PULLED ME INTO POLITICS

When I sat down as a twenty-nine-year-old mom and contemplated what in this world I wanted to leave for my children, I knew I didn't want to leave them an America that continued to slaughter babies in the womb. *Roe v. Wade* was a scourge on the American landscape. At that time, some estimated that an average of three thousand babies were being killed every day in America.

I would find out a few years later that my own husband had been affected by this issue. Before he became a Christian, two of his former girlfriends had abortions. In light of this I was sensitive to the debris in people's lives, both male and female. I couldn't sit by and do nothing about it anymore.

As I considered getting involved in politics, I also thought about the issue of America and Israel's relationship. I knew I didn't want my children to wake up to an America that was not allied with Israel—the only democratic state in the Middle East. This miracle nation promotes freedom and equality and is one of the best friends America has. I didn't want to wake up in a world where we, as Christians, didn't stand next to our Jewish brothers and sisters and defend them. I couldn't just sit back while liberal forces continued to speak out against the covenant people whom God loves. I wanted to elect people who would stand with Israel.

I was also concerned about government spending—which was bad enough when I first considered going into politics but is even worse now. The days of standing and looking at our national debt climb higher and higher must stop. Both political parties are guilty of feeding the fire, and deficit spending in Washington is causing our nation to pay it forward in a horrendous way. This is a bleak reality for our children and grandchildren. Our elected officials must stop the spending spree. We must do something to fix entitlements and to save beneficial federal programs for future generations as well.

These were among the issues I cared most about when I drove down to San Antonio that year for the Texas Republican Convention. It was a trip that would change the trajectory of my life.

THE LEARNING PROCESS

On primary day 2004 I went to my precinct convention after the polls closed at seven o'clock. No one else showed up. I asked the election judge for the paperwork for the Republican Party precinct meeting, filled it out, and voted myself in as a delegate to the senatorial district convention. I then voted myself in as our precinct's delegate to the state convention.

At the county/senatorial district convention a month later, I heard my future employer speak for the first time. It was also the first time I voted on a resolution and debated an issue—with the person next to me, not on a microphone. (I was not that brave.) It was the first time I asked questions and got answers on how to really get involved. That was the day I knew I had to keep stepping out, even though I felt awkward in this new system that I didn't quite understand yet. There was something in this for me on the other side of my fear.

A month later Pastor David connected me with another young woman, Laura, who had attended the same seminar at their church. She also was a first-time delegate to the state convention, and we decided to travel there together. I left the boys with Tim and traveled around three hundred miles from Dallas to San Antonio to the largest political convention in America—larger than the national convention at that time.

Peggy Borchert asked Laura and me if we wanted to testify in front of the platform committee against school choice vouchers. We were to make the point that we were worried about state mandates and concerned that control would follow the potential dollars given. Laura declined, but I quickly replied, "Sure!"

All I remember about that night in front of the platform committee was that I sat next to a Messianic Jewish rabbi who wanted the Republicans to add stronger language to their Israel plank, specifically on the fact that Jerusalem was Israel's true capital. And I remember that it was late—maybe nine thirty at night—when I finally got up to testify.

I was overly passionate about my issue at the time and was nervous in front of those thirty-two delegates, as well as the crowd gathered around the committee. It was not a textbook performance by any stretch of the imagination, but it got me started.

At that moment I could never have imagined that in 2020 I would serve on the state platform committee and then would be nominated by Robin Armstrong, our Republican National Committee representative from Texas, and David Barton, historian and founder of WallBuilders, to represent Texas on the national platform committee. Though the convention was canceled that year because of COVID-19, being elected as a national delegate from my congressional district and to the national platform committee was an honor I will never forget.

One step leads to another, and nineteen years later I look back and realize all that God has done in and through me since then.

A MANDATE FROM GENESIS TO REVELATION

As the body of Christ, we must get moving in political arenas. Are we the answer to the ills in this nation or not?

I believe that the church *is* the answer and that our complacency in our culture and our communities has gotten us where we are today.

What are the issues we care about as Christians? What are we doing about them? Are we just sitting on our couches binge-watching Netflix or Amazon Prime while our nation goes down the toilet?

Are we waiting for Jesus to come back while we keep our heads in the sand?

I believe the Bible is crystal clear from Genesis to Revelation that we have a mandate from God:

> Then God said, "Let Us make man in Our image, according to Our likeness; let them have dominion over the fish of the sea, over the birds of the air, and over the cattle, over all the earth and over every creeping thing that creeps on the earth." So God created man in His own image; in the image of God He created him; male and female He created them. Then God blessed them, and God said to them, "Be fruitful and multiply; fill the earth and subdue it; have dominion over the fish of the sea, over the birds of the air, and over every living thing that moves on the earth."
>
> —GENESIS 1:26–28

Notice that we were made in God's image. We were made to create, to produce, and to invent—in other words, to be entrepreneurs. It is in our DNA to be fruitful. God put us in the earth to "be fruitful and multiply; fill the earth and subdue it; have dominion over the fish of the sea, over the birds of the air, and over every living thing that moves on the earth."

That does not seem like a passive faith to me. It sounds like a big job that we get to partner with God to accomplish here on earth now—not just sometime in the future in heaven.

When we jump over to the Book of Revelation, the final book in the Bible, we see the same idea:

Now when He had taken the scroll, the four living creatures and the twenty-four elders fell down before the Lamb, each having a harp, and golden bowls full of incense, which are the prayers of the saints. And they sang a new song, saying: "You are worthy to take the scroll, and to open its seals; for You were slain, and have redeemed us to God by Your blood out of every tribe and tongue and people and nation, and have made us kings and priests to our God; and we shall reign on the earth."

—REVELATION 5:8–10

There are three powerful pictures here that inspired me to live my life on purpose.

First, we see the "golden bowls full of incense, which are the prayers of the saints." God doesn't consider prayer a side item on a checklist of things we should do. It is the eternal work between the divine and His creation. There is nothing more important for us to do on earth as citizens of heaven than to partner with Jesus our great High Priest who "always lives to make intercession" for us (Heb. 7:25). In this scripture in Revelation, we see the depth of His care over these prayers. He keeps them in golden bowls before Him.

Next, we see the powerful identity Christ has given believers through His blood that was shed at His death on the cross. Ultimately He became "the resurrection and the life" (John 11:25), and we now live in His resurrection power (Gal. 2:20).

He has redeemed His children out of every "tribe and tongue and people and nation." He has made us different than the world (i.e., unbelievers). He has set us apart and made us righteous and holy before Him. Our power as Christians doesn't come from our talents, gifts, or money; it comes from our lives being set apart for Him.

Our eternal fruit on this earth is in direct relationship with how set apart our lives become. How far will our faith take us and to what depth of adventure will we go to know Jesus in our lives?

Then we see one of the truths that stirred Martin Luther to break away from the Catholic Church, sparking the Reformation: we have been made "kings and priests to our God; and we shall reign on the earth."

Luther knew it was important for the people in his day to have the

Holy Bible in their own language. It was not good enough for the priests to have it only in Latin. The people needed it in German in order to walk with God effectively. This monk caught hold of the idea that we, as ordinary believers who put our faith in a holy God, can stand before Him, talk to Him, and read His words for ourselves.

We are called as kings and priests, and ultimately we will reign not just in heaven but also in the New Jerusalem on the earth. I am planning on leading a whole city and being the mayor of a town in the kingdom, so I guess I should start practicing now.

It is not unholy to advocate, speak up, and be educated on the issues of our day. Of course, there are some solid moral issues that should unite us together as the body of Christ. In other areas, however, I have found that most of the issues I have studied throughout the years are not as black and white as I originally thought. This means that people of faith may stand on different sides of an important national or state issue. For example, even though I testified so passionately against school choice voucher programs as a young mom, I now hold some different views about it. There are options I am now open to, like education savings accounts controlled by the parents. The devil is in the details, but if these accounts can be used for homeschooling, tutoring, and more without government control, then I believe we must look at all options to get children out of failing public schools.

Even in our debates and our differences, it is still noble for people of faith to reach opinions and to fight for what we believe in.

GOING BACK TO COLLEGE

Coming home from that state convention in 2004, I decided to approach my husband about going back to college because I felt I had found my calling.

Since Tim and I were on Dave Ramsey's Financial Peace University plan and were snowballing our personal debt away, he told me I had to pay cash for each class. I convinced Tim to let me take one class: American government. I then transferred my Bible school credits to Dallas Baptist University, a four-year Christian school.

I was all in on every level, and after three and a half years, I finally graduated magna cum laude with a bachelor of arts in political science. My motto for those long years was "He who endures to the end shall be saved" (Mark 13:13).

MY DAD'S INFLUENCE

While in college I got into political activism. After graduating, I then landed my job as a campaign manager for Congressman Hensarling. My father, a former pastor, questioned whether I was doing the right thing. He was concerned about my path and challenged me often on my thinking.

He reminded me that when I was nine years old, I sat on the front pew of our Seventh-day Adventist (SDA) church for three weeks listening to his Revelation seminar on the end times. He remembered my note-taking as a child, my attentiveness to look up every scripture in my own baby-blue Bible, including Revelation 22:14: "Blessed are those who do His commandments, that they may have the right to the tree of life, and may enter through the gates into the city." I recalled reading that verse and thinking about the tree of life and what it looked like. A few weeks later my dad baptized me at our church. His passion for the Bible and belief in me drove my awareness from a young age that God had a distinct call on my life for teaching the Word. It was a generational calling that my father had prayed for.

Although he grew up in the SDA church, my dad (who looked a little like Elvis when he was younger) went through some years of rebellion and wandering from his faith in high school and beyond. He "found Jesus" during his time in the US Army while watching Billy Graham on TV. It was the first time that he truly felt that God cared about him and that he really connected his faith to his life's purpose. In a typical foxhole prayer, my father asked God to keep him out of Vietnam, and by some miracle, as a medic noncombatant, he didn't end up having to go. His call to the ministry followed. Though he never did pass Greek at Andrews University in Berrien Springs, Michigan, he did become an ordained pastor with the SDA church.

I was born on August 17, 1974, while my dad was studying for the ministry. Somehow my mother agreed to his crazy idea of naming me Bunni Nicole, after the nickname of one of Billy Graham's daughters, Ruth "Bunny" Graham. My dad had held on to the name for years, thinking it was cool. Two years later in September, my sister, Sunni Michele, came into the world. We girls grew up as fourth-generation Adventists on each side of our family.

My father always had his share of weaknesses. Even as a pastor he fought depression, but he never stopped reminding us all that salvation was found in the finished work of the cross.

He always told me that I could be anyone I wanted to be or do anything I felt called to do. His main request was that I follow Jesus. My father was one of the reasons I pursued a deep relationship with God in the first place and became an adventurer for truth like he was.

After nine moves by the time I was twelve years old, we landed in Arlington, Texas. My dad had a life-changing experience with the Holy Spirit and resigned from denominational ministry to work for the James Robison Evangelistic Association.

THE CHAMPION

My sister and I continued in SDA schools even after my dad's shift to the more charismatic side of the body of Christ. But my life changed forever one day in the dark auditorium of the Dallas Convention Center as I sat listening to a man named Carman preach the gospel through his songs.

My eighth-grade mind was full of thoughts of boys and Top 40 hits by George Michael and Debbie Gibson, and I wanted nothing much to do with my father at the time. A youth leader from our SDA church loved Christian music and listened to everything—not just Adventist music. He invited me and a few other youths from our church to go to the convention center for a free concert on Carman's Radically Saved tour.

In my entire life I had never been around Christians who were not Adventists—that is how sheltered I was. I don't think I had even had a conversation with anyone who was not an Adventist. And there I was, surrounded by throngs of worshippers who went to church on Sunday, and amazingly to me (since I grew up with a different perspective), they seemed to love Jesus.

As Carman sang his hit song "The Champion"—a wild ride of drama, speaking, and singing that detailed the death, burial, and resurrection of Jesus—it hit me: I was lost.

I might have experienced God from time to time when reading His Word—like I had in fifth grade while reading a psalm in the woods—or listening to all the Bible stories that I had grown up with. But I didn't *know* Him.

In that darkened auditorium among thousands of people, Jesus captured my thirteen-year-old heart. I was never the same again. Tears ran down my face as I confessed my sins, told Jesus I wanted to worship Him forever, and gave my life completely to Him as my Lord and Savior.

The victory had been won for my soul. Jesus was the Champion.

On Fire for God

The next fall I had an experience with the Holy Spirit that marked my life so much that I spent my sophomore year writing what must have seemed like doctoral dissertations to my SDA Bible class teachers. I eventually mailed a seven-page letter to my Adventist church asking them to drop my membership, and I asked my parents if I could go to public school for the first time in my life. (Later in life my husband and I sent our kids to an Adventist school for a season. We have had so many great relationships with our brothers and sisters in this church, and I have even led worship or shared at several SDA churches.)

My mother, while remaining in the Adventist church, was incredibly understanding of my faith journey and encouraged me every step of my life—through all the twists and turns. As a gifted administrator, leader, and consistently positive person, she never balked at my quick decisions but trusted me to follow God wherever that might lead. No one has been a more consistent cheerleader for me than my mom in every season of life.

My junior and senior years at Martin High School were spent witnessing to anyone who would listen—specifically the kids in the theater department, whom I loved and was extremely concerned for. I was one of the radical students who hosted prayer and worship gatherings in the middle of the grassy knoll outside the cafeteria doors at lunchtime and the Bible club after school.

Also during those years I got involved in a local Christian theater. Sharing the gospel through theater became a passion for me. In fact, sharing my faith became a way of life. I was on fire for God.

Thankfully I had great mentors who shaped my life. Mark Jobe, father to the now-famous worship leader Kari Jobe, became my youth pastor at the nondenominational Restoration Church. This amazing pastor and his wife, Sandy, had to sort through all my theological questions—from Saturday versus Sunday worship, to the fruit and gifts of the Holy Spirit, to the importance of the unity of the body of Christ, and so much more. I was on a relentless search for biblical truth, whether it led me to what I wanted to hear or not. Several of my SDA friends even went on the journey of discovery with me.

As a senior in high school I led my first person to the Lord through a theater show called *Judgment Seat.* In the show I played a young teenager who was killed in a car crash with her family and had to stand before the judgment seat of Christ. The show ran for four weekends. At the end of each show we had an altar call and prayed for people to receive Jesus. I led a fifteen-year-old girl to Jesus the first weekend, and I was instantly addicted. The change on her face from hopelessness to sheer joy changed the passion of my life. No longer was I just looking to go to college to study theater, to write, and to speak, but I wanted to carry the power of the gospel with me into it all.

I wrote and directed a play called *True Love* that we performed at my local church. Many teenagers were touched by that show.

After high school I planned to go to the University of North Texas (UNT), a liberal arts university in Denton, Texas, where I had been accepted and had received a small scholarship for theater. My initial plan was to major in theater and writing, live in a co-ed dorm, and minister to all the starving artists on campus over the next four years.

But God would not let me go too far away from His Word, and as the days dragged on, He kept pulling me ever so slightly toward a different vision.

JOURNEY TO BIBLE COLLEGE

After my high school graduation that summer, I got a job as a window washer. I was broke and desperately needed money.

I worked hard, but in my spare time, I couldn't stop reading the Bible and weeping at what I was reading and experiencing. A few friends, including my new boss from the window-washing company, invited me to a couple of Bible studies where I discovered people who had a passion for the Word of God like I did. They were young professionals who loved to debate the Bible, dig deep into expository studies on certain books or topics, and worship and pray. At first I felt silly crying all the time over my Bible, but then I just rested in this physical expression of my heart before the Lord. Something told me that everything was going to be okay and that God would work all this out for me. He was moving in my life.

God's next move came in the form of a late-night conversation with my older friend Todd, whom I met through my theater group. He was the friend who invited me to Pastor David Halvorson's church, where I eventually met my future husband. I don't know whether Todd became my friend because he sympathized with this young girl who couldn't stop asking questions about everything theological or because he too needed a friend.

Todd reminded me half of the apostle Paul and half of John the Baptist. He loved to write long Pauline-type epistles and enjoyed never-ending conversations with me, even when I tried to cut them off. Todd also liked to speak the truth—sometimes with a hard bent. He didn't know how to do anything in moderation. He was a part of all three Bible studies I attended that summer, so we saw each other everywhere.

One night Todd came over to my mom's house to help me figure out my class schedule at community college. I had already dropped my plans to go to UNT. During that summer of weeping over my Bible, something had changed—I had changed. I was being broken.

I confessed to Todd for the first time that I had lost all my passion and vision for seeking higher education at all. I was coming to understand that I was finding my identity in my theater abilities and in being one of the top sopranos in my high school choir and my youth group worship team. I wanted to be a playwright to make a name for *myself*, not really for the sake of Jesus. My tears that summer were God's way of breaking me of myself and my vision for my own life so that He could give me His vision.

We stayed up till after midnight talking. The next morning, he invited me to visit his Bible school, so I went with him on the first day of the semester at Christ For The Nations Institute. Kevin Jonas, father of the future teenage heartthrobs the Jonas Brothers, was leading worship that morning, and it was incredible. God met me in such a real way. I knew I was home.

This is where I was supposed to be for the next two years, and I knew that I was not supposed to sing a note, write a script, or act in a show while I was there. I needed God to redefine me with His Word. This was my breaking season.

MY DAD'S POSITION

Years later, my dad didn't want me to leave what he considered to be the call on my life doing worship or teaching the Bible to go into politics. He had understood my work in business, working beside my husband. He loved Tim and our two boys, Israel and Ben, so much, and he knew my priority was my family. But in the back of his mind, my dad felt that I was called to preach the gospel in some way, and he was going to keep encouraging me to that end.

My dad grew up in a denominational setting that was very apolitical. I don't remember politics being discussed much in our home growing up. I do remember my sister and I rewriting the words to the song "Oh, Benjamin Harrison" from a Disney movie called *The One and Only, Genuine, Original Family Band*. We replaced the names Benjamin Harrison and Grover Cleveland in the song with those of our new favorite candidate, Ronald Reagan, and the Democratic candidate, Walter Mondale.

I am pretty sure my parents voted Republican, at least in presidential election years. I know they didn't vote for President Jimmy Carter in 1980, and I am sure they voted for Reagan's reelection in 1984. I never recall them discussing any primary race, local election, or political issue other than the racism we discovered in our white SDA church in Vicksburg, Mississippi, in 1986.

My dad somehow had the idea that Christians couldn't get involved with politics without corrupting themselves with the evil that was in that world. He believed it was a corrupting game. I told him politely that I believed he was wrong.

Politics—the necessary process of certain people getting what they want in government—is not evil or wrong. It is necessary.

I would even go so far as to consider it a godly struggle. If the church does not speak up when our government is redefining marriage, sanctioning the legal killing of unborn children, running up debt into the trillions of dollars, and printing money to cover up the effects, I believe we are in disobedience. We have failed miserably in this area to fulfill God's call on our lives to protect and "have dominion" (Gen. 1:26) over the earth—specifically in the nation where we are placed.

Deep down, my father knew I was in the will of God, but like so many other Christians, he struggled with the idea of believers in the political world. And he was genuinely worried about me, as any normal father would be.

It wasn't until years later when he was on his deathbed that my dad came around.

THE GOSPEL IS ALWAYS PREEMINENT

In any job or activity that we embark on as believers in Jesus—in all of our lives—the gospel should always be preeminent.

We engage with government to protect our liberties in America, whether that is our First Amendment rights (free speech and religious freedom), our Second Amendment rights (our right to bear arms), or any other passion that compels us to actively participate in this national conversation. Yet this does not mean that while we engage in those activities or interact with people in this area, we cease to be Christians. We do not stop loving or praying for people. When God opens the door or when the

Holy Spirit prompts us to share the hope we have in the gospel, we are commanded to open our mouths.

> Now then, we are ambassadors for Christ, as though God were pleading through us: we implore you on Christ's behalf, be reconciled to God. For He made Him who knew no sin to be sin for us, that we might become the righteousness of God in Him.
>
> —2 CORINTHIANS 5:20–21

Though we engage in politics to protect liberty and to strengthen America (one of the leading nations that funds the sharing of the gospel all over the world), we cannot use that as an excuse to not share the story of Jesus. America's strength is found in the hearts of her people, and if her people are not healed, set free, revived, and grounded in the Word of God, then we lose the ultimate power of what makes us great as a nation. We must see God transform people's lives each and every day.

Sharing the story of the death, burial, and resurrection of Jesus and how it has changed our lives is the greatest thing we can do in this generation. Period. Only Jesus can save, and only Jesus can change someone's life. If we don't share Jesus with others, we are hiding our greatest instrument for change in our nation.

> For I am not ashamed of the gospel of Christ, for it is the power of God to salvation for everyone who believes, for the Jew first and also for the Greek.
>
> —ROMANS 1:16

THE OPEN DOOR TO JAMES' HEART

The last full campaign I ran in my political career before embarking into full-time ministry was the reelection of US congressman Michael Cloud in the Twenty-Seventh Congressional District of Texas. A strong believer in Jesus, Michael had been a media director at his local church, Faith Family Church, for over ten years. He and his wife, Rosel, are genuine believers.

I hired a campaign assistant named James. This twenty-year-old young man came running into my life with a passion to get the job done.

With his Libertarian bent James was constantly wanting to debate my established social conservative beliefs, but he was also zealous to make a difference and to help wherever he could. I put him in charge of our yard-sign project in thirteen counties. He went out every day all over the district, putting up big four-foot-by-four-foot signs that read "Michael Cloud for Congress."

One early evening in August, James wandered into an outdoor campaign fundraiser we were holding in Wharton County, stumbling as if he was going to fall over. He had hit his head with a large, metal T-post driver while putting a metal stake into the ground. The young man was not doing well.

He staggered up to me and said, "I don't feel well, Bunni."

I instructed him to go lie down in the host's pool house. Thirty minutes later I went to check on him, but he was not doing better. Now worried that he might have a concussion, I asked the event host where the nearest hospital was and learned that it was in Victoria, about forty minutes away. I told the congressman that I was leaving the event in the hands of our other campaign assistant, Nicole, and was going to take James to the hospital. Instantly Michael said, "Let me see James." He left all the guests and went straight over to his campaign helper. Without delay, he asked James if he could pray for him before sending us on our way.

James came from a broken home. He grew up without his father being much of an influence in his life, and his mother had done the best she could. I realized soon after getting to know this young man that he didn't have much formation growing up and needed a lot of love and wisdom imparted into his life.

As we drove down the country highway, James was staring out the window at the clouds when he said something that surprised me. "Bunni, I think God is up there looking at us; don't you?" This opened a huge door for me.

"I absolutely believe God is near and cares about each one of us, James," I replied.

With a deep look of reflection on his face he asked, "Bunni, did Congressman Cloud just pray for me?"

"Yes, he did, James."

James then made this statement that floored me: "I think that was the nicest thing that anyone has ever done for me."

One simple act of kindness from a sitting member of Congress to one of his campaign helpers—one quick prayer from a humble man of God—and James was changed. Now I got to share the good news of God's love with him. I had a responsibility as a follower of Christ. I couldn't leave this open door to James' heart without filling it with the truth.

On the way to the hospital that day, I shared with James God's deep love for him, my testimony (from pastor's kid to salvation), and my husband's testimony of coming out of seven years of drug addiction as a young man. Then I shared the simple gospel message.

I left James with another prayer, asking God to reveal Himself to this young man.

I couldn't go into the hospital with him because of COVID-19 regulations at the time, but I promised I would check up on him later that night. He walked in, found out he didn't have a concussion, and was back to work the next week putting up more signs.

BRINGING THE GOSPEL WHILE BLOCK WALKING

Over the course of the next month, I had many conversations with James and his girlfriend, Kobi, building on what I knew God was doing in their hearts. God was drawing this intellectual young man from a broken home. Kobi, who was studying to be a teacher, was also being drawn by God's love. They both needed acceptance and validation, and God was the only One who could speak destiny into their hearts.

The first weekend of October, we decided to take a group of volunteers to northern San Antonio to knock on doors for one of Congressman Cloud's best friends, Rep. Chip Roy, who was in a very competitive race.

Chip was running his first reelection campaign after being elected in 2018, the same year that Michael had won and I had lost. Wendy Davis, a former state senator and darling of the liberal media, was running against this outspoken conservative congressman, and she was raising a lot of money. An extreme defender of a "woman's right to choose," she had become famous in our state years before when she led a filibuster on the floor of the Texas Senate to delay a vote on abortion legislation. The pro-life community did not want her getting anywhere near Congress.

That weekend the Cloud campaign hosted around thirty-five people who knocked on doors and told the people in Texas' Twenty-First Congressional District the differences between Chip Roy and Wendy Davis. On Sunday morning, it would be too early to block walk, so I asked Congressman Cloud if we could do a little nondenominational church service with simple worship and a couple quick devotionals for the people attending. They were not required to come to the short service, but if they wanted to get a little inspiration, they could. He agreed.

Nicole, my other campaign assistant, led worship with her guitar. Then Scott Bauer, one of the congressman's best friends, and I split up the time to share thoughts from the Word of God.

As I had prayed earlier, I knew more and more that God wanted me to share how the gospel impacted my life even while I engaged in politics. Following that, I shared the simple message of God's redemption plan. My perspective was that whether our volunteers were Protestant, Catholic, or not yet believers, we all needed to remember that this story is what ultimately changes lives. I treated them all like they knew the truth, but a few were hearing the story of God's love for the first time.

To share the gospel, I used the New Testament scripture references imprinted on a multicolored wristband created by a friend, Kyle Lance Martin, for his ministry, Time to Revive. Color by color in about a fifteen-minute format, I taught these truths:

- Romans 3:23: "For all have sinned and fall short of the glory of God."

- Romans 6:23: "For the wages of sin is death, but the gift of God is eternal life in Christ Jesus our Lord."

- Romans 5:8: "But God demonstrates His own love toward us, in that while we were still sinners, Christ died for us."

- Ephesians 2:8–9: "For by grace you have been saved through faith, and that not of yourselves; it is the gift of God, not of works, lest anyone should boast."

- Romans 10:9–10: "If you confess with your mouth the Lord Jesus and believe in your heart that God has raised Him from the dead, you will be saved. For with the heart one believes unto righteousness, and with the mouth confession is made unto salvation."

I shared how a few years back, through the ministry of Time to Revive, I was reminded how to share Jesus simply with people. At the time, I was overwhelmed with the number of people I encountered in America who didn't know or understand these beautiful truths. I exhorted everyone that politics in and of itself would not save America.

"Our nation needs Jesus above everything else," I concluded.

At the end of the little service, one lady walked up to me with tears in her eyes. She let me know that she was Catholic and thought she had strong faith but that I had personalized Jesus to her in a new way. It made a big impact on her. I told her that faith isn't just an ascension to knowledge; it is truth that transforms. I prayed for her, asking God to change her life even more.

Then Kobi came up to me. "Bunni, can I have one of those bracelets? James would like one too."

"Absolutely," I said, giving her the two on my wrists.

Kobi then said the words I had gotten so used to hearing on the streets of America over the last few years: "I have never heard that before."

America needs Christians to be engaged in politics and government, but above everything else, America needs the good news of Jesus. Jesus demonstrated His love for us by dying on a cross and desires to bring us into relationship with Him every day. Kobi and James heard the message.

A few weeks later when I traveled from Dallas back to Victoria, where the campaign was happening, I asked if I could take them both to dinner. I didn't know that it was James' twenty-first birthday. That same day he had also been accepted into the US Navy, which he had been pursuing for a long time.

That night—in a loving, motherly way—I took them both through the Bible from Genesis to Revelation, making sure they had the full picture of the love of God. I didn't give them the speech that they might have expected to hear on Christian TV programming. I didn't tell them to come to Jesus just to get destiny and purpose. I told them that God would be their Father, one whom they both desperately needed and who loved them deeply. I also told them that joining the people of God would mean driving on the other side of the road from the culture. It would mean abandoning sin and might mean that we'd all need to prepare for suffering and persecution for our faith as disciples of Jesus.

After telling them all that, I asked whether they wanted to accept Jesus and make Him Lord of their lives. Each of them looked me in the eyes and said enthusiastically, "Yes!"

That night in the parking lot of a Japanese restaurant in Victoria, Texas, James and Kobi prayed to God on their own and asked Jesus to come into their lives and be their Lord. Standing in a circle, holding hands, and praying with tears running down our faces, we were all changed. Their lives were set on a new course, and my heart was impacted again.

For all of us in the Cloud campaign that year, Election Day 2020 was a happy day. The congressman won reelection, as did his friend Rep. Chip Roy—but we were more excited that James and Kobi had come into the kingdom of God.

A year later, after James survived boot camp, Tim and I celebrated James and Kobi's wedding with them. I was honored to be a part of the service as their spiritual mom, as they called me. All of us celebrated this new journey for this young couple—their love for each other and their love for God.

SEVEN WEEKS TO SEE JESUS

My dad, Jack Colclesser, lived his last seven weeks like he lived his entire life—sharing the finished work of the cross with anyone who would listen.

In the fall of 2014, my father, who was still young at only seventy-one, was swimming with his new wife, Penny, in their pool. He suddenly couldn't move and was stuck in the water; paramedics had to come and get him out.

He had suffered stroke-like symptoms, and a few days later they found a giant glioblastoma, a fast-growing brain tumor, in his head. When he had started going blind in one eye the month before, he thought it was just his eyesight getting weak. His other eye had already been blinded by a retinal detachment. Yet this time, we found out, the brain tumor was causing the blindness.

Dad had surgery to see how big the tumor was, but the doctors already suspected he would not live long. After the surgery, their prognosis was that he had six to twelve months to live. When my dad came out of ICU, he informed my sister and me that he was "going to see Jesus soon" and told us not to worry another minute about him.

We, on the other hand, were not handling it all that well. We spent a few days in Florida with him and Penny and then flew home to figure out life. I was in the middle of the general election of 2014, but thankfully Congressman Hensarling was running only against a Libertarian candidate who had neither raised nor spent a dollar. I am forever thankful for the day Jeb called me and said, "Bunni, we just got the Wright Amendment overturned, and there are flights going out of Love Field now to Orlando. Get on one of those and work from Florida. The campaign is fine. Family first."

If Jeb hadn't made that call, I don't think I would have made the trip to spend a week with my dad. If I hadn't gone, I wouldn't have seen him alive again.

During that week with my dad, I spent a lot of time sharing stories with him. He was spending every minute he could talking to every nurse about the Lord, doing marriage counseling with his main caregiver and her husband, and telling everyone how excited he was to see Jesus soon.

This was the week I really drilled down with him on all my stories from my career. I told him about my friendship with Jeb and about other elected officials that I had met and ministered to, as well as the Bible study I was leading with state and congressional staffers.

I told him what a privilege it was to walk with these candidates and elected officials, to encourage them and help them reach their goals for the sake of the nation. I told him about my expectations that the fruit of my life would bear out something special for our nation. I told him about my daily desire to bring light into government workers' lives with my joy, optimism, and faith in Jesus.

I laid out the message to him that I was truly sharing the gospel and discipling leaders in my own way. God had called us to disciple the nations. What better way to start than through our national leaders?

My dad understood. He rested. He spoke into my life again regarding my identity in Christ and God's call on my life, reminding me of my note-taking on the front pew of his church, the seven-page letter to the Adventist denomination, the sermons I had preached at our house church, the songs I had written, and the discipleship books I had penned that were almost ready for publishing. Then he said this: "I know wherever you serve, Bunni, you will change the world. The congressman is blessed to have you."

I left him on a Friday to fly back to my family after a week of being gone; he passed away the next Tuesday. He had just turned seventy-two.

I wish he had seen me run for Congress. I wish he had seen James and Kobi come to Jesus or listened to me tell all my stories of walking with Jesus each day in politics. I would have loved to recount them to him over the phone or in person. Many times when I was speaking during the campaign, especially when there was a large crowd, I imagined my dad in the great cloud of witnesses cheering me on.

> Therefore, we also, since we are surrounded by so great a cloud of witnesses, let us lay aside every weight, and the sin which so easily ensnares us, and let us run with endurance the race that is set before us.
>
> —HEBREWS 12:1

He would have been extremely proud of me.

SALT AND LIGHT

God has called us to be salt and light. What better way than to shine the light of truth into situations that arise in politics? What better way to be salt that preserves than to see the good in people, not just the bad and the ugly?

For me, politics is not evil, and I don't believe the Bible teaches that it is. It is systems and organizations that are pushing against each other trying to get their way. Yes, there are people who do evil things in politics—as in every industry in our culture. Yes, there are evil systems and backroom deals and moral choices that make my stomach churn. But if we, as believers in Jesus, are following our consciences, staying in the Word of God and using it as our compass, and staying humble in this unique seat of power, God can do so much through us in this world.

I have seen this truth time and time again, and I want to continue to encourage the body of Christ to get involved and in some small way be the truth in the middle of politics.

In the end, politics and government are full of people. People who need Jesus. People who need examples of salt and light in their institutions, vocations, and governmental systems so they can walk with Jesus too. Everyone needs the Lord, and the gospel is always powerful—whether we share it with an elected official, a candidate, a young staffer, political activists, or our neighbors next door.

Politics is not inherently evil. Light is stronger than darkness. Jesus has called us to carry His light wherever we go. We can't leave it to someone else—it is our duty. We are called Christ followers for a reason. We are supposed to follow in His footsteps, even if it means going into government.

> Then Jesus spoke to them again, saying, "I am the light of the world. He who follows Me shall not walk in darkness but have the light of life."
>
> —JOHN 8:12

Now it came to pass, as He was praying in a certain place, when He ceased, that one of His disciples said to Him, "Lord, teach us to pray, as John also taught his disciples." So He said to them, "When you pray, say..."

—LUKE 11:1–2

If Jesus—who was perfection on earth—had to run away to the mountainside to be alone with the Father, how do we think we can survive all the noise that clings to us daily without running to Him? The consistent quieting of our souls enables us to hear God's still, small voice and magnifies His power through us. It is only in the place of prayer that we can find Him and be found in Him.

Chapter 4

TEACH US TO PRAY

AMERICA IS CONSUMED with constant and distracting noise. Our culture is oversaturated with opinions, talking heads, clickbait, social media, entertainment, music, and more. This noise consumes our thoughts, minds, and souls, keeping us from being able to hear from God or at times to even think straight. Anxiety is at an all-time high everywhere in our society—from teenagers to grandmas.

All throughout our nation this noise is attacking the souls of people who are attempting to live their lives in peace. Those of us who love the news and politics wonder why everyone is not staying up on the latest happenings like we are, but most people are desperately trying to stay away from fear.

Those of us who are trying to protect America's first principles and our constitutional rights and don't want to see our nation spiral out of control morally or fiscally have a double problem. We need to know what is happening in the world, but that means we have to immerse ourselves in the twenty-four-hour news cycles and publications such as the *New York Times*, *Wall Street Journal,* and our local papers—not to mention podcasts, blogs, Twitter, Signal, Gab, and more. It is hard not to get bombarded by so many media sources to the point of saturation.

Since we refuse to ignore it all or to rely solely on a Facebook feed for our news, it means that we must work hard to sort through information, prioritize news, and discern what is valuable. It also means we have to work hard to not let news completely consume our hearts and lives.

DEHYDRATED

During my time at Dallas Baptist University while studying political science, I barely opened the Bible. Instead, I was diligently reading my textbooks and being a busy business owner, college student, and, most important, wife and mother. I let everything else fill my days. I didn't read the Word of God or spend any real time with Jesus. All this was while I was leading worship every week on Wednesday nights and Sunday mornings at a local church. The travesty of that season was that I was leading Christians into the presence of God, but I hadn't spent any time in His presence myself.

About a year into my job with Jeb, after constantly drinking from a fire hose of new information, things reached a crisis point in my personal life, my marriage, and our church life. I woke up one day and realized I hadn't cracked open the Good Book to take in God's life-giving words for a very long time.

"As the deer pants for the water brooks" (Ps. 42:1), I started gradually feeding myself the Word of God again. It was hard at first. When you have been away from the "water brooks" for a time, you don't realize how dehydrated you are.

At first I started every day with a prepared Bible study and then began rereading whole books of the Bible. A year later I started to write my own discipleship training manuals. I had been revived.

During this same season of renewal, I had been walking our neighborhood and felt the Lord impress on me that Tim and I should open our home to whoever wanted to come over that needed ministry or fellowship. We were craving real fellowship and community, and we knew that others were too. Tim and I started inviting everyone we knew to come over for food and fellowship on Friday nights. Ten years later we were still meeting every Friday night.

We started this gathering with a simple dinner. I cooked for everyone; then after dinner we worshipped. I was a worship leader, so it was easy for me to just sit down at the piano or pick up my guitar and start leading everyone in songs. Soon we moved to dinner, worship, and then prayer each week.

A year or so later we started sharing the Word in turn, and this little gathering of a few close friends developed into a vibrant home gathering. After five years it became a house church with elders and then became a fellowship of three house churches called Reality Community. This gathering would play a critical part in my walk with God, the spiritual growth in our family, and our ministry to others through our careers.

ROMANIAN PRAYER ROOM

Five years into this weekly gathering in our home, I went to Romania with my spiritual mother, Helen. Mike and Helen Lambert had become elders and leaders with us in our weekly community. God was on the move.

Cornel Bistrian, a dear friend whom we'd supported off and on while he and his wife built a Christ For The Nations Bible school in Cluj-Napoca, Romania, came to our home one night. As Cornel shared his story, Helen and I both caught a vision to go to Romania and help at the Bible school. We talked to our husbands about it, and they enthusiastically encouraged us to go. Soon Helen and I were headed over the ocean to give Cornel and Dorina a week off from ministering to over one hundred Romanian students.

That week in Romania changed my life. It shifted everything in my career and ministry.

The shift began in a Romanian prayer room. On Tuesday and Thursday mornings the students were encouraged to come together for prayer—it was not required but highly suggested. Cornel asked Helen and me if we would help them lead the prayer meeting, and we were honored to do so.

In that long, upper-floor room of that Romanian Bible school, I was reminded of who I really was. I remembered the hungry Bible college student I had been at eighteen, when I drove to school early every day to pray with the African students who really needed breakthrough from God. I remembered their fervent petitions, their meditations and prayers from the Scriptures, and their passion for more of God's presence in their lives. They had left everything—including their wives and children—to come to Bible college in America. They were going to make sure they touched God during that season. For them, that quest started in the prayer room early each morning.

Now, here I was, reliving that passion for prayer. This time it was showing up in the form of young Romanian Bible school students who didn't have much in terms of material possessions but who had much of God.

Many students kept their milk outside their windows because the entire school had only one small refrigerator to share. The students came from small villages all over the former communist nation to be trained in ministry for their area. Many were in Cluj going to a state university during the day to please their parents, but at night they were digging into the call of God on their lives. These kids were desperate for God, and it made me realize something: I had been Americanized. I was self-sufficient. I was a powerful campaign manager for a United States congressman. I had gifts and talents galore, but in that room, I needed God. "Blessed are the poor in spirit, for theirs is the kingdom of heaven" (Matt. 5:3).

Cluj, Romania, was where I began my journey to recalibrate my life—not just in the Word of God but in the place of prayer. It was where God humbled me again like He had in Bible school, so many years ago. I had put away my singing, acting, and writing while at CFNI so I could find my identity not in my talents but in Jesus. When I became successful and fulfilled in politics, I was at a spiritual breaking point again. I had forgotten who I really was.

Just as He had from the beginning of my relationship with Him, God wanted me to find true prosperity and dependence at His feet.

NATIONAL PRAYERLESSNESS

I have seen two serious issues repeatedly in the modern American church as it relates to our prayerlessness. First, we forget that we can talk to God—that He is a real person with real feelings and that He really cares for us.

What is prayer? Basically, it is talking with God.

Having a relationship with anyone without talking with him or her is impossible. Talking but not listening to someone is also a problem.

Relationships have to involve two-way communication, and this is just as important with God as with our fellow human beings. We talk, and more importantly, we listen.

In Luke 11, the disciples had spent months with Jesus. They had seen Him heal the sick, feed more than five thousand people with just a few loaves and fishes, and impact people's hearts and lives forever. It is fascinating to me that they didn't ask Jesus how they could follow in His footsteps and do all those important works. Instead, they made a simple request: "Lord, teach us to pray."

They knew instinctively that His power came from somewhere. His ability to do miracles and healings couldn't be taught. The power that flowed from Him came from His relationship with the Father.

> Now it came to pass, as He was praying in a certain place, when He ceased, that one of His disciples said to Him, "Lord, teach us to pray, as John also taught his disciples." So He said to them, "When you pray, say..."
>
> —LUKE 11:1–2

Jesus instructed them to make time to pray. He said *when* you pray, not *if* you pray. Then Jesus Himself, God in the flesh, gave these weak disciples an indispensable outline for praying to the Father in what we call the Lord's Prayer.

The American church must start again at the beginning. We must go back to simply talking with God. We need to remember that we can't survive a year, a month, or even a week in a prosperous place in our souls if we don't start talking to Him on a regular basis. It doesn't have to be complicated; we just need to be consistently in need of Him.

Second, we forget that we can regularly talk to God about our national burdens and about specific people—even government officials, people in the news, and, God forbid, our enemies. We know something is not right in our nation. When we watch the news and see corruption, debauchery, or injustice in our cities, we shudder. As believers we have God's heart for our nation, and we wonder what is happening to the land that we love. What is happening to the foundations of truth, kindness, and just laws that we know were sewn into the fabric of our nation from the beginning? We are worried and concerned—as we should be.

We see lawlessness springing up everywhere while prideful leaders prop themselves up as the national saviors. Our children and grandchildren are feeling lost, alone, and overstimulated; they are overcome with deception as they abandon truth.

Why do we see it all? Because the Spirit of God is *in* us. If we are Christians and have been born again by the Holy Spirit, then we have the Holy Spirit inside us, and He will "teach [us] all things" (John 14:26). When we study the Bible, we find truth and wisdom. Our discernment is heightened. We know deep inside that things are not right in America. We start being concerned about the generations who will follow us, so we begin looking for solutions to our national crisis. We are awake and know that something must change.

The question then arises, "God, what would You have us do?"

We must begin with the most important act: prayer! We agree with God's heart for our nation and the problems in it. We take our burdens for America to the feet of Jesus.

After almost two decades of political activism and political jobs, I have seen many horrible national problems. I have seen members of Congress who can't get their heads around even a tenth of the issues. I have seen few people with solutions, and I have seen what the pressure of carrying these immense problems can do to individuals. The pressures and burdens can consume and destroy well-meaning people from the inside out.

As Christians we should have discernment. We should be the ones who are sensing what is really happening in our nation. We cannot, however, let what is happening—no matter how real the issues are—eat us up and spit us out.

Anger and fear concerning what we see—the injustices, lawlessness, national failures, and worldly corruption—can cause us to want to fight back and rush in with solutions. That is the nature of God in us: the God of justice and the God of order. Yet we cannot solve anything without Him. We can't overcome and fix all the problems in our flesh. We can't do anything without His grace, and we can't constantly carry the burden of it all in our hearts and minds.

Over the years, I have seen sweet brothers and sisters in Christ (who I know follow God) be consumed by the news of the day and the latest crisis in our nation and then lose touch with the heart of God regarding it. We can't let the burden overtake us, though we must still engage with it. The only way to engage and not be overtaken is to bathe the battle in prayer.

We are called to engage in hard things like politics, business, education, and media. We are called to get our hands dirty. While we actively engage, we must also roll these heavy burdens onto God's big, capable shoulders. It is a dichotomy that God orchestrates in His kingdom: He puts us in the sandbox to play, but He is the one who is really building the castles out of our weak and fragile designs.

We *get* to pray. We get to be a partner in His story. It is so exciting that He lets us be a part.

God has plans for America just like He does for every nation on the earth:

> The LORD brings the counsel of the nations to nothing; He makes the plans of the peoples of no effect. The counsel of the LORD stands forever, the plans of His heart to all generations. Blessed is the nation whose God is the LORD, the people He has chosen as His own inheritance.
>
> —PSALM 33:10–12

Then we have the simple command of the Lord that we should pray for all in authority over us so that we might live quietly and peaceably.

After the apostle Paul charges young Timothy, his spiritual son, to "wage the good warfare" (1 Tim. 1:18), he writes this important passage for all of us:

> Therefore, I exhort first of all that supplications, prayers, inter-cessions, and giving of thanks be made for all men, for kings and all who are in authority, that we may lead a quiet and peaceable life in all godliness and reverence. For this is good and accept-able in the sight of God our Savior, who desires all men to be saved and to come to the knowledge of the truth.
>
> —1 TIMOTHY 2:1–4

Prayers and the "giving of thanks" for people in authority over us—whether our police officers, mayors, Congress members, or president—is a holy thing. God desires for them all to be saved and to "come to the knowledge of the truth." This is His perfect will spelled out for us. When we pray for our leaders and ask God to intercede, we are truly leaning on Him in the way He intends for us.

This is our highest calling as American Christians. We have been awakened for a purpose: to bring supplications, prayers, intercessions, and thanksgiving before the King of kings on behalf of our "kings." This should not be a religious afterthought. It should be part of our lifestyle.

We live in a critical time in history. Let us petition the Lord for His will to be done, for all people to be "saved and to come to the knowledge of the truth." That is what we do with these deep national burdens—we throw them back to Jesus and partner with Him in the place of prayer. He will get all the glory from our obedience.

TURNING OFF THE NEWS

After returning from Romania that year, I decided to turn off the constant drip of news coverage. I had a small TV on my desk that I switched back and forth between Fox News and C-SPAN so I could follow what was happening on Capitol Hill and the rest of the country while I worked.

When I got back to my office, I put the TV away and stopped my daily consuming of talk radio shows as well. Just like that. I then enjoyed the quiet.

I didn't put my head in the sand. I continued to stay informed, but I did it in a strategic way, cutting out as many of the voices that were filling my thoughts as I could. Over the course of the next few months, I realized that I could hear God exponentially more clearly.

I set up email alerts from The Hill, Fox News, and other state and local publications so that I could remain connected. But during the day I turned on worship music or listened to scripture being read while I worked. In between phone calls and emails, I could breathe, and my head was clear. Even though I was still engaging, I was not being consumed by the onslaught of the messages.

As I look back on that decision—over a decade later—I have never regretted it. I personally believe it is one of the reasons that many of these stories came to be.

God loves to speak to us. He wants us to see His "will be done on earth as it is in heaven" (Matt. 6:10). He wants us to hear His voice, but we have to be diligent about setting boundaries for our lives, cutting out the noise when we know we must.

FINDING GOD IN THE WOODS

When I was ten years old, our fifth-grade class went to an outdoor SDA school in the Kentucky–Tennessee area. During the fall, we spent five days with our teachers away from our parents at what was otherwise a summer camp location. It was a year after my dad's Revelation seminar where I had sat on the front row listening intently.

Since the beginning of the year, we had looked forward to the extended overnight camp, which was created in the hope that we would discover something about science and nature that would stick with us. The instructors also added a spiritual element by teaching on creation and the importance of the Bible.

One afternoon when the weather was perfect, they gave each of us a notepad and instructions to go into the woods and find a place to "spend time with God" in the nature He created, though we were not to go too far away from the adults at the camp.

We were instructed to find one psalm, then read it, think about it, and talk to God about it.

I wandered, probably further than I was supposed to go, until I was in complete solitude. Seeing no other kids around me, I found an old log to sit on. I had spent hours sitting in trees reading as a kid, so I wasn't worried about bugs or anything else. I turned randomly to Psalm 27. I read it once. I read it twice. Then it happened. Tears started welling in my eyes (as would become a pattern in my life) as I read these words:

> One thing I have desired of the LORD, that will I seek: that I may dwell in the house of the LORD all the days of my life, to behold the beauty of the LORD, and to inquire in His temple. For in the

time of trouble He shall hide me in His pavilion; in the secret place of His tabernacle He shall hide me; He shall set me high upon a rock.

—PSALM 27:4–5

I felt God. I just breathed in His presence. This went much deeper than hearing the Bible stories in Sabbath school and trying to apply those stories to my young ten-year-old life. God was touching my heart and letting me know He was near.

I wrote down on the notepad a few things about what Jesus was speaking to my young heart. If this was what reading the Bible was like, then I didn't want to forget the feeling.

WAR-ROOM WOMAN

The first week I started as the new campaign manager for Congressman Hensarling, I received a call from his regional representative in Athens, Richard Sanders. Richard had been so sweet to me as an intern. When he occasionally called the Dallas office to talk to one of the staff members, he always made a point of lingering on the phone with me for a few minutes, asking me questions and getting to know me.

Now that I was permanent staff, he reached out to welcome me to the team.

We met that first week for lunch, and this good-hearted East Texas man, who loved people and had a heart of service, welcomed this new girl to the team. Over a three-hour lunch, Richard gave me the rundown of everything I needed to know about the offices and the congressman and his family, as well as how they liked to do business at a higher caliber than most government offices. Because of the insights Richard gave me on just that one day, I was a better employee.

Richard grew up in a family of nine children, which included two cousins being raised by his parents and seven biological brothers and sisters. He played football in high school and college, and he was a great family man with two daughters whom he adored. He was an entrepreneur as well as a political operative and relationship builder like few I have ever met.

Having run unsuccessfully for Henderson County judge in 2001, Richard was then recruited by a young man with thick, brown hair named Jeb Hensarling to help him run for Congress in the Fifth District of Texas. From that point on, this gentle giant never left Jeb's side. He became a wealth of information and relationships, and he truly had a servant's heart. In later years, Congressman Hensarling acknowledged Richard as one of the best colleagues he ever served with.

After eight years of serving as Jeb's regional representative all over the rural counties of our district, Richard tried again to run for Henderson County judge. This time he was successful.

During his tenure Richard listened carefully to people and sought to impart the vision of their individual responsibility for finding solutions. His approach empowered people, countering the belief that the government was the answer to all their problems and difficulties.

The moment of testing and truth came shortly after he took office as county judge. In early December 2011, the county government received a letter from the Freedom From Religion Foundation regarding the manger scene on the courthouse lawn, "stating that since the manger scene is the only seasonal display on the grounds, it is an endorsement of the Christian religion, and therefore unconstitutional."[1]

Judge Sanders responded, "We've got an array of decorations and feel that we are in compliance with federal law. We're not pushing any religion down anybody's throat. These are holiday decorations we enjoy. If there was a groundswell against it in Henderson County, it would be different. But everybody I've talked to in Henderson County has been very positive."[2]

Four pastors then organized a rally in support of the county officials' decision to keep the manger scene, and five thousand people congregated in Athens on the courthouse lawn.[3] This was especially notable given that the population of Athens was less than thirteen thousand people at the time. The show of support was an amazing sight, and Athens, Texas, made national news because of it.

The political courage Richard and other officials displayed in the face of these challenges even led then Texas attorney general Greg Abbott to respond with a letter supporting the town and the county officials.

Coming off a great local and state victory, Richard then had another enemy knock on his door: cancer.

One day, I got a call from Phillip Smith, our regional representative who had taken Richard's place, saying they had found colon cancer that had metastasized to four places in Richard's liver. He had stage IV cancer.

"Does the congressman know?" I asked Phillip.

"Yes, he was one of the first people he called," Phillip replied.

There is something about crisis in our lives that teaches us to pray. The situation with Richard was the first time in my political career when I didn't care what people thought of me. If I looked like a crazy Christian to them, so what? I was on a mission to save my friend from destruction.

Years later Richard's wife, Kathy, told me she remembered everything about that day when I marched into Richard's hospital room after his first surgery. I had written out six to ten healing scriptures on small index cards. I began praying them every day for Richard, and I directed him to do the same thing. I had other passages for him and a passion to see to it that the devil would not take my friend's life.

I felt like Miss Clara in the movie *War Room* who would not stop praying until she saw answers to her prayers. I was relentless, and Richard and Kathy knew I was serious.

Praying with boldness over Richard as he lay on the hospital bed that day, it hit me that prayer is not just a casual thing we do when we meet crisis. Effective prayer is to be an extension of our lives every day as we walk with God. Jesus' disciples discovered what Jesus already knew: if they learned to spend time with the Father, the Father would rub off on them.

Though my community of political friends was in crisis in that moment, I believed a miracle was coming. To be clear, a lot of people were praying for Richard's healing. He lived another four years—way past the time that any doctor thought possible.

Through the years that I knew Richard, he was never in a hurry when he was with me. He was always full of hope and treated me like I was the most important person in the room. He treated everyone in his life exactly like that. Let's just say that every prayer I prayed for him was worth every minute.

PRAYER THAT LED TO A CAMPAIGN

In October 2017, Tim and I took our son and future daughter-in-law, along with some other young people, to a prayer gathering at the National Mall in Washington, DC. The gathering was led by Lou Engle of TheCall and David Bradshaw of Awaken the Dawn. For three days we joined in 24/7 prayer and worship over America from tents for all fifty states and eight regions. Then on the last day, we met together for an extended prayer meeting. From eight in the morning till five in the evening, we prayed facing the Capitol with the Washington Monument behind us.

We prayed for women and men to rise up and be who God created them to be. We prayed for an end to abortion in our generation. We prayed for a breakthrough in the body of Christ across racial and denominational lines. We prayed for our inner cities. And we prayed for laborers to be sent into the harvest fields of America.

Less than six weeks later, I was running for Congress.

Representative Hensarling announced his retirement from Congress on a Thursday. Immediately after I sent out the email to our lists, I called state senator Bryan Hughes, a strong conservative in the district (in Mineola). He was my top pick for a replacement, and I was confident that he would be Jeb's pick as well, though we had never had that conversation. Having been close political friends for over ten years at that point, Bryan and I talked for a long time. I had my talking points and my case ready. Senator Hughes, in my mind, was supposed to run for Congress. He had the perfect combination of a conservative policy record; a loving, outgoing personality; and a boldness that was unmatched in our movement. I told Bryan that I needed to know by Monday. If he agreed to run, then I would be all in with him as one of his consultants for the race.

While waiting for Bryan's decision, I heard through the rumor mill, talk radio, and Twitter that state representative Kenneth Sheets and Allen West, the former congressman from Florida who now lived in Texas, were looking at the race too.

That weekend Corey Russell (one of my ministry friends and mentors in prayer) was coming to town for some speaking engagements. I determined that for a few days I would not worry about Jeb's replacement.

Rather, I would pray, fast, and trust that God would raise up the right person. My plan was to follow Corey around for the weekend, listening to his messages and setting my heart on the Lord.

The burden I felt that weekend—to intercede for the people of that district, for Senator Hughes, for the Hensarling family, and for the nation— was unlike anything I ever experienced before or since. It was deep, like I was carrying something that was uniquely mine to pray. I had knowledge of the district and the players who would be involved in this race, and I knew what the activists were looking for. I knew the needs and how to best pray for the right person in the right role. As the main political consultant who knew the district well, I certainly would have a part to play in this race. I desperately wanted this seat to be filled by the right person.

On the following Monday morning Bryan called. He told me quickly and directly that he didn't feel called to run for Congress; it just wasn't for him. He felt he could do more for Texans in the state legislature in Austin than he could in Washington, DC, with all the gridlock. It wasn't the first time I'd heard that sentiment.

I was devastated; I was so convinced that Bryan was the answer for the Fifth Congressional District that I didn't have any backup candidates. Bryan was supposed to be the one. The only other conservative senator in the district (who was currently one of my clients) was Bob Hall, a seventy-five-year-old running in the primary race of his life. He decided not to do it. The rest of the state representatives in the district didn't have the conservative credentials to quickly galvanize support in all seven counties.

The only other person I could think of with all the needed qualities was county judge Richard Sanders. However, Richard was in recovery from cancer and still weak, and he was slowing down in his career. When Richard graciously declined, I started talking to Jeb's current regional representative, Phillip Smith.

Phillip was another person with the charisma and governmental knowledge to make it happen in such a short time. He didn't have the fundraising experience I did, but I figured if I helped him, we could get it done. Phillip weighed it hard, but with two children still at home, he didn't want to take the risk.

I then heard through the grapevine that state representative Matt

Schaefer was looking seriously at the race. Matt was also a current client of my firm, but his state house district was not directly in the congressional district, though it was in the East Texas media market. Since he was chairman of the Texas Freedom Caucus, I hoped that if Matt took a poll, he would come up with at least a 20 percent to 25 percent favorable name recognition in the congressional district.

About a week after Jeb announced his retirement, I called Matt and his wife, Jasilyn, to talk it over. I couldn't wait. Every minute counts when congressional seats open without an incumbent running. Matt and I both knew what would await him in Washington if he chose to run, and he wasn't willing to raise his kids on a part-time basis.

By Friday, I still didn't have a candidate, and I was getting frustrated. I was talking regularly to my friends Kevin Brannon, state senator Van Taylor (who was running for Congress in the Third District), and Bob Pipkin with Club for Growth (an influential limited-government, free-enterprise advocacy group in Washington, DC). They all trusted that I was one of the leading experts on the district and thought I understood what kind of candidate the conservative movement needed. While all these conversations were happening, I was still feeling the burden to intercede for the district and for the right person to find his or her place in this race.

One evening I walked into the living room, and my husband commented, "What are you going to do? Are you about to throw yourself on the tracks in front of a moving train?" That was his way of not asking the *real* question—one that remained in the empty space between us: Was I going to run?

I hadn't even told Tim that every potential candidate I talked to kept turning it back on me, saying, "Bunni, you should run!" At the end of Senator Hughes's conversation with me, he had said, "Bunni, you are the one who really carries the burden for Washington, DC. You should run. I would support you 100 percent."

Late that fall night, when I finished going back and forth with Matt and Jasilyn for over an hour, Jasilyn also ended the conversation with "Bunni, I think you are the expert on what the district needs, and you have the heart for it. You should run!"

That Friday, now over a week since Jeb announced his retirement, Bob Pipkin called for his daily check in. I don't know why, but something in my heart said I should tell him my story, so I did. I described my journey from being a pest control business owner to a restaurant owner to a college graduate at age thirty-two while homeschooling my boys to being the campaign manager for the incumbent to now having built one of the largest GOP consulting firms in the state with thirty-two clients. At the end of that ten-minute narrative I said, "Bob, what this district needs is a person who has small business know-how, is an executive leader, is a solid conservative with a record in the movement, and can raise the money to get it done in such a short window of time."

I paused to take a breath, and Bob quickly jumped in. "Bunni, the Club has supported candidates with a profile similar to yours—a small business background and a record of advancing conservative principles. You should meet with the endorsement committee if you're serious about running. I'll be happy to put you in touch with them."

I got off the phone and sat still, staring at the wall in front of me from behind my large antique desk at my consulting firm. "What just happened?" I thought. "I can't really be thinking about this. Am I really thinking about this?"

I remembered a meeting I'd attended a few days before with twenty other leaders and political activists who had come from all over the district. Their agenda was to meet and discuss the kind of candidate they were looking for to fill this important seat in Congress. I promptly pulled my notes from the meeting out of my purse.

Someone who knows the Constitution. *Check.*

Someone who knows federal public policy. *Check.*

Someone who has a record of being a consistent conservative in some tangible way. *Check.*

Someone who could mobilize support in all seven counties in a short amount of time. *Check.*

Someone who understands the average person, the struggles of small businesses, and the needs of everyday Americans. *Check.*

Lastly—and the main thing everyone in the room was concerned about—a conservative who could raise the money to get their message out quickly and who could win. *Maybe.*

Could I do that? I was a political consultant and fundraiser, yet would donors potentially believe in me? "I can't believe I am thinking about this. I am crazy!" I thought.

I then made my way to the front door, walked outside, and called four people to vet this crazy idea: state senator Van Taylor, Kevin Brannon, Brenda Pejovich (Jeb's treasurer for his first race), and state senator Bob Hall.

STEPPING INTO AN ADVENTURE

Later in the afternoon I got home in time to prepare for our church meeting. I told Tim about the conversations. We were both weighing it all reluctantly.

That night at our house church, the fellowship knew that I was burdened about the district and Jeb's retirement. They asked if they could pray for Tim and me at the end of the meeting. Gathering around us, our friends and spiritual community prayed about the salt and light that our family had become and for God to bring our light out further than He had done ever before. Mike Lambert, our spiritual father who was currently living in Israel, prayed over the phone that God would provide the right candidate for the Fifth District of Texas—the way He had called David while the young man was out watching his sheep, strumming his harp.

"Could that be me?" I wondered.

When we finished praying, I felt even more uneasy. Then my phone rang. I had forgotten to turn off the ringer before church started, so I quickly picked it up and saw that it was a political friend who knew about the search I was on. Within a few minutes that person encouraged me to run, told me that they would financially support me if I did, and laid out a potential plan to victory for me. I was stunned.

What in the world was happening? I never saw it coming.

In a matter of two weeks, God had called me to step into an adventure with Him that would radically shift everything in my life. At that moment I knew that if I didn't run, I would be disobedient to the call of God on my life.

The next day I showed up at my boss's door and asked him for his endorsement. Though it would be a few more weeks before I would give the formal announcement, I knew I was running for his seat in Congress.

JESUS' KEEPING PRAYERS

I pray for them. I do not pray for the world but for those whom You have given Me, for they are Yours. And all Mine are Yours, and Yours are Mine, and I am glorified in them. Now I am no longer in the world, but these are in the world, and I come to You. Holy Father, keep through Your name those whom You have given Me, that they may be one as We are. While I was with them in the world, I kept them in Your name. Those whom You gave Me I have kept; and none of them is lost except the son of perdition, that the Scripture might be fulfilled.

—JOHN 17:9–12

One of the Bible's descriptions of Jesus is that He is our great intercessor. If you have ever met a person who is called to be an intercessor, you know the power of that calling. The true intercessors I have met are single-minded, steadfast, loyal, faith-filled, zealous, and tenacious. They keep going in prayer even when everyone else around them gives up or couldn't care less about prayer.

Jesus is the ultimate intercessor for us. The night before His death, He was thinking about His disciples. He was praying that God the Father would keep them steadfast. He was praying that they would not be moved. He was declaring over them that He would keep them through His name.

His prayer continues even today as He stands at the right hand of the Father.

But He, because He continues forever, has an unchangeable priesthood. Therefore He is also able to save to the uttermost those who come to God through Him, since He always lives to make intercession for them. For such a High Priest was fitting for us, who is holy, harmless, undefiled, separate from sinners, and has become higher than the heavens.

—Hebrews 7:24–26

I have prayed these passages over my life constantly, and they give me so much comfort because I know He has me. He had me during that race for Congress, and He has me now in my new season. He won't let me fall so far that He cannot reach me. He is praying for *me* day and night, all the time interceding to the Father that I will be kept in Him. He will not lose me! He will not let me go!

Jesus, the great intercessor, has supernatural keeping power.

Many times we elevate sin and the devil in our minds; we meditate on the deep and great darkness that we are constantly fighting. We elevate the noise in our culture with its bad news and crisis points. We may think that all this is too big for God to handle.

We all have struggles and feel the power of evil, but Jesus is bigger than our flesh, our selfishness, and even the external warfare within our culture. His keeping power is greater than the power of the enemy. When we feel weak, He is strong.

I love the picture of Jesus as the great intercessor standing up, doing warfare for us—telling the devil, "Get away from My kids that I have redeemed. I have them! I bought them with My blood. They are Mine."

If Jesus is continually praying for you and me, why wouldn't we want to join with Him in those prayer meetings? Every moment of every day I can hear His heart and His prayers. I pray alongside Him for myself and my family, for others, and for our leaders and our nation. Jesus is constantly praying for His church—His body. As I get closer to His heart, my heart cries out more and more for His church to come into the fullness of everything Jesus wants us to walk in. His heart is beating for us. He is praying for us.

Jesus is also continually praying for lost and hurting humanity. The closer I get to Jesus and pray His prayers, the more I hurt for humanity and for the lost sheep. I feel His heart and His love for people more.

Do we trust that the great Intercessor can keep us in His love?

Do we trust Him enough to spend some of our time joining with Him in prayer for the church and the harvest of people yet to be found? What about the critical issues in our nation and our elected officials who are putting their lives on the front lines of the battle?

Interacting with the person of Jesus is *prayer*. He is real. Will we ask Him to teach us to pray?

Keep your heart with all diligence, for out of it are the issues of life.

—Proverbs 4:23, MEV

When our hearts are corrupted, everything is affected. The content of our souls will eventually come out of our mouths. If we don't deal with the root cause called sin, we will lose our testimony, our effectiveness, and the fruit that waits for us. Applying the truth to our own lives is the only medicine that can heal. Ultimately the highest calling in our lives as Christians is to be like Jesus.

Chapter 5

THE ENEMIES OF OUR SOULS IN POLITICS

EVIL IS MANIFESTED more clearly in politics than in many other professions. The shades of gray seem to be darker. Ethics are twisted to produce the results that politicians desire.

We know instinctively that lies and deception are not morally right, yet we see these activities in campaigns all over the country. Some candidates tell half-truths and make up stories as they are pitted against each other in close races. Voters need to do their research to look past the lies and make careful, well-thought-out choices.

What I call whisper campaigns—backstabbing friends spreading rumors and false facts about someone to try to sway a race—are not healthy for politics or life, but they are common occurrences at all levels of politics. Obnoxious pride and power's lure can corrupt individuals, families, and organizations to the point of manipulating elections and buying influence.

We see the destruction caused by unhealthy politics every day when we watch our favorite news channels or read our local and national newspapers. Seeing the plethora of stories where so-called leaders are attacking each other, it's a wonder any sane human being would want to get involved in politics.

But there comes a time in the world of government and politics when enough is enough. Even when we see the worst of such destructive behavior in campaigns, we expect there to be some sort of civility after people are elected. As citizens we hope these officials will try to be respectful to each other in a working environment, despite their disagreements. We hope they will be honest about their positions on bills and issues. There are codes of conduct—official and unofficial—that leaders are expected to adhere to in their legislative bodies and local communities.

If a legislator says he or she will vote for something and then does the opposite, that member loses credibility with both their leadership and other members. If a council member promises to do something for an interest group in his or her city on a local issue but doesn't follow through, that council member should probably expect to have a strong opponent in the next election. We as citizens expect some sort of ethical behavior from our public servants. Sometimes it happens; sometimes it does not.

So how are we supposed to deal with our hearts, especially as believers, when engaging in the dirty, mudslinging world of politics?

We know we must be engaged if our nation is ever going to get better. But how many of us really want to get in the mud pit?

We need Christians to be candidates who run for office, staffers who work on issues, and parliamentarians who enforce the rules. Christians make great judges, congresspeople, and city managers. They make good legislative staffers, political activists, and citizen lobbyists—but only if they can live honorable, upright lives.

Working in and with government through the years, I have often felt like I needed to take a bath to wash off all the muck and mire from the day. I have imagined getting under a giant shower head and letting the water of the Word of God cleanse me from all the dust I have picked up in this political journey. Too often the dirt is unavoidable. The war comes to us in this arena, whether we want it to or not.

Over the decades I have identified three major enemies of our souls in the political arena: pride, anger, and fear. The devil himself is our ultimate enemy, but these expressions of his nature try to make us ineffective and steal our fruit. We must proactively go to war against them in our souls.

PRIDE

For if anyone thinks himself to be something, when he is nothing, he deceives himself.

—GALATIANS 6:3

The first day I got my new business cards showing that I was the campaign manager for Rep. Jeb Hensarling, my heart naturally filled with pride. I had worked so hard to get there—night school for three and a half years, countless conversations with political operatives asking questions to gain wisdom, and many hours of volunteering. It had not been an easy road to get that title, but the day had finally arrived. I had created these cool linen business cards, printed with blue and red lettering and the congressman's campaign logo. They came to my front door, beautifully crafted in a box of five hundred.

After carefully opening the box, I took out a card and felt the edges and even smelled them. I was proud that as a mom, wife, and former business owner I had made it. I was in politics full time. I was the campaign manager for a United States congressman.

When I went to church and people asked me how I was doing, I said, "Great! I am the campaign manager for a US congressman now."

"Wow! Amazing!" they'd exclaim.

I loved passing out my cards, making my new job known, and hinting to others in a subtle way that I had *access*.

It is clever how pride sneaks into our lives and how quickly it enters political activity. I have seen sweet, humble believers suddenly think really highly of themselves after getting their pictures taken with the governor or obtaining a legislator's cell phone number.

Pride displays itself when we try to cut others out of our spaces of influence, keep others down, and constantly compare ourselves with other people. Eventually what is in our hearts will come out. It will manifest through our aggressive or condescending comments, whether spoken or written, to others. It will come out in our cutting remarks on social media or in slight attacks against others behind their backs.

When pride rises in my own heart, I will eventually identify it, though it might take me a while to get there. At times, I have heard myself commenting about someone else and shuddered at the absolute horror of what I said. I have occasionally had trusted Christian friends in politics call me out on a prideful statement. (Thankfully, that has not been too often!) If we don't identify pride in our hearts and deal with it, this enemy *will* take over. Whenever we see it, we must confront it.

Have you seen someone you know get involved in politics and then become such an ugly, horrible person on social media that you don't even want to be around that person anymore?

Through the years I have seen activists who love God and love country—people with good hearts—get called into this arena. But then ten years down the line, they become such hateful people that I want nothing to do with them, even if we are engaging on the same side. This should not be! Unfortunately, it happens because we don't remain diligent in dealing with the pride that so easily fills our souls when engaging in politics or media. Many times in my career, I have had to take my heart to task in this area and war against pride in a real, clear way.

One Sunday I knew my heart was cold and full of pride. I needed to worship, so I went to a megachurch in my area. At the end of the message I was the first person at the altar, kneeling before the Lord. No one there knew me, and I didn't care. I knew I needed to get this pride out of my heart by any means possible. The physical act of kneeling before the Lord broke something open inside me.

When I am feeling like I am better than others because of all the powerful people I walk with, I have to remind myself that I am here only because God has enabled me and empowered me by His grace. To combat this enemy, oftentimes I go into a public place and begin talking with someone, asking how I can pray for him or her. In this simple act of obedience, whether I feel it or not, the chains of pride come off my heart as I share the gospel with the person before me. As I do so, I am reminded that I, too, am saved by grace through faith.

ANGER

> Let all bitterness, wrath, anger, clamor, and evil speaking be put
> away from you, with all malice.
>
> —EPHESIANS 4:31

Many of the same people in politics who have been eaten up by pride
have also had anger eat their lunch. These two enemies like to move
together, devouring whomever they get their claws into. Pride is more
subtle than anger and usually comes first. Anger feeds off pride.

Many times we get angry at another person when we think we could
do better than him or her. Other times we get angry when someone takes
advantage of or hurts another person or makes an unrighteous stand.

As we look at our national political climate, it is right to get angry at
real injustices, but then it is all too easy to direct that anger to individuals and attack them with name-calling. It is not good to react in a spirit
of anger, forgetting that they, even in a fallen state, were created in the
image of God. We forget that God still has it in His heart to redeem both
them *and* the situation around us. Carrying burdens on our own, in our
own strength—even righteous indignation—can cause anger to take over
our souls. This is another reason why getting into a quiet place with Jesus
for solitude and reflection with Him when we are fighting against injustices is so important.

Anger can start as a small root of bitterness that then becomes a well-
spring of pain and hurt. We get offended by words spoken, actions taken,
or votes cast or by being overlooked or unacknowledged. This bitterness
can start small but if not dealt with can consume our hearts to the point
that it colors everything we do.

It took me a long time to deal with all the hurt and betrayals I experienced during my campaign for Congress. I had to work through the
anger and keep going to Jesus in prayer. I knew I was free when anger
stopped spewing out of my mouth every time I talked about the race.

Anger cannot reside in our hearts for long if we want to go forward
in our lives and work to bring true change. One thing I have learned in
politics is that an enemy I have today will most likely be an ally with
me in another fight. So I must keep the door of my heart open and walk

forward quickly. That lesson has helped me in many other aspects of life as well.

FEAR VS. FAITH

> Fear not, for I am with you; be not dismayed, for I am your God.
> I will strengthen you, yes, I will help you, I will uphold you with
> My righteous right hand.
>
> —ISAIAH 41:10

Politicians play on our fears. From text messages and emails to those slick mailers, they tell us that we must get involved because our country will fall apart if we don't. The bad guys will regain control, and then what will we do? Or they highlight this or that policy that will take away our freedoms. Though there is truth in most of these political statements, in the long run fear will never motivate people to action the right way. People who began their journey into politics or government out of fear aren't typically involved for long. And if they are, they are not pushing consistently in the right direction. They are being led by the leash of fear.

On the other hand, those motivated by conviction, revelation, and hope get their hands dirty in civic engagement and do incredible things to impact their communities. The right motivation matters because it impacts the way our souls react when we are in the fight. If we are being controlled by fear, we will always react in fear.

When push comes to shove, political people who are led by hope and faith have a better chance of responding the right way during a hard situation. Their choices may hurt their careers in the short term, but in the long term they will keep their testimonies intact by having the clarity to see things through to the other side.

Fear is short-term thinking. Hope is long-term thinking.

What is true in politics is also true in life. Fear may motivate someone for a short victory, but faith and hope are the only things that will sustain a person for the long haul in this journey called life.

As a political consultant I always had to ask myself what was motivating me: "Am I being motivated by facts or fear when making this decision?"

I have seen members of Congress being pushed against their own consciences on a hard vote but then making the right choice after being confronted with this simple question: Are you being motivated to vote this way out of fear? Analyzing the state of our hearts will help us identify where faith is—or is *not*—and lead us in our choices.

Following faith and hope brings joy. Following fear brings destruction in government and life. The most successful national leaders who motivated the nation for change were people such as presidents Ronald Reagan and John F. Kennedy. Though completely different from each other, they moved America through hope and faith, not fear.

We also can't let fear hold us back from stepping out and choosing a hard path. I once knew a young woman who stepped into a political club and was asked to become president of that club less than a year later. If that young woman had operated in fear, she would have said no. But faith says, "Why not? Let's go for it."

After only a year into my new role as Congressman Hensarling's campaign manager, our chief of staff, Dee Buchanan, asked me to take on all our major donors, not just the smaller ones I had been working on. He asked me to take over all aspects of the campaign even where other contractors were working. I was still new, but I could learn. I wasn't going to let fear hold me back. I had to take the thoughts of fear and turn them into thoughts of faith.

Fear told me it would be hard to befriend millionaires and maintain relationships with the congressman's largest donors. But faith said, "Surely it's not that hard. They are just people who put their pants on one leg at a time."

Fear told me it would be too hard to learn social media and marketing. Faith said, "It is just technology. I can figure it out."

Taking on the added responsibilities helped our campaign's bottom line and my future career path as a political business owner and candidate myself. Thank God, I was motivated by faith that day and not fear.

WORKING THROUGH UNFORGIVENESS

After my campaign for Congress, my husband took me to Disney World for a week to start the recovery process. I rode It's a Small World repeatedly and watched automatons of the American presidents recount our history. I swam around the pool at the hotel and stared at the palm trees waving overhead while lamenting, "What am I going to be when I grow up?"

When we got home, I spent a week on my couch reading my Bible and trying to give my vocal cords a break. I then went back to work to rebuild my company.

On July 15, the Federal Election Commission (FEC) quarterly reports were filed from our race that had ended in May. It was then, for the first time, that I came face to face with how angry and hurt I was.

During the final days of our campaign, I was consumed with watching every penny. Tim and I had loaned the campaign $20,000—a sacrifice from our own savings—and I wanted to make sure I got that money back for our family. I made sure the last expenditures were covered and ended the campaign having raised over $970,000 with $3,000 left over. But from the FEC report, I discovered that soon-to-be Congressman-elect Lance Gooden had not even paid for his runoff. His consultant (who had hidden his involvement) had floated all the invoices for Lance's TV, radio, and mail buys until after the race. His fundraiser had also floated most of her invoices and did not even bill him till after the runoff. They were betting that he would win and then pay them later, guaranteeing a strong relationship on the back end. Unfortunately, this is how it works many times in politics. "You scratch my back, and I will scratch yours."

I had outraised my opponent by $200,000. Here was the hard truth I was now having to swallow: I had paid for my runoff completely while his consultants floated him to victory. Unfortunately this practice is legal, and these vendors, as well as my opponent, were absolutely within the rule of law doing what they did. It still felt so unfair to me. The injustice of being someone who had done everything right yet couldn't win crushed me in that moment.

"I won't get over this quickly," I thought.

That fall, I helped my friends Van Taylor and Ron Wright win their seats in Congress. I also watched from afar as another soon-to-be friend, Michael Cloud, won a seat in South Texas. As much as I wanted to see my friends sworn into Congress, I couldn't make myself go to Washington to their swearing-in ceremony.

After the general election in November, I collapsed. I was spent from those two campaigns and from helping the rest of my clients that year. I still hadn't slowed down enough to really deal with my heart in relation to my race earlier in the year. I was now planning another mission trip to Romania—praying and trying to prepare messages for the two Bible schools I would be visiting, as well as for the churches where I would be ministering. The key word here was *trying*. I was getting nowhere. My heart was so messed up.

In desperation I visited a prayer room in Dallas. As soon as I entered the room, I collapsed into a chair. I wanted to run. I didn't want to stay for the two-hour prayer session, but I knew I needed to be there. I wish I could tell you that I cried or felt the presence of God in that room or forgave everyone instantly. I did not. Instead, I prayed while pacing alongside a wall. I sat with my Bible in my lap, staring at the words with a fog over my eyes. I felt lost. I felt full of anger—and, may I say it, even *hate*.

I knew I had to keep going to those prayer meetings, so I showed up from six o'clock to eight o'clock morning after morning. I pressed through until I could finally look at the ugliness in my own heart. I whispered prayers for God to expose it all and then rip it out of my soul.

We don't have a choice about which injustices come against our lives. I wish we did. Life happens and we get hurt; we get sideswiped in the moments we least expect it. Vicious rumors about my family had been passed around in East Texas via texts and secret Facebook groups while TV ads had portrayed me as a liar and people who I thought were friends turned against me. But it was *much* more than that. It was my anger over the seeming injustice in the FEC report that was keeping me in bondage. I knew there was only one path to healing: I had to run to Jesus. Nothing like walking with imperfect people will cause us to run even harder after a perfect God.

After showing up for two weeks in that prayer room, I found the answer to my heart's problem: I had to let the pain go.

For those two weeks, I prayed for Lance Gooden, the man who had funded the super PAC against me, and the people who had said horrible things against me. I interceded on their behalf—not because I liked them in that moment but because I knew I had a divine command to do so. I laid down my pride, my anger, my fears, and my own thoughts and justifications, and I prayed.

Finally, my heart began to crack open; I could feel again. Tears of healing began their work.

Soon I was off to Romania.

When I returned from my trip in December, I found a Christmas card waiting for me in my mailbox. It was from my previous opponent. It was just a general card sent to all the voters in the district, but their family was so cute, and I was personally starting to heal. I set the card on my desk and prayed.

I prayed for the Gooden family every day after that. Most days I didn't feel anything, but I kept at it—praying for them until God began to fill my heart with love for this precious family.

Love allowed me to move forward.

MOVING OUT OF BITTERNESS

> Looking carefully lest anyone fall short of the grace of God; lest any root of bitterness springing up cause trouble, and by this many become defiled.
>
> —HEBREWS 12:15

The next August, I was down in South Texas working for Rep. Michael Cloud when he told me about his trip to Israel with now congressman Lance Gooden and Lance's wife, Alexa. As he shared about the incredible experience and his appreciation for all his new colleagues, I said, "You know what? I need to throw a party for Congressman Gooden and help pay off his debt from our runoff."

As soon as I said that, tears began running down my face. In the presence of Congressman Cloud and his wife, Rosel, another layer of pain fell off my heart. I now just needed permission to throw that party.

Rafael Cruz, the father of Sen. Ted Cruz, was in South Texas head-lining a few fundraisers for the Cloud campaign. I found an ally in this man who was not afraid to love extravagantly. He loves many things—the Word of God, America, freedom, pastors, his friends, and his family. He also loves to walk early in the morning and frequently reminds all his friends, including me, not to eat processed carbs or sugar. He is preparing every day, by the grace of God, to live to be 125 years old, and I am con-vinced he will get there.

This incredible minister of ministers is not afraid to speak his mind concerning what is right and wrong as he travels our nation. Motivated by his deep love for the body of Christ and his love for America, Rafael lives with abandon. We had developed a friendship through the years, as he was a regular speaker for my political candidates and elected officials.

During my runoff Rafael got permission from Senator Cruz to head-line a couple of fundraisers for me. In his lively style, he solidified many dollars and votes for me in Dallas and Kaufman Counties. I think Rafael knew all along that I was a genuine believer who shared many of his same passions. I never hid my love for Jesus, especially around other believers who were as passionate as I was.

At dinner that night in South Texas, I said, "Rafael, I looked up Lance's campaign debt, and he still owes around $40,000 from our runoff. He still hasn't gotten that paid off yet. I have an idea. What do you think about me throwing him a party to help pay off the rest of his debt?"

Without hesitation this seasoned man of God said, "Sounds like Jesus to me, Bunni. You sow in this season to reap in your next season." Rafael's confirmation was key for me in that moment. Now to get my husband on board.

"Heck, no!" Tim said when I told him my idea. He was adamant. I knew what we had both gone through, and I understood that it was a miracle that I was even thinking about this.

I waited and continued to pray. Then one night a couple of weeks later as Tim watched Congressman Gooden on Fox News, he shouted to me from the other side of the house. "Hey, tell my congressman he is doing a good job." The door was open, and we were both beginning to find freedom.

I texted Lance, saying, "My husband wants me to tell you that he is proud of your service. You are doing a great job."

He immediately replied, "Thanks, Bunni. That means a lot."

"Any chance we could meet for lunch or coffee when you are in the district one day?" I texted back.

"Sure, I'd love that," he texted. "Let me get my team to schedule it."

Around two weeks later Congressman Gooden and I were sitting in a Dallas restaurant for lunch, catching up on our families like old friends and talking about everything politics in Texas and Washington, DC. I told him how his voting record had been amazing since taking office and that, as a constituent, I was extremely proud of him. I then reminded him of my husband's praise.

"That really blessed me when you sent me that. Please give Tim my regards," Lance said. "I think these races are always harder for the spouses than the actual candidates. We are political animals who are used to this mess, but they are not so much."

I agreed. It had been hard for Tim.

At the end of lunch, Lance asked a normal question: "Well, before we leave, what can I do for you?"

I have heard this question through the years from many of the congresspeople I have worked with to help tie up the conversation and finish a meeting.

I held my breath and just went for it. "Well, Congressman, I don't need anything from you in the traditional sense, but I would like to see if you would let me hold a fundraiser for your campaign and help you pay off the rest of your debt from our race."

It took everything in me to not break down in that moment, as I knew the tears were starting to well up in my eyes.

Knowing I was struggling, I am sure, Congressman Gooden said humbly, "Bunni, I would be honored if you would do that for me."

When I got in the car, I broke down and wept. One more chain of bondage was being broken off my heart.

THROWING CONGRESSMAN GOODEN A PARTY

As soon as I got home from my lunch with the congressman, I went to work. I pulled up the list of donors who had helped me over a year and a half before and compared them with Lance's current donors. I called my former finance chairman, Brenda Pejovich, and my former finance vice chairman, Brint Ryan, to ask if they would help with my plan. Brenda was willing to host it at her house and give money, and Brint was willing to lend his name to the invitation, since he had already maxed out financially to Lance. My next call was to Jeb, who was graciously willing to attend. I then called all my former campaign staffers. I even called Congressman Cloud, telling him that the party was on and asking for two weeks off, unpaid, from work. This way I could get the event to the goal that I was shooting for in the time frame.

On election night in 2018, I had called Lance to concede the race when I knew we had lost, but now my heart was finally at the real place of concession. In political circles, it is not unusual for a former opponent to endorse a candidate, but only occasionally have I seen a former opponent host a fundraiser for the other person. For me and my team, it was something deeper, not just being politically nice.

That night in December 2019, after calling all my previous supporters, we raised $35,000 and helped Lance pay off his debt by the end of the year. Many of my former staff were there. My former boss was there, and most importantly, Jesus was there as we honored the winner and the good work Lance had been doing in Congress. For me this act of obedience cut off the last chain of offenses, bitterness, and unforgiveness from around my heart.

WATCHING OUR SOULS CONTINUALLY

People ask me all the time how I have endured all these years in politics. It is an ugly sport at times, but as an activist, consultant, campaign manager, and then a candidate, I have persevered. How have I survived and kept moving forward?

The answer is this: I have dealt with my heart—not perfectly but continually.

We cannot let offenses, bitterness, and unforgiveness take us out or stop our advancement. The enemies of our soul in politics cannot be the things that define us for the long term. We cannot let the trials, pains, and injustices of life steal our hope for the future. Pride, anger, and fear cannot be in the driver's seat of our heart. Our purpose and our future are too important to stay trapped in all the enemy's devices.

Every person on this planet will be confronted at some point with disappointments, failures of their leaders, abuses, persecutions, or some sort of suffering. The strength to endure and overcome comes from one posture alone: on our knees and in radical obedience to what the Lord tells us to do. This is how we conquer these spiritual enemies in politics and in life. This is how we yield to the work of God in our lives. The goal is ultimately not to be right but to be like Jesus.

"Now My soul is troubled. What shall I say? 'Father, save Me from this hour'? Instead, for this reason I came to this hour. Father, glorify Your name." Then a voice came from heaven, saying, "I have glorified it, and will glorify it again."

—JOHN 12:27–28, MEV, EMPHASIS ADDED

Many times we struggle with the idea that God still speaks today. Can God speak through us? Remember—God spoke to Balaam out of the mouth of a donkey. God spoke to a young boy named Samuel giving him a word for the priest, Eli. God spoke to the apostles Peter and John on their way into prayer to heal a lame man. God has a way of using simple vessels who come to Him with open ears. He loves to show His love to people by revealing to them that He sees them. All it takes is for willing vessels to step out and be His mouthpieces on earth.

Chapter 6

CAN GOD SPEAK TO POLITICIANS?

W E HAVE THIS backward idea that what happens in church is sacred but what happens in the rest of our lives is secular. This division of our hearts and minds is what hinders us from being free to walk with God wherever we go. We minimize His power in the places that we don't consider sacred.

Does God reside only within the four walls of a church? Does He have to use a preacher to open our hearts to His Word? Can His precious written words not spring to life for us in the midst of our mundane lives—in our careers, around a water cooler, or even on an airplane with a member of Congress?

We limit God's involvement in our lives every day when we tell Him how, when, and where He can move through us. By not inquiring of Him in every circumstance, we hinder the partnership that we were created for from the beginning. The prayer that Jesus taught us to pray says, "Your kingdom come. Your will be done on earth as it is in heaven" (Luke 11:2).

When we live out biblical Christianity, heaven impacts earth through our lives as we walk with God. Remember how God walked in the Garden of Eden with Adam and Eve? Yet then rebellion formed in their hearts, they chose to disobey, and sin entered the world.

Wasn't the sacrifice of Jesus on the cross the breakthrough needed to bring us back into relationship with our Creator?

Yes, Jesus reconciled humankind back to that intimate walk with God as in the garden. Hearing God speak now is as simple as being open to

His still, small voice in our hearts and letting His Word reign supreme in every part of our lives. "To him the doorkeeper opens, and the sheep hear his voice; and he calls his own sheep by name and leads them out" (John 10:3).

God loves to speak, but the question is, Are we listening?

You Will Have Your Own Field Soon

During my ten years of working for Congressman Hensarling, I rarely traveled with him, though every now and then we had an event that did require travel.

The year was 2012, an election year, when Jeb and I went to San Antonio together for a rare out-of-town fundraiser. Sitting on a Southwest Airlines flight next to my boss, I was reading my Bible where I had left off the day before, the story of the faithful servant in Luke:

> And the Lord said, "Who then is that faithful and wise steward, whom his master will make ruler over his household, to give them their portion of food in due season? Blessed is that servant whom his master will find so doing when he comes. Truly, I say to you that he will make him ruler over all that he has."
>
> —Luke 12:42–44

Jeb, in an unusually chatty fashion, started a conversation with me. Staffers' rule of thumb is to leave an elected official alone if he or she is working, resting, or deep in thought but to go with it if *he or she* strikes up a conversation.

At that time, as the House Republican Conference chairman under Speaker John Boehner, Jeb was the fourth most powerful Republican in the House of Representatives—an assignment he began in 2011. (He used to laughingly tell his constituents that it was the most powerful position in the House that didn't get a security detail.) Being the head congressman responsible for the GOP caucus's communications, talking points, and media strategies was an extremely demanding job. Jeb not only needed to grow his own campaign's war chest but was also responsible for raising more money for House Republicans. It was also his job to counsel the members who couldn't help themselves and went off script from the messaging his team generated.

It was exhausting, and the stress lines on Jeb's face had started to show. On top of that, he had to manage two groups of staffers: his own regular staff and an entirely different office of staffers who served the other members. Dee Buchanan, Jeb's chief of staff (and the man who had hired me), helped run the conference operation, while the new chief of staff, Andrew Duke, managed Jeb's staffers and gave me oversight when needed on the campaign side.

One advantage of Jeb's leadership post was that he was one of four leaders who met together every week to hammer out plans and tactics for the other GOP members. Jeb was known around the Hill as a solid conservative leader who wasn't afraid to speak his mind to the Speaker, but he did it behind closed doors. He didn't air anyone's dirty laundry in front of the media. He was measured and thoughtful and did everything with purpose and tact.

That day on the airplane he was struggling. Being the most conservative member at the leadership table, Jeb was continually hearing the frustrations from the rest of the conservative sections of the conference. He wasn't personally frustrated about policy; for the most part everyone at the leadership table agreed on those issues. Rather, he was frustrated with Speaker Boehner's tactics. I could see the weariness on his face.

As Jeb shared his heart, I just listened. I gave him plenty of space to say his piece. When he finished, he seemed resigned to the fact that he didn't know where he wanted to go in leadership next—whether to stay as the conference chairman for the next term and potentially work his way up the food chain to be Speaker or to simply get out of leadership altogether.

Looking down at my Bible, I was reminded of the verses I had read just a few minutes before. But now they took on a whole new meaning. Without fanfare these words came out of my mouth: "Sir, I was just reading the passage about the faithful and wise steward, and I know God sees your faithfulness to the Speaker. What you are doing is right for what God has called you to. Just keep honoring Boehner in public and speaking your convictions behind closed doors. You are being faithful to watch over his field well, but soon God is going to give you your own field to take care of."

As soon as I said it, I knew it was a word from God. I couldn't have thought that last statement up on my own.

That was September 2012. I will never forget it. I had never had a conversation with Jeb on his desires or potential plans for the future. I didn't even know what his real options were. It is one thing to be a Christian hearing from God in a church setting, but it is another great adventure to have God show up on the job.

A few months later, on January 3, 2013, Rep. Jeb Hensarling was elected by his peers to take over as chairman of the House Financial Services Committee, which oversees the nation's housing and financial services sectors, including banking, insurance, real estate, and more. As chair of this powerful committee Jeb could make his own agenda and work on his own policy incentives.

The man got his own "field."

He served faithfully in that field for six years (three terms) until his retirement from Congress at the end of 2018.

God Loves Israel and Lee Zeldin

In 2017 I was using my consulting firm to help other members of Congress such as Sean Duffy (WI-7), Andy Barr (KY-6), Mia Love (UT-4), and a young member named Lee Zeldin (NY-1), who had first come to Dallas in 2016. At that time he was one of only two Jewish Republicans in Congress, and I was extremely excited about his impact in the nation's capital.

Working in pro-Israel activism with the American Israel Public Affairs Committee (AIPAC), I had gone to Israel in 2015 with their educational foundation alongside a group of pastors and Christian government leaders. I was now even more enthusiastic to get Christians involved in standing up for our greatest ally in the Middle East.

Some of my Jewish friends in Dallas had hosted this then freshman member for a reception in their home. I was completely impressed with his intellect and military service. He was still serving in the Army Reserves, even as a member of Congress.

Now I was helping Congressman Zeldin with his fundraising around Texas. We were on our first trip together, flying from Dallas to Houston for our second event of his Texas trip. Besides the delight of his getting me into the USO's special lounge area in the airport, I was thrilled to be working for him. Lee had an incredible work ethic. He was never afraid to call any potential donor that I asked him to contact or phone a constituent in his district who needed his help. Lee was a workhorse. I knew this leader was going to make a significant impact on our nation. He was motivated!

On the flight we started talking about Israel. Even as a member of the Jewish community, he had never traveled to Israel until he went on a members' trip with the American Israel Education Foundation (AIEF)—the foundation arm of AIPAC.

As a Christian who has studied about Israel and the Jewish roots of my faith for years, I was having fun educating this member of Congress on all things Israel. He was fascinated that Christian people like me who loved the Jewish people and the land with such conviction existed. I could tell he was captivated by the conversation.

That is when I got to tell him about God's love for the Jewish people. I talked to him about two passages that specifically detail God's faithfulness to His people, who had floundered in their commitment to Him. Their unfaithfulness didn't keep Him from continually fulfilling His covenant with them.

> Thus says the LORD of hosts: "I am zealous for Zion with great zeal; with great fervor I am zealous for her."
> —ZECHARIAH 8:2

> Therefore know that the LORD your God, He is God, the faithful God who keeps covenant and mercy for a thousand generations with those who love Him and keep His commandments.
> —DEUTERONOMY 7:9

As we talked for over forty-five minutes, he got more and more passionate about the topic. "Bunni, I have always understood the concept of being pro-Israel and its importance militarily—and of course I am

Jewish—but what you have just shared with me is a much bigger picture." He paused and then said, "Perhaps it is a perspective that I should reflect on more. I think maybe an evangelical Christian such as yourself might have just as much passion for the land as we Jews do many times."

As we finished, I thought about the apostle Paul's words in Romans regarding God's plan for the people of Israel and His heart for them. Paul reminds the people of Israel that Moses said, "I will provoke you to jealousy by those who are not a nation" (Rom. 10:19).

God was meeting me again on a Southwest flight as I shared His faithfulness, His love, and His covenant with this young member of Congress from New York. I thanked God for a job that enabled me to speak into the lives of so many leaders in our nation.

Years later, Congressman Zeldin went on to run for governor of New York against Kathy Hochul, picking up more votes in New York State than any GOP candidate since Nelson Rockefeller fifty-two years earlier[1] and helping flip two congressional seats to the Republicans in New York.[2]

RON WRIGHT FOR CONGRESS

After my loss for Congress, I reluctantly wandered back into my office and faced my staff.

The hardest part of the campaign for me was the stress I had put my husband through and the collateral damage to my company and team. We still had thirteen clients to get through the general election, and we had a lot of work to do. Unfortunately I was hemorrhaging money, so I couldn't afford to keep all nine of us on the payroll. Half the team had come onto the campaign with me at my request and were now out of jobs. It was excruciatingly hard for me to face them in our boardroom that day. These employees were not just friends; they were family. I had already cut two full-time employees and now had to cut four more. That left just the beginning core business team to start the process of rebuilding.

My twenty-eight-year-old superstar, Ian Stageman, who completely ran my company while I was on this adventure, had persevered and was a better leader because of it. Glonda and Mike Mooney, my first hires in 2015, had helped me build a statewide donor database, had managed

Senator Hall's and Congressman Hensarling's accounts, and were ready to begin again. When I moved everyone else—Ashley, Susan, Bethany, and Colette—over to my campaign for Congress, these three faithful friends kept my company going, serving our clients day in and day out.

That fall, our goal was to get the rest of our clients over the finish line. Sen. Van Taylor needed to be elected to Congress from Collin County. We wanted to see state senator Bob Hall recoup his losses from a contentious primary and win his general election. We had to get our Fifth Court of Appeals candidates reelected, along with Commissioner Andy Nguyen in Tarrant County. We were also working with a New Jersey born and bred attorney, J. J. Koch, to win a seat as a Dallas County commissioner. We had all of this on top of our out-of-state clients: Rep. Ted Budd (NC-13), Rep. Andy Barr (KY-6), and others for whom we still had scheduled events.

This group of clients was nothing compared to the operation we had run just six months before. My adventure for Congress had inflicted some deep collateral damage to my livelihood, as well as to the people I walked with day to day.

A few days after going back to work, I got a call from Ron Wright. Ron was running for Congress in the Sixth Congressional District, covering a part of Tarrant County and all of Navarro and Ellis Counties. He was now the Republican nominee in a pretty safe Republican district, though the electorate had become more Democrat with every election in the years leading up to his race.

The current member of Congress in the district was Joe Barton, who was embroiled in a sex scandal involving illicit text messages to a woman who was not his wife.[3] He was not running for reelection because of this hit to his reputation, as many local leaders felt he had somewhat damaged the Republican brand in the district.

When the seat came open, Ron Wright not only had an illustrious career working as the Tarrant County tax assessor-collector but had also worked as the chief of staff for Congressman Barton years before. In addition, Ron had served on the Arlington City Council in the district, and his record of service on numerous nonprofit boards and city boards set him apart. Recognized as a servant leader in his community, Ron also had a strong record of standing up for family values and good governance, and he had the conservative battle scars to prove it. He had led the effort to keep strip clubs out of Arlington, and as the tax assessor-collector he put "In God We Trust" on the official letterhead for the county tax office. This caused an uproar from a vocal minority that thought those offensive words should not be on official government documents, let alone on our national currency. Ron stood his ground, claiming that if it was good enough for our US currency, then it was good enough for his office.

When Ron decided to run for Congress, the conservative movement in the Sixth Congressional District was united behind him for the most part. He just had to raise enough money to get his message out and run against ten other people, including a formidable candidate named Jake Ellzey—a US Navy fighter pilot who completed tours in Afghanistan and Iraq. In the primary Jake had been endorsed by Rick Perry, our former Texas governor and US secretary of energy under President Trump, making the race a little more competitive. Ron got through the primary on top and then pulled out in front during the runoff with a close win of 52 percent to 47 percent.

Going into the general election, Ron's campaign was almost broke from his hard-fought primary runoff. But now he had another competitor: a liberal Democrat from rural Ellis County. Hiding her liberalism behind her gun ownership and country talk, Jana Lynne Sanchez, a political consultant herself, was a formidable candidate. Ron knew the district was changing and had to take the race seriously. He had to raise money and raise it fast, but he personally hated doing it.

Ron hired me and my firm in July 2018, less than two months after my runoff loss. I knew the only way to help him get over his dislike of making donor calls was to personally coach him through it. With limited staff resources I threw myself into a new mission to see Ron Wright get to Congress.

When I was young, our family moved to Arlington, about two miles from Ron's house. I graduated from Martin High School in a South Arlington neighborhood, so it felt natural for me to drive to Ron and Susan Wright's middle-class home there in my old stomping grounds. I first helped him call all his previous donors, and then we reached out to new potential donors for his campaign. We were successful and got it done. We even planned some big events in August and September in all three counties.

During that season, so soon after my race, I was trying to find a new cause and to get it through my head that my life was not over. I now had a job to do—to help my friend.

Then it happened: the reason I was there.

A REASON I LOST

One day Ron's campaign manager, Micah, rushed him to the hospital. In excruciating pain, Ron thought he had kidney stones. However, he and his wife, Susan, soon discovered that he had cancer. He had a small tumor in his lung and spots on his liver, so the doctors declared it stage IV.

It was a deep blow to all of us, and I was only one of two people outside their family who knew the situation. The day Ron and Susan told me the news, they also let me know how much more they needed my help. Micah and I did everything we could to make Ron's and Susan's lives easier in the process. The next day I was in the prayer room, covering them in prayer and trying to make sense of it all.

It was a tough year for Republicans in the midterm election cycle. It was the first election since President Trump had taken office, and we were trying to keep Nancy Pelosi from coming back into power. Paul Ryan was currently the Speaker, and after much disappointment in not getting Obamacare overturned, the House was hanging by a thread.

It was too late for Ron to get off the ballot, so he had to continue—the Democrat candidate couldn't win this important seat and hurt the balance of power in the House. Ron had won his runoff but now was sick, and it was jeopardizing his ability to serve. I had lost my runoff and so wanted to serve my district but was unable to. It didn't seem fair to either of us.

Then a scripture came to my heart, and I began praying it over Ron's life:

> Bless the LORD, O my soul; and all that is within me, bless His holy name! Bless the LORD, O my soul, and forget not all His benefits: who forgives all your iniquities, who heals all your

diseases, who redeems your life from destruction, who crowns
you with lovingkindness and tender mercies, who satisfies your
mouth with good things, so that your youth is renewed like the
eagle's.

—PSALM 103:1–5

Again, I was consumed with intercession, and it continued through that
general election. I carried Ron and Susan in my heart every day and cried
out to God for Ron's life to be sustained. I prayed Psalm 103 over Ron as
I sat beside him making calls. I drove him around to donor meetings and
watched as he looked like he was going to faint in the Texas heat during our
campaign kickoff in Arlington.

The chemotherapy caused him to lose over twenty pounds, and many
times it made him lose his train of thought. It was not fun. Yet this brilliant man would quickly get back on track and keep pushing forward.
Thankfully he didn't lose his hair, and no one figured out the situation.
We pressed on, asking the citizens of the Sixth Congressional District to
#BacktheBowTie—the man with the conservative record and a love for
every color and pattern of bow tie.

I will never forget one donor meeting when I took Ron to a big high-rise
in Dallas. Because of his treatments, he sometimes had memory lapses. In
the middle of the meeting, he completely forgot his campaign messaging
points. As he stared at a potential donor with a blank look on his face, I
quickly realized what was going on and stepped in to engage her in conversation. "Ron believes exactly what I believe," I said. "The same principles
that I ran on and have based my career on—fiscal conservatism, a strong
military and border security, and standing up for our families and communities—are how Ron separated himself in the primary from his opponents. He has an incredible reputation in his community, one that unifies
everyone around the cause, and that is one of the reasons he will be a great
member of Congress. You can trust him to serve well."

Ron quickly regained his thoughts, picked up the conversation, and
closed the deal. The woman promised to get us at least two maxed out
checks from her boss and his wife. In the elevator Ron turned to me and

said, "Bunni, thank you. You saved me in there. I wouldn't be making it without you right now."

I believe God in His sovereignty knew that Ron and I were supposed to be working together in that season.

The night before the election, Ron called me at home. He wanted to thank me for all my hard work, focusing so much time and attention on his race and helping to carry him through during that difficult time. It was in that moment that I expressed what I had been feeling for the last few weeks: "Ron, helping you win this seat in Congress is one of the reasons I lost my election. It has been an honor to stand beside you, believing for your healing and seeing you make your way to help our nation. I wouldn't have missed this adventure for the world."

Ron Wright's general election victory in 2018, so soon after my runoff loss in May, was one of the highlights of my career. But it took me losing a race for Congress to get there.

RUNNING FOR REELECTION

The next July, after serving in Congress for seven months, Ron called me, rejoicing that he was doing well but wanting me to know that he was going to tell the world about the battle he had been fighting. He wanted to thank me again for keeping his secret, praying for him and Susan, and walking beside them through this incredible trial. He was so full of joy and thankfulness and was having the time of his life serving his country in Congress, and he was going to announce, a few months later, that he would run for reelection.

The next day Ron told the public, "Anyone who has gone through chemo knows what it's like. There have been days God picked me up and carried me because I didn't have the strength."[4] It had been a long hard battle, but Congressman Wright had "maintained a busy congressional schedule of constituent meetings, active committee participation, and votes in Washington as well as the important work in the district." He had "no intention of slowing down."[5]

Ron served out his first term well and won reelection in 2020. Unfortunately the cancer came back with a vengeance during the last few months of the year. On February 7, 2021, after he and his wife, Susan, contracted COVID-19, Rep. Ron Wright was the first member of Congress to pass away from the virus that had taken over our nation. He had a compromised immune system, and it hit him hard. He was sixty-seven years old.

I will never forget my time with Ron—his strong faith, his warmth and humor, his love for people, and his service to our nation. My short season of walking with Ron Wright will forever be in my mind as a divine appointment for both of us. During that season I revisited why I had been called into this political work in the first place: to be Jesus to others in times of need.

Even politicians need God to speak to them.

No Partiality

God can speak to us all in multiple ways. He can cause a scripture to jump off the page at just the right time or use a friend to encourage us. He can send a dream to speak destiny or a divine appointment to walk us through a challenging time.

"God shows no partiality" (Acts 10:34). He can speak to all of us.

Out of His eternal love, He desires to walk and talk with us. This love is why Jesus came—born of a virgin, leaving His heavenly home to become a baby in a manger and to live a sinless life with a community of fallen people. As Jesus went to the cross, His whole vision was to restore us to a relationship with the Father and to bring humanity back to the garden.

> Father, I desire that they also whom You gave Me may be with Me where I am, that they may behold My glory which You have given Me; for You loved Me before the foundation of the world.
> —John 17:24

We can't discount the voice of the Lord in our lives—to speak to us or to use us to speak to others. God will walk with us, talk with us, and use us in others' lives as long as we are sensitive to His presence and His voice.

His presence can go into a room with us as we sit beside someone who needs our help, or He can provide encouragement and wisdom through us to someone on an airline flight. We must only be obedient to take Him with us—making sure everything in our lives remains sacred.

Then the eleven disciples went away into Galilee, to the mountain which Jesus had appointed for them. When they saw Him, they worshiped Him; but some doubted. And Jesus came and spoke to them, saying, "All authority has been given to Me in heaven and on earth. Go therefore and make disciples of all the nations, baptizing them in the name of the Father and of the Son and of the Holy Spirit, teaching them to observe all things that I have commanded you; and lo, I am with you always, even to the end of the age." Amen.

—MATTHEW 28:16–20

There is a famine in America of the Word of God and real discipleship. Truth is not often discussed, community is not experienced, and we are unable to be honest with each other about what is going on in our lives behind the scenes. Discipleship is found in interaction and longevity of relationship, teaching others to be true to themselves and before God. The goal is to see the people we love fulfill the call of God on their lives regardless of all the curves in the road.

Chapter 7

DISCIPLING THE NATION

AFTER JESUS' RESURRECTION and before He left His disciples, He spoke a clear mandate to these future world changers: "Go therefore and make disciples of all the nations" (Matt. 28:19).

In this mandate no one was exempt from the task of *going* and the task of *making disciples*. Even the people listening to Jesus that day who doubted weren't exempt. Jesus didn't ignore them; He empowered them as well (Matt. 28:17). He empowered everyone on the mountainside whether they were full of faith or not. Their power to make disciples was found not in their own abilities or talents but in Jesus, in whom "all authority has been given...in heaven and on earth" (Matt. 28:18).

Believe me, God knew what He was getting with these weak people. Thomas had doubted Him, Peter had denied Him, and the rest had hidden themselves waiting it out. These were not the mighty men of valor who looked like they would turn the world upside down. It was Jesus' authority and power that would sustain them for the work ahead. And it did. The early church spread the good news far and wide, telling everyone about Jesus' resurrection. It was not up to them—it was up to *Jesus* to get this work of discipleship done. They had to simply obey. Even as He expanded the mandate from their little parcel of earth in Judea and Samaria to the ends of the earth, it was still His power that would enable them.

> But you shall receive power when the Holy Spirit has come upon you; and you shall be witnesses to Me in Jerusalem, and in all Judea and Samaria, and to the end of the earth.
>
> —ACTS 1:8

Jesus took the pressure off these fishermen to change the world on their own and put it on Himself and the power of His Holy Spirit. This power is still available to us as modern-day disciples of Jesus. If we think we will change the world in politics or government in and of ourselves, we are deceived. We cannot do anything without His wisdom and strength. If the people of God with the Spirit of God are not impacting our world with the truth and wisdom given by Him, then what do we really have? Nothing. Politics alone will not save America.

God's promise to us today is the same as it was to the disciples on the mountain before Jesus was glorified and went into heaven: "Lo, I am with you always, even to the end of the age" (Matt. 28:20).

As believers in Jesus engaging in a world of political activity, we must know that God loves the people of our nation more than we do. He wants to see discipleship happen in individual lives even more than we do so that they will change organizations and government systems.

Americans are not exempt from the command of discipleship. We are to go everywhere: to our city council chambers, our school boards, our state houses, and even one of the darkest places on the planet—Washington, DC.

Depending on who are in the seats of power, our government has the opportunity to become better or worse. We have a responsibility to affect change, but it starts one life at a time and one heart at a time. Our nation is only as good as our leaders and our participation in our government. In other words, our nation needs discipleship from top to bottom.

Breakfast With James Robison

In 2009, *D Magazine* published an article with the headline "Jeb Hensarling: The GOP's Most Powerful Nobody." The publication said the "Dallas Congressman is a rising leader among congressional Republicans and a voice of fiscal conservatism."[1] It was a great piece on my boss's career from 2002 to that point. I bought a ton of copies and mailed them to potential donors around Texas. As I did this, one person kept coming to mind: James Robison.

Reverend Robison, the evangelical leader who had meant so much to my father and then to me, was someone I had been wanting Congressman Hensarling to meet for a while. I went online and found Robison's home address. (I have my ways.) Then I sent him a copy of *D Magazine* along with a note from the congressman. Robison called my cell phone the next Saturday morning. He didn't seem to remember our connection because he left a message wanting me, as the congressman's campaign manager, to know that he would love to meet Jeb Hensarling.

Working with our scheduling team, we arranged a breakfast meeting for James Robison and Jeb Hensarling. I didn't go to many meetings with Jeb because we did most of our campaigning and fundraising through events and phone calls, so I had to lobby my way into staffing this one.

As a member of Congress with biblical beliefs about life, marriage, and religious liberty, Jeb voted accordingly, but he didn't want his career defined by these issues. He mainly highlighted his record in the fiscal conservative lane. Because of this he didn't pursue religious media and had no real reason to meet Robison before then.

As a preacher who consistently shared the gospel as an evangelist, James Robison could not escape a bent toward the political world. He had been a key spiritual leader to President Ronald Reagan and other national government leaders. James operated in love and wasn't afraid of being defined by his connections with politicians. I felt James would be a good connection for my boss.

We arrived at a hotel near the DFW airport. It was a crisp morning in early November, and I looked forward to a good, hot breakfast buffet. I was thrilled that after just two years on the job I was getting to introduce my former boss to my current boss. Of course, I doubted that James Robison would even recognize me.

After extending a formal welcome, Robison asked us if we wanted to get some food.

"Sure," I replied.

As we stood across from each other at the buffet station, James said, "Bunni, do I know you? Your name sounds familiar, and you look familiar."

"Yes, you do, sir, though I won't expect you to remember. I worked for you at LIFE Outreach over twelve years ago when I was in Bible school at Christ For The Nations. I was also a part of Restoration Church, where you attended. As a teenager I spent a night at your house at a slumber party with your daughter Robin. Mark Jobe was my youth pastor at the time."

"Wow, Bunni, that is amazing," James responded. "I knew you looked familiar. How in the world did you get here working for a member of Congress?"

"It is a long story, sir, but maybe one day I will get to share it with you. Just know I am called to politics. I'm a missionary to America."

This booming evangelist and mountain of a man just laughed. "Yes, I would really like to hear that story sometime."

Sensing that I was trying to not monopolize the conversation as a staffer, James moved on to converse with Jeb. They talked for over an hour about the congressman's career, about his work as the voice of fiscal conservatism in the House, including his fight to get rid of congressional earmarks, and then about Jeb's family. About forty-five minutes into the conversation, James pulled out his phone and read Jeb a message he had received from his oldest daughter, Rhonda, earlier in the year around Mother's Day. In the message she had thanked her mother and father for her faith and relationship with God. James then stopped and looked Jeb straight in the eyes—as if Jeb were his television audience—and said pointedly, "Jeb, you are going somewhere in Congress. Soon you will be in leadership. But I want you to always remember that there is nothing more important than your wife and your two precious children. They might, or might not, look at your life years later and thank you for your work in Congress. But they will look back and thank you for giving them Jesus." Reverend Robison continued, "I can see that you are a man of deep faith, Jeb, but you must give them your faith. Don't let them get out of your house without knowing God. Always remember that first things are first—God, family, and then your country."

Jeb wholeheartedly received this man of God's empowering words. James ended the meeting by praying over Jeb and thanking him for spending some precious time with him for the purpose of encouragement. On my way home I got a text from Jeb: "I am not sure of the overall purpose of that meeting but thank you!"

Thirteen months later, on January 3, 2011, Jeb's peers voted him to be

House Republican Conference chairman, the fourth most powerful position in the House. Still, in the sixteen years of his career, Jeb prioritized his wife and family. He never forgot that they were his *top* priority.

A TRUE FRIEND

For almost as long as I have been involved in politics, I have known Van Taylor. A graduate of Harvard College and Harvard Business School, Van grew up in Midland, Texas, in a family of means. Even so, both of his parents were extremely down to earth. With his career in real estate investment banking and service as a marine in Iraq, Van had always dreamed of going to Congress. His story separated him from other potential national candidates.

Having joined the Marine Reserves while at Harvard Business School, Van signed up for another term to serve his country after watching the Pentagon burn on 9/11. During Operation Iraqi Freedom he participated in the rescue of thirty-one wounded Marines—evacuating and safely transporting them to medical treatment. For this and other missions, he won many military decorations, including the Navy Commendation Medal, the Combat Action Ribbon, and the Presidential Unit Citation.

After returning from Iraq, Van married Anne Coolidge—the woman who had written him a letter every day while he was in combat—in 2004. He had reached the rank of major before leaving the Marine Corps Reserve.

In 2005 and 2006, when he and his wife were newly married, Van ran a very organized campaign in the Seventeenth Congressional District in central Texas against Chet Edwards, a Blue Dog Democrat. He was convinced he could win the congressional seat but came up short.

I met Van in 2007, after his first race for Congress and after I had landed my first political job with Jeb. My friend Sarah Rozier, who worked with Congressman Hensarling in Jeb's Dallas office, had also worked for Van during his race against Chet Edwards. Even though Van lost that race, Sarah had deep respect for his work ethic, passion to serve, and love for America.

Van was the first donor in every new election cycle to "max out" (give the federal annual limit of $5,000 to a campaign) to Congressman Hensarling. Van would call me on the day after the election to give his money. He began studying Jeb's career and showing up to events I hosted for my boss. Van and I became friends.

Then living in Plano, a city in Collin County, Van was asked to run for the Texas State House in 2010. He won the runoff and was sworn in early when the incumbent stepped down earlier than planned. Four years later, Van won a seat as a Texas state senator when Ken Paxton vacated the position to run for Texas attorney general. I have always had such great respect for Van's conservative record and for his temperament in working with colleagues. The man could get things done legislatively; he would learn about a problem and go try to fix it.

When I decided to start my own firm in 2015, the first new client I landed was my friend state senator Van Taylor. Within two months he had helped me sign up two more state senators: Sen. Bob Hall and Sen. Konni Burton. Van's belief in me as a consultant pushed my little firm forward and our friendship to a new level.

No one liked to banter back and forth about politics more than Van Taylor and me. One year he watched, I believe, every ad for Congress from every incumbent and every challenger in the country. He was a political animal. I couldn't make fun of Van, though, because while I was running for Congress, I used to relax at night by watching ads from around the state. I think I watched every grassroots ad and debate by what I had hoped would be my colleagues in the Texas delegation: Chip Roy, Michael Cloud, Dan Crenshaw, Ron Wright, and Van Taylor.

Van and I became friends over our love for politics. But in working together, we also connected over our families, our friends, our conservative beliefs, and our hopes and dreams. As an Episcopalian, Van approached his faith with a little more reserve than I did, but I never shied away from being authentically myself.

Every time I had a major shift in my life, Van Taylor was there supporting me wholeheartedly—from starting my firm, to stepping away for a season to run for Congress, to downsizing my firm, to launching my nonprofit, Christians Engaged. The man has always been there asking how he could help me. I am very thankful for him in my life.

When Van Taylor won his race for Congress in November 2018, I was so happy to finally call him Congressman. I was fully invested in Van's career. Even after I dissolved my firm completely, we kept in contact with each other.

My first assistant, Sable Coleman, became Van's district director when he served in the state house and state senate and then when he went on to Congress. My friend and former colleague Margaret Smith went to work with Van after Jeb's retirement. Emma McIlheran, my intern for three years and the daughter of Mark and Cherri McIlheran, who hosted the home group where Tim and I first met, went to work for Congressman Taylor as one of his main caseworkers, rescuing American citizens out of Afghanistan through his office. Congressman Taylor's team—from his chief of staff, Lonnie Dietz, to all the rest—were great professionals and dear friends. His office was top notch. He was attempting to fix a broken Washington, and we were all cheering him on.

LONELY PLACES

Washington, DC, is a lonely place. The longer elected officials stay, the smaller their circle of friends becomes. So many times, friends and colleagues who had once been close start to drift away as more and more of their time gets taken up with their work for the country.

I try to explain this reality to Christians every day, giving the analogy that our elected officials are like missionaries. We have a responsibility not only to elect good representatives and send them to these places of influence but also to stay in their lives with support, friendship, and prayers.

Praying for them and their families is essential. Encouraging them when they stand up boldly and vote according to biblical values gives them even more courage to do it again. Holding them accountable when we perceive that they are drifting off the path is critical—but we must do it the right way, respecting their offices and ensuring we have all the information, including their own perspectives regarding votes they took or decisions they made. Keeping their confidences, being trustworthy friends, and not saying one thing but doing another give these public servants assurance that they can trust our word.

We see this loneliness in the church world as well, as members wander around without real connections, accountability, or mentorship. We have gotten so far away from simple devotion to Jesus with each other—real discipleship and friendship. This must change.

In church culture a good pastor and church leadership will try to make inroads into people's hearts, keeping doors open for the purposes of allowing the gospel and truth to impact their lives. Real discipleship brings truth when needed and provides the balm of compassion and mercy when humility is found. Walking beside another person and sharing life with him or her is one of the greatest joys and privileges we have. We come alive when we are giving. Every believer should have people who disciple and feed into his or her life, and every believer should have someone or many others whom he or she is pouring into.

This is how we become a life-giving river, not a stagnant pond. Rivers carry vegetation, minnows, and salmon—forms of life. As we become channels of blessing, encouragement, and the truth of God's Word, we bring healing and life to others around us. "Everything will live wherever the river goes."

> And it shall be that every living thing that moves, wherever the rivers go, will live. There will be a very great multitude of fish, because these waters go there; for they will be healed, and everything will live wherever the river goes.
> —EZEKIEL 47:9

Revival looks like something. In revival we find our first love and go back to the simple devotions of prayer, worship, and meditation in the Word, and then we inspire and empower people around us to go deep in God and become the leaders they are destined to be. In the end they will come alive and realize that they are here to know God and make Him known.

Watching Christians attack elected officials on social media through the years has made me want to speak up even more—to teach activists how to walk beside these people in power and impact their lives and votes for good, not to be cut out of their lives.

If our friends yelled at us nonstop on our social media pages, would we listen to them or block them from any other communication? Why do we think our elected officials are any different? Why would we think yelling in public forums, even online, would make them listen to us? Some ways to communicate are effective, and some are not. In the end, if an elected official is not doing what we perceive is right, we have an opportunity to vote him or her out in a primary or general election and work passionately for another candidate who we feel would serve better.

ENDEAVORING TO KNOW HIS EVERY WORD

During a contentious primary in 2022, it came out two days before the election that Congressman Taylor had been privately struggling for the last year. Van issued a statement to his supporters on March 2, 2022:

> About a year ago, I made a horrible mistake that has caused deep hurt and pain among those I love most in this world. I had an affair, it was wrong, and it was the greatest failure of my life. I want to apologize for the pain I have caused with my indiscretion, most of all to my wife Anne and our three daughters.[2]

When Congressman Taylor ended up with 48.7 percent on primary day—under the 50 percent threshold to avoid a runoff—he chose, for the sake of his family, to suspend his campaign instead of continuing. This decision essentially made Keith Self the Republican nominee for the district.

I have never been prouder of a friend than I was that day. This man had served his nation relentlessly for so many years, but now he was choosing to serve his God and his family above everything else.

As a close friend with this state and national leader for years, it broke my heart, and I carried many regrets of my own for a while. What if I had reached out more when he was in DC? Had I prayed enough for him and his family? Had I been faithful to carry the Word of God to him as a friend? Where had I dropped the ball?

It was a key reminder to me that our leaders—even those we look up to as our conservative warriors—are not infallible and need us in their lives. Over the course of the next year, Van worked diligently to restore his family, to spend precious time with his girls, and to repair the breaches in all his relationships. He read the Bible daily, coming to depend on God like he had never done before. He sent me text messages of different passages he was reading, as I sent him some of my favorite passages, and we kept in contact over the phone. I walked with several of his team members as they planned out their next career moves.

On January 2, 2023, as Congressman Taylor was leaving office, he issued a statement to his past supporters. I believe it is a beautiful picture of the power of the Word of God and how God always pulls us back into relationship with Himself, yearning for the best for His children.

> Over the last ten months, I have done much soul searching and reflecting on past actions, but more importantly on what lies ahead. Reading the Bible every day has brought peace and hope. I can honestly say I did not know God's love and grace until I endeavored to know His every word. Every day my faith grows as I work to rebuild trust in my family. I am grateful for God's forgiveness and my family's love and understanding.[3]

Van's story had only just begun as he discovered his true identity: a son of God, a loving husband, and a giving father.

WE NEED EACH OTHER

Discipleship takes relationship building, and we need each other to remind us who we really are. Our God is in the restoration business. If we don't have any level of relationship, how can we speak into each other's lives? If we don't show each other compassion when we fall, how can we demonstrate the nature and character of God? If we aren't diligent to reach out and spend time with each other, how will we know how we are really doing behind all the facades?

Many times over the years, I have needed friends to speak truth to me. No one is exempt from needing correction and encouragement, and none of us knows the totality of God. We are constantly learning and growing. If we are not, there is something deeply wrong.

When we go through challenging seasons and even periods of sin, we need truth and perspective, but we also need compassion. We must remind one another as Christians that the only thing that empowers us to do anything good is the power and authority Jesus gives us. We are some very weak people, but God makes us strong. If we daily turn to Him for His love and "His every word," as Congressman Taylor said, then He will keep us on the right path of fruitfulness and purpose for our lives.

I have cherished the conversations with people whom Tim and I pastored for years—friends we have walked with and leaders we have encouraged. Every word we speak as believers—whether in a car, on a phone call, in a text message, or in an office—can be a teachable moment where God's Word transforms or encourages someone to walk with Him more.

Discipleship doesn't have to be complicated. It can take the form of Bible studies, small groups and gatherings, or, most effectively, conversations around meals, on lunch dates, at coffee breaks, or even while walking the halls of Congress with a friend.

Discipleship is reminding each other of God's truth and His love for us—day in and day out. As Christians we are called to impact America one heart at a time, even one elected official at a time. We all must come to the place where we say, "I have decided to follow Jesus" and walk that road of surrender together, encouraging each other along the path. True joy is found in knowing Jesus, in each other, and in giving of ourselves so that others might live.

The greatest hope He could ever give us is found in Jesus' closing remarks to His disciples and to us as well: "Lo, I am with you always, even to the end of the age" (Matt. 28:20).

Now, Lord, look on their threats and grant that Your servants may speak Your word with great boldness.

—ACTS 4:29, MEV

Boldness comes from somewhere deep. It doesn't just appear out of nothing. We gain courage as we experience God's faithfulness yearly, weekly, and daily. It is being able to answer the question "Am I being true to who I am, and am I doing what I am supposed to do?" We are bold when we are familiar with God's voice and decide to obey it repeatedly, gaining rewards through our faithfulness.

Chapter 8

BOLDNESS LIKE JOAN OF ARC

I N MAY 2021 my nonprofit ministry, Christians Engaged, was denied tax-exempt status. We quickly became a national story and a dramatic example for conservative and religious media to highlight as the target of what appeared to be an oppressive Internal Revenue Service. The IRS seemed to be targeting conservatives again, not unlike the days of Lois Lerner back in 2013—but this time Christian organizations were in their sights.

With the help of our friends at First Liberty Institute we pushed back and took on the IRS, making national headlines in the process. In just a few weeks I was on Fox News three times. We were the top Sunday story on Breitbart, and we saw our story covered by many Christian and conservative publications, including *Charisma* and *Decision* (Franklin Graham), and even a more liberal publication, *Newsweek*.

In June 2021 the Victory Channel aired an episode of *FlashPoint* in which Charlie Kirk, founder of Turning Point USA, said, "This is a big deal. This is for every single church watching right now. They could pull your tax-exempt status because they could say that if you preach the gospel, you're basically trying to politically intervene on behalf of the Republican Party. They are now going to go after religious institutions and be able to say that if you do not preach what we want you to preach, you don't get the tax benefit."[1] Later that year, on November 7, 2021, Pastor Robert Jeffress of First Baptist Dallas preached a message called "The Church in the Kettle," highlighting our story as an example of courage.[2]

It hit me later how bold our board of directors was during that season. The courage didn't come out of a vacuum, though, as we had all been prepared through years of engagement. Our deep rest in God came from having gone through other adventures that had prepared us for that moment. I'll share more details on this story later, but one person texted an encouragement to me, saying I was like a modern-day Joan of Arc. I laughed and commented, "I don't really plan on being burned at the stake."

Still, it made me think about how much courage that young seventeen-year-old must have had to lead an entire army into battle and to convince the king of France that she had a word from God. In her generation, this young "Maid of Orléans" was known for her bold stand and leadership.[3]

What is the difference between zeal and courage? Human zeal can move people to action and get them fired up, but when we see real courage in action, it is another story altogether. Zeal doesn't have a cost associated with it—courage does. Young liberal college students can say whatever they want to say in their passion, but if their parents are covering their bills and they don't have to worry about losing their jobs, they probably won't feel the potential effects of their words. It is another thing altogether to consider how they would change their lifestyles to really affect the world around them. As the old adage says, "Actions speak louder than words."

Courage and boldness are knowing that what we do and say will affect everything in our lives yet choosing to do it anyway because we deem it to be right. The cost must be counted, because together courage and zeal can cost you your life.

> Then He [Jesus] said to them all, "If anyone desires to come after Me, let him deny himself, and take up his cross daily, and follow Me. For whoever desires to save his life will lose it, but whoever loses his life for My sake will save it.
>
> —LUKE 9:23–24

MOUTHING OFF TO WBAP

As a young person my first exposure to politics was when my friend Greg Hobgood took me to a Pat Buchanan rally in 1992. It was the spring before I graduated from high school. I couldn't even vote yet, since I wouldn't turn eighteen until August, but I was still excited to go.

As the former White House communications director for Ronald Reagan and political commentator and writer, Pat was running in the primary against the current president, George Herbert Walker Bush. He was campaigning to the right of President Bush on social issues and American foreign policy and highlighting Bush's "Read my lips: no new taxes" line as a broken promise.

Standing there waving my "Pat Buchanan for President" sign and cheering, I was inspired. I was young and zealous for sure. In the car on the way there Greg had told me why he was supporting Buchanan. I began rehearsing in my head the three-point message I could use to defend myself to my mom, who might question my attendance when I arrived home.

As we were leaving, Greg and I saw a reporter from WBAP 820 AM, one of the leading talk radio stations in Dallas-Fort Worth. We walked toward the reporter to see whom he was interviewing. Seeing us, the man from WBAP quickly approached me, not Greg, and asked whether I would give a quick interview from a young woman's perspective. "Why are you supporting this conservative hardliner against the softer, more moderate incumbent president?" he asked.

I recycled Greg's talking points and gave a passionate appeal for everyone listening to go vote for Pat Buchanan in the 1992 Republican primary for president. Greg was not too happy about getting upstaged by a girl whom he'd brought with him—one who didn't know anything about politics—but we laughed about it on the way home.

As I look back on that incident, I can say that rally got me interested in politics. But as I tell young people all the time, zeal is different than courage. Though I was zealous because of the new information I had acquired, real courage is not just mouthing off to an audience, even in my young eloquent and passionate way. Remember, I wasn't even old enough to vote in that primary. Again, it was a real-life example of zeal over true courage. I would discover real boldness and courage later on.

HEARING AND OBEYING

> You will be brought before governors and kings for My sake, as a testimony to them and to the Gentiles. But when they deliver you up, do not worry about how or what you should speak. For it will be given to you in that hour what you should speak.
>
> —MATTHEW 10:18–19

Jesus spent quality time with His disciples raising them up to be the men He desired them to be. Here was the King of kings in human form pouring His life into twelve men. This was not a microwave process by which these men would be ready to reach the world overnight. It would take time. Jesus was giving them time to be with Him, so He invited them to go on His journey, to share meals, and to see His works. It was that time, day to day with their Master, that would produce the fruit of boldness and power in their lives.

In Matthew 10, Jesus told His disciples, in essence, to not worry about what their testimony would be when He brought them before powerful world leaders, because He would give them the words. Their responsibility was just to learn to hear from Him.

It can be a scary process for us to think about what sacrifices we need to make to follow Christ. In God's providence He doesn't show us the full picture from beginning to end. He wants us to trust Him for our daily bread. We wonder what will happen to our lives if we really believe this and act on it. What kind of suffering will we have to endure?

But Jesus wanted His disciples to focus on what He had been teaching them all along: how to hear the Father. Jesus did only what He saw the Father doing (John 5:19), and He knew that obedience was the only thing that would get His friends through the next season of their lives and turn them into world changers. They had to learn to hear the Father and obey God quickly. It was this obedience that would turn the world upside down.

THE CALL FROM KEVIN MCCARTHY

As I was on my way to a meeting in Washington, DC, at the end of my primary and right before my runoff, my phone rang. I jumped out of the rideshare and answered it, trying to sound cheery. "This is Bunni."

"Bunni, it's Kevin McCarthy. How are you doing?"

"Well, I am doing great, sir. How are you?" I stumbled, trying to get my head around the idea of the majority leader of the House of Representatives calling me on my cell phone.

Leader McCarthy went on, "I hear your race is going incredible. Way to hit it out of the park on fundraising. Do you think you will have the resources you need to get your message over the finish line?"

"I believe so, Mr. Leader. We are running a strong campaign. I am relentless when it comes to a finance plan."

"I am sure you are," he replied. We continued chitchatting for a few minutes, talking about my work with many of the legislators in the caucus, including Congressman Hensarling. Then he cut right to the point: "Bunni, I hear you are thinking about pledging to the Freedom Caucus. You know they don't have a woman, and they badly want a woman in their ranks."

There was a lot of debate internally during my campaign about whether I would join the Freedom Caucus if I were invited. Personally I had discussed it with a multitude of counselors, including Jeb, but hadn't made up my mind yet. If I decided to go that route, it could potentially create a target on my back, causing some leadership to cut me off from significant funding during the runoff. It could also cause more problems in fundraising later in my career in DC, since corporate PACs and other major donors were not fans of the Freedom Caucus.

Initiated by a group of nine Republicans, including Mark Meadows and Jim Jordan, in 2015, the Freedom Caucus was a step farther right than the Republican Study Committee that Jordan had chaired previously. Though Jeb had always been sympathetic to their cause and voted almost as conservatively as they did, he didn't feel that joining them was the path he was supposed to take.

In earlier years the Freedom Caucus—a by-invitation-only gathering of members (who didn't even publish their membership)—had worked to overthrow Speaker John Boehner and pushed the GOP leadership to be more conservative on some key issues. For the most part they had been successful in taking on Boehner. Congressman Meadows and the rest of the caucus forced a vote for a more conservative member to be Speaker. Jeb had been part of their discussion about potential Speaker candidates, but ultimately his friend Paul Ryan stepped up. Though Paul was far from being a Freedom Caucus member, the conference saw him as someone who could bring the factions together and lead them forward.

During my race in 2018 the Freedom Caucus was trying to find its footing and relevance in the middle of the Trump administration. Under Obama the caucus had been a powerful factor in pushing the Republican leadership to be bolder. Now it was mostly aligned with the executive branch and with the House Republicans, which were in the majority; they were all working to govern together. Though the Freedom Caucus was in a place of limbo, it still had strong members in its ranks whom I desired to fellowship with and learn from, as I aligned with them on fiscal and social issues. Yet the House Republican leadership saw the Freedom Caucus as a thorn in their side most of the time, and they didn't necessarily want to see the caucus's numbers grow—thus the reason for McCarthy's call.

After a few minutes of talking with Leader McCarthy, I understood what had prompted this sudden call. I was about to walk into the office of Club for Growth—the fiscal conservative PAC led by former Indiana congressman David McIntosh. I imagine McCarthy had heard about my visit through the political grapevine. Though he and I had not yet met, I was a front-runner in Texas' Fifth District, and he wanted to see where I stood. What the leader didn't know was that I had been deeply aligned with Club for Growth for a long time. I helped them keep an eye out for potential candidates and believed in the cause of limited government, which they championed, to my core.

Asking for the Club's endorsement and help was going to be a big step for me, but I was prepared. I knew at some point in the conversation they would ask me whether I would consider joining the Freedom Caucus— not as a requirement for their endorsement but as a gauge of how much these issues really meant to me. They were looking for new members who would take a stand. I had weighed the question thoroughly and had now made my decision. I had even shared it on a panel of local candidates in Dallas County the week before. If the Freedom Caucus asked me to join their ranks, I would accept.

Though I knew I wanted to join this group of conservative members, I also had a healthy respect for the majority leader. He had a strong record and had worked hard on fundraising around the nation and keeping a diverse Republican conference together, which was extremely difficult. He had done well as the majority leader under Speaker Ryan, and I thought he would make a good Speaker.

Recognizing that the GOP leader was calling for a reason and that my answer could be potentially fatal to my campaign (at least in terms of funding support from certain sources), I knew I was in a critical moment for my career. The man on the other end of the phone could get upset and work to put money and resources into my opponents' campaigns.

Then came his inevitable question: "Bunni, are you planning on joining the Freedom Caucus?" to which he boldly added, "Jeb didn't need to join them to be effective, and neither do you."

I understood Kevin McCarthy's point of view; I was not a novice on the points. I even believed that for others it might not be a good fit to join the Freedom Caucus. But for me it was—I had made my choice. Was I going to Washington to please others or be true to myself? I needed God in that moment.

Without hesitating, I answered, "Mr. Leader, I know you don't know me very well, but I hope you have heard around town from my federal clients about my reputation in the conservative movement. I have been a great team player as a campaign manager for ten years. I want all of us to win at every level. I am also an avid fundraiser, so I understand the goal of winning and keeping the majority. I will be pledging to join the Freedom Caucus if they invite me, but that does not mean that I will not do the hard work for the team, pay my dues, and work for the American people."

There, I had said it. He knew. But hopefully I had taken the sting out of the bite.

"Sir," I continued, "I would love the opportunity to meet you face to face later today while I am in town to tell you my story, my commitment to this nation, and why I did not make this decision lightly. It is the right fit for me personally, and if I get the honor of representing the people of the Fifth District in Congress, I have to stay true to myself."

With that, Leader McCarthy told me his team would work on getting us together later that day and ended the call.

I walked into Club for Growth and won their support if I happened to make the runoff. Later that afternoon I spent an incredible and memorable hour in Majority Leader Kevin McCarthy's office as we bonded over our love for America and our desire to push conservatism forward. I walked out with huge respect for him that has continued to this day.

I had not expected that spontaneous call, but God had known it would happen. And He gave me the words at just the right time. He had already given me years of political wisdom to live out my convictions and to do it with grace toward others.

180-DEGREE TURNS

My life has been a constant series of 180-degree turns. It has happened so much that I have often wondered whether I am led by the Spirit or just impulsive.

God often leads us by our desires that are being conformed to His desires. As born-again believers, if we are walking with God, then we are continually asking Him to conform us into His image. Our fleshly, carnal desires will increasingly fade away as a desire for His kingdom rises within us. The psalmist tells us to delight in the Lord "and He shall give you the desires of your heart" (Ps. 37:4).

If I have learned nothing else in walking with God for decades, it would be this: I must move with my heart and convictions. He speaks many times through the godly desires He places deep inside me. He has a way of sanctifying my thoughts and dreams through the fire of His Word and His presence. If my heart is moving in another direction from the current path I am on, I have to submit my heart to Jesus and seek Him for clarity—daily. If the new direction aligns with the Bible and I am taking it to the Lord, then I can trust it.

When my heart is going after a selfish desire, something to promote myself, I will find that His Spirit is not in that. I must stay in continual fellowship with Him and check my heart repeatedly. If I stay before the Lord in prayer and in His Word, He is faithful to craft my desires into His desires. He is faithful to move me in the direction that will cause me to grow and become more like Him—even if it looks a little impulsive at the time.

For example, I was heading to the mission field in Latin America but then got married to my best friend and started a family. I was helping my husband and growing successful businesses but then went back to college and got into politics. I worked morning to night to build a successful political consulting business when all of a sudden, out of nowhere, I was running for Congress.

Now, after ending my race and after getting Ron Wright and Van Taylor both elected to Congress, I was ready for another 180-degree turn.

GOD, I AM DONE

It was the second week of January 2019. I went to the prayer room again one morning for a six o'clock worship set. The worship team was singing, people were praying, and I was on the floor whispering these words: "God, I am done. I don't know what those words even mean, but I am done."

I wasn't telling God that I was done with politics. I didn't want to quit helping candidates, but I was done with my consulting company. We had revenue of over half a million dollars in 2017 before I ran for Congress. I knew I could rebuild it, but I didn't want to. I was ready for some sort of shift. I was tired of the responsibility of running so many clients and carrying a big payroll. My heart was no longer in it.

After my race I fasted from speaking to rest my vocal cords. During my fast God began to place a vision in my heart for a movement of Christians who would learn government and politics but also pursue change for the nation in the right spirit. I scribbled down pages of notes, not knowing what I was writing. After a few months the thoughts began to culminate around three simple words: *pray, vote,* and *engage.*

At the end of the two-hour prayer room session, I prayed, "I just want to go back to running one member of Congress so that I can serve one vision and be able to connect with You more and do more ministry. Can You help me figure that out?" I wrote this prayer down in my journal and then walked out the door. I was seeking God to know His desire for my life, which I hoped was the same as *my* desires.

A few hours later that same morning I got a call from Rep. Michael Cloud.

CLOUD FOR CONGRESS

As I mentioned before, being the complete political fanatic that I was, during my race I often relaxed before bed by watching debates and keeping track of news regarding Texas' other six Republican open congressional seats in 2018. I was especially fascinated by a race in the coastal bend of South Texas with an Oral Roberts University graduate named Michael Cloud.

Michael was a former media director at Faith Family Church in Victoria, Texas, and the owner of Bright Idea Media. He continued to gain steam in the race for the Twenty-Seventh Congressional District. I watched the video he had made in which he physically ran to announce his run for Congress against the incumbent representative, Blake Farenthold.

To the outside world it may have looked like a fool's errand, but this former seven-year GOP chairman of Victoria County and member of the State Republican Executive Committee thought his grassroots volunteer jobs could translate into a seat in Congress. With a group of faithful friends who believed in the call of God on his life, Michael raised $23,000 in a living room in September 2017, simply by asking humbly for their help. He went out in faith—running.

A few months later it came out that a sexual harassment incident had been filed against the incumbent and that he had paid for the settlement with taxpayer funds from the US House's human resources department, then called the Office of Compliance.[4] Blake Farenthold's problems became national news in December 2017. Soon afterward, the congressman resigned and withdrew his name from the upcoming race.

Michael Cloud didn't have a lot of resources but could inspire people toward good governance. He became one of the front-runners in a six-person, open-seat primary and ended up in a two-person runoff. Going into the 2018 runoff, Michael's primary vote totals were behind those of Bech Bruun, the chairman of the Texas Water Development Board. So just as it was in my race, he had some ground to make up. Michael and his team built a grassroots army that was getting people's attention. Yet Brunn, a young, energetic leader who had grown up in Corpus Christi, knew many of the deep pockets in the area and was able to galvanize donors and key influencers around his campaign. It was becoming a fight.

The strength of the Cloud campaign was its incredible grassroots team in all thirteen counties of the district. With his media experience Michael was able to put together inexpensive videos that connected with the average voter in South Texas. His messaging communicated his conservative values and heart for service, and it paid off. Michael Cloud won the GOP primary runoff by 61.1 percent to 38.9 percent but then had to win a crowded special election for the rest of Farenthold's expired term. With Republicans and Democrats both running at the same time, it made the special election tricky. Thankfully, Bech Bruun endorsed Michael and helped pull the Republicans together.

Michael Cloud won that race on June 30, 2018, just one month after the runoff, and immediately took office. Though he still had to run a fourth race in November for the general election, "Mr. Smith" was now going to Washington.

It was a brutal schedule in 2018, but the Cloud family and their grassroots team—working on a shoestring budget—pulled it off, winning four elections in one year. They ran by faith, and God blessed it as He brought in the cavalry to help. Michael Cloud was destined to be in Congress.

WE BOTH LOVE JESUS

I met Michael at the state Republican Convention in 2018, only three weeks after my loss and after his win in his own runoff. He was in the middle of the special election and wasn't slowing down. I wandered around that year's venue, the Henry B. González Convention Center in San Antonio, wondering how my activist friends who had seen me at every convention since 2004 would receive me.

The loss in my congressional race was so fresh that at one point I broke down as I walked through the halls with Lonnie, Senator Taylor's chief of staff. I felt like a fool. Friends and activists from all over the state kept asking, "What are you doing here? I didn't think you would be here." I got sick of hearing it. I'd reply, "We are family. Of course I am here. There is much more work to be done." On the other hand, young women would come up to me and thank me for being a shining example. One minute I felt like a hero for Republican women everywhere, and the next I wanted to crawl into my bed at the hotel and never come out.

Just before the congressional luncheon that was held at every convention, I was in the VIP room greeting elected officials from all over the state. When I saw Michael Cloud, my self-pity was suddenly overcome with boldness, and I went right up to him and stuck out my hand. I was thrilled to meet this humble man that few people knew about at the time. I could sense his heart in the videos I had watched of him and in his speeches on the campaign trail. I was so excited for his future in Congress.

"Michael, it is such an honor to meet you! I have been watching all your videos," I exclaimed.

We talked for about five minutes while his campaign consultant looked on.

Then I closed with this thought: "Michael, you are from ORU. I am from CFNI. We both love Jesus. If there is ever anything I can do for you, please let me know."

That was it. I was blessed to have met him and was believing for this man to have a strong Christian testimony in Congress.

Almost seven months later my phone rang. It was Congressman Cloud calling me on the exact day I had said, "God, I am done!"

In a quiet yet bold tone, Michael said, "Bunni, I woke up this morning thinking that I would really like to work with you, but I am not sure exactly where I need you. I am still trying to figure out all the pieces. Maybe you can help me." He laughed in that nervous way that endears him to others, and I knew I had found the one member of Congress I wanted to work for.

Two days later we boldly jumped into a new adventure together as we both signed agreements for me to be his general consultant, campaign manager, and Texas fundraiser. Michael Cloud was my new Jeb Hensarling.

I was ready to settle back into an old routine of running just one campaign, but this time it would mean running back and forth from Dallas to Victoria, five and a half hours away from each other. Either way, I was doing another 180-degree turn in my life. Some people around me were concerned that I was downsizing my company, but I knew deep inside it was where God was leading me.

A CABIN IN VICTORIA

Victoria, Texas, is a rural community of God-loving and America-loving people. These patriots had pulled their community back together after Hurricane Harvey, a Category 4 storm, caused $125 billion in damages to the Coastal Bend and Houston in 2017. The community became tighter than ever as neighbors helped each other rebuild and revitalize the area.

This sentiment showed up in their smiles and warmth, even to a girl from Dallas. I fell in love with this little city of around 65,000 people where, unlike Dallas, I could get anywhere in ten minutes. I found nice restaurants on the Guadalupe River, neat shops downtown, and my favorite hangout next to the campaign office: Jason's Deli. I discovered the parks, their small family zoo, and the welcoming churches in the area ranging from large to small congregations.

Trying to live and work in both Dallas and Victoria was a small chore at first, but Rosel, the congressman's wife, mentioned the idea of my using a small cabin at Son Valley Ranch. The Clouds' friends Glen and Cherylnn Dry had a ministry that owned this beautiful ranch that included a western-style church building, beautiful fishing ponds, and three small cabins they built after Hurricane Harvey. At the time, they used the cabins to care for needy families. The property even had a donkey named Ethel—fitting for a Republican consultant who was attempting to love all people.

One of these little cabins became my new home away from home anytime I was down in Victoria. With a tiny living room, a small kitchen, one bedroom, and one bathroom, it was a perfect fit for me. It was also a great symbol of my life going from a high-profile congressional race and a fast-paced consulting firm to near obscurity.

I was usually in town only when the congressman was home for an extended week or a long weekend. During the August recess, however, I was there for close to three weeks. Tim met me for a quick weekend getaway in San Antonio during that long stint to help make it work.

The words of seventeenth-century monk Brother Lawrence came alive to me in that cabin as I read one of my favorite books again: *The Practice of the Presence of God*. I committed to the Lord that I would enjoy walking with Him whether I was in the halls of Congress or in a little cabin in Victoria, Texas, serving someone else. I was determined to be happy and to walk in joy and peace.

My dad used to ask Tim and me all the time, "How's your courage?" It was his way of encouraging us. He always wanted to point us to the simple answers. There is something about simplicity that brings us back to what really matters, and in the stillness of that little cabin, I found my courage again. I read my Bible and spent extended times in prayer around my busy job.

Within only four months Congressman Cloud's chief of staff, who had been on the Hill for over twenty years, told me, "This is one of the best political organizations I have ever seen." That was a real compliment. Through all of it my soul was healing.

It was spring of 2019 when I went to work for Congressman Cloud. Soon after that, we had a pastor's meeting in the district. Even though I hadn't planned the meeting, the congressman asked me to attend. About forty pastors were there, and at the end they gathered around Michael, praying and thanking God for raising him up to this place of influence. I enjoyed the gathering and marveled at the respect these spiritual leaders had for Michael.

Then, all of a sudden, tears started welling up in my eyes. Deep disappointment filled my heart. "Why have I not been raised up to stand with him in Congress?" I thought. "Why am I here, far away from the people I should be leading?"

I wasn't jealous, but I knew deep disappointment was still in my heart. It was a wake-up call that I had more work to do. I continued asking God to heal every part of my soul. I knew I was in Victoria for a reason.

In the stillness of the cabin that week, God again spoke courage to my heart, telling me He was not done with my story. He was only beginning.

DIGGING A DEEP WELL

Responding to God in obedience is not something that comes naturally to us.

Unbelief, doubts, fears, and worry vie for control in our lives. But God is always trying to take us to a deeper place in Him. This dependence on Him and His Word can't be built in our walk by just going to church on a Sunday morning or feeding only from secondhand bread we receive from a preacher in a pulpit.

We must discover our individual walks with God without leaning on the crutch of someone else, or we will never grow. Learning to feed ourselves, not just parrot talking points from someone else, will create a voice in us all our own. We must build fellowship based in the Word of God among a community of believers, but we can't stop there. We have to learn to "drink water from [our] own cistern, and running water from [our] own well" (Prov. 5:15).

Paul indicated that the washing of water by the Word is the means of purification for the church:

> Husbands, love your wives, just as Christ also loved the church
> and gave Himself for her, that He might sanctify and cleanse her
> with the washing of water by the word, that He might present

155

her to Himself a glorious church, not having spot or wrinkle or
any such thing, but that she should be holy and without blemish.
—Ephesians 5:25–27

Maturity is found in daily dependence on Jesus—letting His living
water wash over us to cleanse us and then digging a deep well within our
own hearts and souls from which we have something to draw. Courage
comes from that place of deeply knowing God, not from a shallow
Christianity that operates from a dehydrated place. We must dig deeper
wells.

Sharing the Vision—Christians Engaged

One day in July 2019 I was down in Congressman Cloud's district, and I
finally got up the courage to talk to him about my vision for a new ministry. It had been birthed in my heart and was growing on paper. Though
I didn't have a name for it yet, I had twenty pages of notes that I had consolidated around three main points.

These were the main weaknesses I had identified in how the body of
Christ in America interacted with its nation and government—and the
three places where I could give help to an uninvolved church: *pray, vote,*
and *engage.*

- *Pray.* My heart was burning to teach the church not only
  more about intimacy with Jesus but also about the power
  of intercession, specifically how to pray for America and
  our elected officials.

- *Vote.* My own experience running for Congress showed
  me how few Christians vote in primaries. The sixteen
  churches where I spoke during the race hadn't seemed to
  understand the processes and the importance of voting
  regularly. I was desperately trying to figure out how
  to motivate and educate Christians across denominational lines to vote in every election, even local races and
  primaries.

- *Engage.* Helping Christians get the practical political education they needed to work with local, state, and federal
government and to walk with Jesus at the same time was
my passion. There was a vacuum of civics education. My
desire was to encourage Christians to become engaged by
explaining the political parties and teaching them how
to interact with elected officials and impact government.
There was also a famine of good Bible teaching on the
hot-button issues of the day, though people searched for it.

I had shared the vision with Trayce Bradford, a friend and former
client, over lunch one day. "If Trayce gets this," I thought, "I might have
something." She was so excited about the vision that she agreed to step
down as president of Texas Eagle Forum, a nonprofit that motivates and
activates conservatives in Texas, to become the vice president of whatever
I was going to call this organization.

After months of healing, I felt an urgency from God that I couldn't dis-
appear forever into a cabin in Victoria. My next step was to discuss this
with the congressman. Could I continue to run his political organization
and start a nonprofit ministry up in North Texas on the side?

This might have seemed like too much to take on, but I knew what I
was capable of. I had helped run house churches for over ten years while
working for Congressman Hensarling. I also had a firm for three years
where I was managing thirty-two accounts at the same time. I knew I was
fully capable of doing both and doing them well.

The day of our conversation was a normal hot day in South Texas. I
was driving Congressman Cloud from an event in Corpus Christi back
to Victoria. After a lot of small talk about the campaign, I started in. I
had to be bold. I shared my vision with him, and he instantly began interacting with me on it. We talked for a full hour. He threw out ideas and
helped me clarify the vision even more. His heart connected with everything I was saying. At the end of the conversation, before we arrived at
his house, he turned to me and said, "Forget about permission. How can
Rosel and I be involved in this?"

When we launched Christians Engaged six months later with a

website and a vision video, Rep. Michael Cloud was my first advisory board member, and soon his wife, Rosel, joined our governing board. We built the foundation of this nonprofit ministry together—a sitting congressman and a woman who had felt lost many days in a cabin in Victoria.

DAILY BREAD

At the beginning of 2020, I was running a full congressional campaign for Representative Cloud (which is more than a full-time job), plus I had just launched the new nonprofit. That first year, even amid the COVID-19 outbreak, Christians Engaged had programs in twenty-seven churches and I publicly spoke over one hundred times. We had begun producing content to awaken the church and lead them into habits of praying, voting, and engaging.

It was an overwhelming year on so many levels for me, but I just kept my head down, did my job for Congressman Cloud with excellence, and then worked another twenty to twenty-five hours a week to grow Christians Engaged.

Ian Stageman, my young assistant at Bunni Pounds & Associates who had run the business for me while I ran for Congress, had continued working for me through 2019. When we decided together to completely shut down the company, he quickly got another job working as the field director of the Collin County Republican Party.

A couple of weeks into January 2020, Ian called. Christians Engaged was less than a month old. He said, "I am not doing the right thing."

Having no peace in his position as a field director, he had decided to quit the job without talking to me first. Somehow, he knew he was supposed to keep working with me. The problem was, we had no money. None. Ian then told me directly that there was no way I was going to run a congressional campaign and a statewide nonprofit all year by myself. The young man was so right. Even though we had less than $5,000 in the bank, I heard the Lord speak to my heart: "You need Ian. Take the leap of faith."

As a contract laborer Ian took a large pay cut to help me with this new start-up ministry. Ian and I stepped out in faith. That first Monday we prayed and asked God directly for the $1,000 we needed to pay Ian's salary that week. At the consulting firm we had started every week with group Bible study and prayer, so it was not abnormal for us to pray together. Now we were doing it in a new ministry, and we were desperate.

I will never forget what happened next. At noon that day a dear friend went to our website and gave Christians Engaged $1,000. It was a miracle.

Week number one was paid for. God gave us a sense of peace; everything was going to be OK. His presence was on this mission, and we were confident that He would provide our daily bread.

BE BOLD. BE COURAGEOUS.

We had our first few churches set and were moving forward with helping pastors present programs to teach their congregations in a very non-threatening way about the importance of prayer, voting, and engaging for America. As a nonpartisan Christian ministry we were not endorsing candidates or political parties. We were educating the body of Christ wherever we found them—in churches, at community festivals, or on social media—to learn about these three keys that we felt could pull America out of its downward spiral.

We believed that the church was the answer to the ills of our nation and that if we could plug believers into praying, voting, and engaging, we could impact everything.

I had a personal mandate that I knew the Lord had given me after my congressional race: find the *awakening* church (not to be confused with the *woke* church that is straying from biblical truth). He was opening the eyes of the awakening church to the fate of the nation, and I felt called to share the knowledge I had been given while also teaching them to walk with Jesus through the muck and mire.

This was my scripture: "Do this, knowing the time, that now it is high time to awake out of sleep; for now our salvation is nearer than when we first believed" (Rom. 13:11). The church was being awakened—slowly but surely. I knew that Christians Engaged was going to play a part in this spiritual awakening and that individual Christians would start impacting their communities one heart at a time. My faith was high!

We were talking to pastors and booking churches, and then COVID-19 hit. Everything started shutting down. We were in the middle of March, and I thought, "How brilliant am I to start a new nonprofit right before this? *Ugh!* How are we going to survive?"

Not only did I have to deal with the stress of the situation on our family, the nation, and the congressman and his team, but now I had to figure out how to keep Ian paid in the middle of a pandemic.

The moment everything started shutting down with church programs, we pivoted and started ministering to people online. God gave us such clarity on how to communicate in a time of frustration. Our tagline for that season was #ChooseHope. We hosted our first statewide prayer call with elected officials and pastors, giving hope to people all over the state. I authored inspiring articles unveiling my own fears and attempts to walk in faith during the pandemic. We started a letter-writing campaign called Letters of Hope, encouraging citizens to send letters to their mayors, county judges, and even Vice President Pence and the Coronavirus Task Force.

I also took advantage of the slowdown to start a project that had been in my heart for years: creating a curriculum to give Christians a starting place for getting involved with politics. To develop it, I started teaching it online through Zoom. This class is now our national signature product— On-Ramp to Civic Engagement.

Less than three weeks into the shutdown, I got a call from a friend with whom I had done street evangelism regularly a few years before. She and her husband had been tracking with what we were doing since our launch. They were not political people, though they were starting to catch a vision for engagement. She shared her heart for the nation, her prayers for the church, and her excitement for the call of God on my life to personally lead this movement. At the end of the conversation, she said, "Bunni, we got an inheritance recently, and God spoke to us this week that we were supposed to give Christians Engaged the tithe from this blessing. It is not much; it is just $21,000."

My jaw dropped; I didn't know what to say. Up to this point a friend's $10,000 gift at the beginning of the ministry was the largest gift we had received. That day on the phone, this precious woman said to me, "Bunni,

God has called you as a voice to this nation. Be bold. Be courageous. Say the things others are afraid to say."

Even in the middle of a national pandemic shutdown, God was speaking to me, reminding me who I was and what He had empowered me to do. The obedience of that couple to speak identity over me again set the foundation of this ministry during a very turbulent time. It also reminded me that relationships that share the gospel together can never be shaken.

COMPLAINING TO GOD

Fast-forward to 2021. I was still working full-time campaigning for Congressman Cloud. Our team had thankfully scared off any potential primary challengers that year, but I had a full plate doing everything for his political operation and running the nonprofit ministry that was continuing to grow.

God had miraculously kept Ian fed and clothed, and that young man helped me make Christians Engaged look professional, even when we were super small. We were faithfully moving forward step by step, but I was worn out and tired of my focus constantly being divided in two. Though I was remaining faithful to my commitment to the Clouds, my heart was in full-time ministry and discipling Christians to impact our nation.

I told Tim, "I need to go away. I am going to go to this three-day Awaken the Dawn tent meeting in Fredericksburg, Virginia. I'm going to complain to God about still having two full-time jobs."

In March 2021 I flew east, stayed in a hotel by myself, and went for prayer and worship every day, spending time on the floor of that huge tent trying to find God. On the third day, I wrote down these words in my journal: "Get happy. Get content. Your breakthrough is coming soon."

That was all I needed to hear from Jesus, so I hopped on a plane and came home.

THE LETTER THAT CHANGED EVERYTHING

On May 18, 2021, eighteen months after applying and two months after I had written those words in my journal, I finally had it: a certified letter from the Internal Revenue Service. It was our official letter concerning our application for tax-exempt status for Christians Engaged.

Like every other nonprofit we had applied for our tax-exempt status when we launched, sending the IRS our website information, our vision, our bylaws, our board members' names, and everything else they needed. We had a great lawyer who set it all up for us correctly, emphasizing our purpose within the constraints of the law to educate people on their civic duties, including teaching on prayer, voting, and engagement.

We never told people how to vote but informed and taught them about the processes. We were not unlike other voter mobilization nonprofits like Rock the Vote or When We All Vote, started by Michelle Obama. These organizations register voters and educate them. The only difference is that we were doing it in churches and teaching the Bible.

In those eighteen months I had worked patiently with the IRS as it reviewed our application. I went back and forth twice with packages of documents and answered every question the IRS agent asked us. Then I waited for almost a year with no response. Eventually I had to open a constituent case with my Congress member and former opponent, Lance Gooden, to get the federal agency to contact us. He was so gracious to help us, and I reiterated how pleased I was with his congressional service.

As an organization we had raised over $100,000 in 2020 (by the grace of God), spending almost all of it on building the ministry around Texas. We were running on a shoestring budget, and our supporters were waiting patiently for their tax deductions.

At last the letter arrived. When I opened it, I was shocked to read the words, but there it was in black and white: "The bible teachings are typically affiliated with the [Republican] party and candidates. This disqualifies you from exemption under IRC Section 501(c)(3)." The IRS was denying our 501(c)(3) status!

"What! Have I read that correctly?" I thought.

The letter went on to say this:

Information you present and on your website is not neutral. You instruct individuals on how Christians should use the Bible and vote the Bible....

For example, you educate believers on national issues that are central to their belief in the Bible as the inerrant Word of God. Specifically, you educate Christians on what the Bible says in areas where they can be instrumental including the areas of sanctity of life, the definition of marriage, biblical justice, freedom of speech, defense, and borders and immigration, U.S. and Israel relations.

It hit me quickly. What could this precedent mean—not only for us but for every Christian organization? I'd thought the Bible was a kingdom document. It was established as the Word of God thousands of years before any political party came into being. How could teaching the Bible be a partisan exercise?

For the IRS to say that biblical teachings were in essence political speech could potentially hurt every Christian nonprofit in America, including churches that discuss their biblical perspective about public issues.

As a fledgling organization we had operated by faith. We had invested all our money into growth, going into churches with no obligation from them and building out resources to educate believers across denominational lines. We simply didn't have the money to file an appeal to the IRS in the less than thirty days allocated to us.

Then my thoughts went to myself and our board: What would this mean to us personally if we appealed this to the IRS? Would fighting this ruling come back to haunt us later? Would this put a target on our backs for audits, whether as individuals or at our businesses?

Thankfully, that same week I was meeting with my longtime friend Lathan Watts at First Liberty Institute in Plano, Texas, to discuss coming on the road with us for the On-Ramp to Civic Engagement seminars we were now conducting in churches. We were getting a lot of questions from pastors and church members on the separation-of-church-and-state issue, the Johnson Amendment, and other topics that I thought First Liberty's team would be the most qualified to answer.

Led by Kelly Shackelford, First Liberty Institute is "the largest legal organization in the nation dedicated *exclusively* to defending religious liberty for all Americans." They believe that "every American of any faith—or no faith at all—has a *fundamental* right to follow their conscience and live according to their beliefs."[5]

After I handed it over to Lathan, our IRS letter went around the office at First Liberty, and he called to tell me they were all amazed that this letter was real. His office even asked for the certified envelope that it came in because the phone number for the agent had 666 in it. (Though Lathan has since moved on to another legal organization committed to religious freedom, he was a key player in getting this case moving for us, and for that I am forever thankful.)

I met with our board and called our advisory board members individually. We all decided to fight the decision and appeal to the scary IRS. All of us had to find a little bit of boldness and courage.

The staff at First Liberty took the case and immediately went to work. On Wednesday, June 16, we filed our appeal with the IRS and distributed a press release to shed a little light on this important issue. And did the light ever shine! This is where the media frenzy started. I was not yet thinking about how God, just two months earlier on the tent floor in Virginia, had told me, "Get happy. Get content. Your breakthrough is coming soon."

A few days later I got a text from one of my friends on the Hill, Rep. Chip Roy, saying, "Bunni, I am on it!" I didn't ask for more clarification. As I thought about it more, I figured it was not very wise of the IRS to take on a former congressional candidate and political consultant who knew *everyone* in the state.

On June 25, Rep. Chip Roy from Texas and Sen. Mike Lee of Utah, along with thirteen other senators and representatives, sent a letter to the IRS commissioner asking him to investigate this case. Rep. Michael Cloud could not be on that letter because he was on our advisory board. Then on June 30, Rep. Kevin Brady and Rep. Jim Jordan sent a letter to the Treasury Department requesting an investigation.

While all this was going on, hundreds of Christians were being awakened from their sleep. I remembered my mandate from the Lord at the beginning of Christians Engaged and marveled that what we had built in faith was now starting to impact the nation. From around America,

Christians were taking our pledge to pray, vote, and engage. We had built a communication system where people could take our pledge and get messages each Monday with a prayer prompt for government. They could also get voting reminders for every election that also taught them how to research their ballots from a nonpartisan Christian perspective and receive a weekly discipleship newsletter on prayer, voting, and engagement with links to our podcast, educational articles, and our newly developed curriculum designed to teach people how to engage.

As I went on more media outlets and our story kept going out, we received emails and phone calls that people were sending letters to the IRS. One man emailed me, "I am sending an angry letter to the IRS right now."

I emailed back, "Do it in the Spirit of Christ," and I laughed, thinking of Jesus turning over the tables in the temple.

People of faith were outraged, but they were moving in the right way to prayer and action. All this was an answer to my prayers. The church was waking up, and God was using a bad situation to make a difference for all our good.

QUITTING MY JOB

The Sunday after the media frenzy had started with our appeal, I woke up with the feeling I'd had when I ran for Congress. There was a huge knot in my stomach that I couldn't shake. I talked to Tim, and he could see it on my face. Over the course of a year and a half, our little ministry had been functioning month to month. At the time, we had only $7,000 in the bank, and I knew I had to step out in faith again.

We had been in over forty churches, had paid for the development of our first online curriculum, and had supplied believers around the state with tons of free resources. Our weekly communications and voting reminders were a lot of work. I was thankful to Ian who helped me run it all. But all of it cost money.

The situation with the IRS was actually good publicity. Word was getting out that the IRS was unfairly targeting a Christian organization. Although this wasn't going to flood our mailbox with money, it did provide an opportunity for me to get the mission in front of some previous supporters who had not yet looked at this mission seriously. I felt a sense of urgency. It was time to take the bull by the horns and really get the ministry off the ground.

God was going before us and providing the opportunity even in the middle of this crazy situation. This was the breakthrough moment for Christians Engaged that I had been praying for. Would I be obedient to follow God or stay in this in-between place?

On that Sunday I started making calls. Later that week I called Congressman Cloud and laid out a plan for me to transition out. It was the hardest thing for me to do, and it was hard for him to hear, but we both knew it was time. We soon came to the agreement that my last full day with the campaign would be June 30, 2021, and my first full-time day with Christians Engaged would be July 1. Ian, team player that he is, accepted the congressman's offer to take over his campaign for a season. I was terrified, but I knew God was leading. It was time to be bold and make the transition to focus solely on the ministry.

By July 1—just fifteen days after our appeal had started—I had $80,000 in cash and commitments for Christians Engaged. God had met me in such an incredible way, giving me favor with so many brothers and sisters in Christ from different backgrounds who believed in me and believed in our mission.

That same day—my first day on the Christians Engaged full-time payroll—I was working from my mom's house in Indiana. We were preparing to gather there as a family for the Fourth of July. Breathing deeply, I thanked God for this new start. I told my mom how thankful I was for this new season, and she smiled. She knew I was happy. I was writing and working with renewed vision when my phone rang.

It was the IRS. The supervisor of the agent who had worked so hard to deny us was on the phone apologizing on behalf of the Internal Revenue Service. I stood there in shock, asking him for his phone number and email to prove that this was really happening to me.

Was the IRS repenting?

The supervisor informed me that Christians Engaged would be receiving its tax-exempt status after all and that we would receive the notice to our attorneys directly after the holiday. God is amazing.

On July 7, twenty-one days after sending our appeal letter, we had our victory letter in hand. I am incredibly thankful that the IRS made this right, but I am even more thankful for our board and leadership who were willing to take on this battle. God strengthened us and gave us a much quicker victory than we could have imagined.

This case demonstrated to all of us—in bright, vivid color—that if we stand up, our republic works. The victory left us all with hope and more commitment than ever before to pay attention to potential threats to our religious liberty and other freedoms. This success was not about us but about every prayer, every letter to the IRS, and every person who shared our story. This victory went to the citizens who had voted into office courageous representatives who stood up and pushed back against government encroachment. Only government can take away our rights, which is why getting involved with our local, state, and federal governments matters.

God worked a miracle in this appeal that we called Christians Engaged vs. the IRS, and He used His people from Texas to Capitol Hill to be light and salt to protect our liberties. Every prayer, vote, and form of engagement matters. Our story gave people greater hope for America.

For me personally, I was thankful for an ORU graduate who stepped out to run for Congress—this man who called me one morning at the prompting of the Lord, who trusted me to run his campaign and a ministry at the same time, and who then loosed me to fly at the right time. I am still overwhelmed with gratitude for First Liberty Institute and our attorney, Lea Patterson, as well as our board of directors and advisory board, who were not afraid to go on this journey with me and fight back together as the body of Christ.

Joan of Arc wouldn't have been a hero if the king hadn't believed in her. She couldn't free France by herself; she had an army. She heard from God and responded by convincing others that she was not just operating in human zeal but being moved by courage. History would later decide whether she was crazy or called by God. I believe Joan of Arc was just being obedient to the One she had cultivated a relationship with, finding courage in the deep well of faith that she had dug throughout her young life. This is where courage and boldness come from. These attributes do not come from nothing—they are cultivated for the right moment in history.

Do you not say, "There are still four months and then comes the harvest"? Behold, I say to you, lift up your eyes and look at the fields, for they are already white for harvest!

—JOHN 4:35

In the political movements, we get so caught up in our debates, our campaigns, and the important issues of our time that we often fail to consider that we are all people whom God loves. Our prejudices are not God's prejudices. He doesn't see people with a label on them. If we open our eyes to the harvest, we will see that individual people, whether they are Republicans, Democrats, Libertarians, or Independents, are souls who are loved by Jesus. His eyes are staring at them with fiery love. He is after their hearts.

Chapter 9

PREJUDICES ON THE RIGHT AND ON THE LEFT

POLITICS DIVIDES. THE entire process requires that we pick sides. Whether we are choosing between political parties, interest groups, or even ideological movements within the same party, at some point we will have to pick a side. As a candidate I had to choose my alliances and decide whether I would go after an organization's endorsement or not. If I pursued one group, it spoke volumes to other groups. If I didn't go after an interest group's endorsement, it also said something loud and clear to them and others as well.

Political activity is divisive, but it doesn't have to be hostile. Like anything in life, operating within government requires that we state an opinion and work within a system that is already functioning. It requires compromise at some level to work within a diverse group of people—whether that is in Congress, in an administration, or at the state, county, or city level.

From the very beginning I have always seen politics as a mission field and have not been afraid to share my faith, minister to people in political clubs or conventions, or even share the Word with elected officials. I have tried to see people as people, though in the heat of political battle that can be extremely difficult.

Even as I have tried to walk in love, God, in His grace, has continued to reveal to me some of my own deep-seated prejudices that have gone unchecked for years. They aren't the ones we normally think of—skin color, economic status, or religious affiliation. The biggest one for me, after almost twenty years in politics, is political affiliation.

RACISM IN VICKSBURG

The last church my dad pastored before leaving denominational ministry was in Vicksburg, Mississippi. In 1985, the Seventh-Day Adventist (SDA) church in our city was racially divided. There was a black SDA church and a white SDA church.

My dad developed a deep friendship with the black SDA pastor in town, and my sister and I played with their three young sons. Our families got together for lunch on summer days, and we tried to be as close as we could. Chaos ensued, however, when my dad decided that we needed to have joint vespers services on Friday nights with the other church of the same denomination in our city. The plan was that one week their members would join us at our church for a Friday night vespers service to worship the Lord, and then the next Friday we would go to theirs. The elders of our white church pitched a fit.

"We are too different," the defectors moaned. My dad had to stand his ground on what he knew the Lord had told him.

Racism was on full display in West Mississippi in 1985, but God was trying to break through hardened hearts to bring His glory to the earth through love. My dad's example has always spoken volumes to me on how to walk against the tide of prejudices. Prejudice is something I have guarded against my whole life—looking to pluck it out of my soul in any form. Though racism still exists all over the world, the modern American Christian also struggles with socioeconomic and ideological divisions. We have seen whole families split over whom they voted for to be president. This should not be.

The heart of God for people is deep. He reaches out to His children despite their behavior, their confusion, their hurts, or even their combativeness with Him. As His followers, we are called to be like Him regardless of how uncomfortable it makes us.

A DELAYED ENDORSEMENT

During my runoff in 2018, I didn't get an endorsement from Sen. Ted Cruz until the night before the election. That night when his campaign manager, Bryan, called, I wanted to throw something at him. It wasn't his fault. He was just the unfortunate messenger.

During the first round of the primary, the senator had supported his district staffer out of Tyler, Jason Wright. Jason was an incredible communicator and a real conservative. Later in the runoff Jason spoke at one of my East Texas fundraisers, saying a line that got a huge laugh: "One day I am going to have to tell my grandchildren that I ran for Congress and lost. But the worst thing I am going to have to tell them is that I got beat by a bunny."

Once Jason was out of the race, I was convinced that Senator Cruz would quickly endorse me—the real conservative in the race—against the more liberal Lance Gooden.

I couldn't support Ted Cruz publicly in 2012 when he first ran a come-from-behind race for the US Senate against our lieutenant governor, David Dewhurst, overtaking him in a GOP primary runoff. I worked for Congressman Hensarling at the time, and he wasn't getting involved in the race. As a staffer I had to stay out. Behind the scenes, though, I was cheering Ted Cruz on and was not surprised by his ultimate victory that year. I saw the momentum on the ground all over the district where I worked. I knew he would ultimately be successful. It was the period when the Tea Party was riding high, and this constitutional conservative who could give a speech like no other rode that wave all the way to victory.

When I started my political consulting firm a few years later, Rafael Cruz—Senator Cruz's outspoken and dynamic father—was a regular guest speaker to get people to come out to the fundraisers for many of my clients. He was extremely helpful to new conservative leaders who were trying to get elected. Rafael and I became friends. Our faith and our passion for our state pulled us together, even in the limited time we spent together as we worked within the movement. It tore me up when Rafael called during my primary, letting me know that even with two friends in the race, he had to support Jason Wright at Senator Cruz's request.

Once it was only Lance and me in the runoff, Rafael was able to secure Senator Cruz's permission to be a guest speaker at two of my fundraisers. I was deeply thankful but still had no movement on a full endorsement from the senator himself. We were hoping to announce it all over the district.

As soon as the runoff started, I pursued the endorsement relentlessly. I finally got a call from the senator's team that he would be willing to meet with me in Houston. Flying to Houston, I felt overly optimistic about the whole process. I already had a great relationship with Wade Miller, one of the senator's key staffers. Wade told me after a local forum that he appreciated my boldness. I also knew Rafael had put in a good word for me.

Even though Senator Cruz and I had met only a few times in passing at events, we had a good rapport. We were together on many legislative races in the state—picking the same candidates. It seemed to me that we were on the same side. After an incredible hour with the senator, I felt great about the vetting process and my answers to his questions. I left him and thanked him, saying, "I would be honored to have your endorsement, Senator. It could make a big difference to drive up a few more percentage points in my favor. I am convinced I am going to win." With his help I had no doubt in my mind that I would win in the end.

After my meeting with the senator at the end of March, and up to the week of the election on May 22, I called his team every week. "Where is my endorsement from Senator Cruz?" I wondered. "I have everyone else in the conservative movement that matters to my district—the vice president and all the conservative state legislators. Why is this so hard?" I am sure Bryan, a friend who like me had served in the trenches for years, got tired of listening to my voice mails.

After all my pursuing, after Rafael's stirring speeches on my behalf, after most of Jason's supporters turned their support to me in the runoff, I still didn't have Sen. Ted Cruz on my side in a public way.

Then I got the call the night right before the election. It was Bryan. "The senator is proud to endorse you, Bunni. Better late than never."

Completely flabbergasted and feeling put out, I whined, "Bryan, with all due respect, what am I supposed to do with this now? The election is *tomorrow*! Early voting is already over. Our last mailing dropped five days ago. How am I supposed to get this great news out to the district? With a text message to the voter file? It is too late."

I was steaming mad. I was hurt.

Bryan, who was just doing his job, replied sheepishly, "I am sorry, Bunni. There was nothing I could do. I am not sure what the delay was."

It had been over two months since I had interviewed with Senator Cruz. I had been in the conservative movement for years. I was a known commodity in the Cruz world, yet something had held up this endorsement. Maybe he didn't think I could win? Maybe he didn't think I was conservative enough? For whatever reason, he had waited for over two months to give me his endorsement, and when it finally happened, it was just before the election. It felt unfair to me.

My team went to work and put out the endorsement on a mass text message to the voters and then in an email to our list. We asked Senator Cruz's team if they would also put it out to their own contacts in the district. They did, but it didn't hit inboxes till three o'clock the next afternoon—Election Day.

I lost by 2,752 votes—a 6 percent difference. It was over.

I was not sure if I believed Senator Cruz's support would have made a difference in that final month, but I had hoped to find out. In the end God had another plan for me, and I had to find my identity in Him alone. I had to move on.

TED VS. BETO

During that 2018 general election (after my runoff), the race that everyone was talking about in our state was Sen. Ted Cruz versus Democrat congressman Beto O'Rourke.

The race was hot and heavy and will not be soon forgotten by Texans as Congressman O'Rourke continuously out-raised Senator Cruz and caused a huge stir around the state. In the third quarter of that year, Beto "was out-raising Cruz period after period, and he posted an astonishing $38 million in the third quarter of 2018—a new record for the biggest fundraising quarter ever in a U.S. Senate race."[1]

Beto went on a tour all over Texas, hitting every one of the 254 counties.

He filmed himself and his team eating at Whataburger and skateboarding around towns looking hip and cool; he became endearing to many.

Ted, on the other hand, was busy in DC breathing out red conservative fire, as always, and trying to stir up his base. It was the midterms, two years into the Trump administration, so the shine was coming off the Trump penny for the suburbanites, especially for the white, educated females who were pulling their whole families out to vote. To those of us on the ground, it seemed that Senator Cruz's campaign took off too late as volunteers scrambled to get Cruz signs up to offset the neighborhoods filled with black-and-white Whataburger-looking Beto signs. In reality, they just didn't have the resources to put into running signs all over the state. The Cruz team was being outspent on every side.

In the middle of Ron Wright's and Van Taylor's congressional races at the time, I was watching the Republicans struggle to prepare against the Beto wave that was coming. You could feel the movement underground. I was still nursing my wounds from my campaign but was also frustrated that so many people couldn't decide whom to vote for in this important senate race.

This was a year before I launched Christians Engaged, but I knew that people around the state were craving simple information. So I drafted a blog post titled "Ted vs. Beto: 10 Reasons Why Every Christian Should Vote Ted." It took me a few hours to write and design the piece. I quoted both candidates on all the issues such as abortion, support of Israel, border security, fiscal policy, religious liberty, and guns. The ten-point guide spelled out the beliefs of both candidates very succinctly. I published it and shared it on my social media accounts. I didn't think about it afterward, as I was consumed with Ron Wright's race at the time.

Two days later I finally checked the blog stats after seeing all the shares on Facebook. I was amazed. It was everywhere. I saw the post on so many of my friends' feeds and in groups I didn't even know existed. It had twenty-three thousand hits in only forty-eight hours.

It wasn't as elaborate as the fundraiser that paid off Lance Gooden's runoff debt, but in a simple way, it helped me lay down my hurt from that last-minute endorsement. My heart had moved in the right direction through that blog post defending our junior senator from Texas.

LOVING HIS FAMILY

Rafael Cruz and I continued to connect regarding our faith, our passion for the body of Christ, and our love for people. From the two fundraisers he had headlined for me during my race to the conversation I had with this man of God over Lance Gooden, his support and wisdom meant so much to me.

A year and a half into our adventure with Christians Engaged, Rafael Cruz joined forces with us, joining my advisory board and using our pledge to pray, vote, and engage at the churches he was preaching in around Texas. His engagement with us added to our impact. He also spoke at our first national Wake UP! conference in 2021.

Backstage, after the two-day conference was over, Rafael mentioned an idea to me. "Let's go on the road together. I want to tag team preach with you," he suggested. This man was becoming closer and closer to me each day. What a blessing he was—praying for our family, encouraging my spiritual gifts, and believing in this ministry that God had put in my heart.

In 2022, we did twelve Awakening Nights together all over Texas and even did a meeting in Pennsylvania. It was such an honor to share my story and charge Christians to be engaged, and it was amazing to hear Rafael sharing his incredible story of coming from communism in Cuba to liberty in America.

Soon after starting Christians Engaged, I was driving home from Victoria one day when I heard the Lord speak to my heart: "Pull Bibi out from behind the shadows of Rafael and Ted. She has a voice for the body of Christ." Bibi Loyola, Rafael's niece and Senator Cruz's cousin, was the Texas outreach director for the senator and was like a daughter to Rafael. Working as one of Senator Cruz's key administrators, she helped her uncle organize his life and manage his schedule. She traveled with Rafael and Ted all the time and served them however she could.

I had known Bibi casually for many years, but as I got to know her more, I saw a deep faith and calling on her life to share Jesus—a call very similar to my own. Having lived through the 2016 presidential campaign, when their whole family had been on the road nonstop, she had helped

Senator Cruz rally support all over the nation. Bibi was an intercessor, a strong Cuban mother, and an encourager. When Ted came in second behind Donald J. Trump in the 2016 Republican presidential primary, the whole family felt the weight of disappointment.

Being obedient, I asked Bibi to be on my board of directors and worked on getting her in front of more people. Every time Bibi opens her mouth within a church, God shows up. She also has become one of my dearest friends, speaking life into me and encouraging me on my journey.

PRAYING FOR SENATOR CRUZ

Senator Cruz is always facing sharp criticism in the news, and sometimes they drag his family into it as well, which I believe should never happen. God has placed such a true love in my heart for Senator Cruz, Heidi, the girls, and their full extended family. They are on the front lines of the battle for our nation. As people of faith, they need us—their fellow members in the body of Christ—to cover them in prayer. My heart has broken in intercession for them many times. God loves them so much, and He has not left them as leaders in our nation to struggle alone.

None of our elected officials are perfect; they all need our intercession. Again the apostle Paul wrote:

> Therefore I exhort first of all that supplications, prayers, intercessions, and giving of thanks be made for all men, for kings and all who are in authority, that we may lead a quiet and peaceable life in all godliness and reverence. For this is good and acceptable in the sight of God our Savior, who desires all men to be saved and to come to the knowledge of the truth.
>
> —1 TIMOTHY 2:1–4

Many times we forget that famous elected officials are real people with real emotions and real families. Part of our mission within Christians Engaged is to call the body of Christ to pray deeply not only for these high-profile elected officials but also for our local leaders, whom many of us tend to ignore. These are the leaders who, regardless of party, are making decisions that affect our lives. Notice that in 1 Timothy 2, Paul makes a direct correlation between our prayers for our leaders and our ability to lead a "quiet and peaceable life" (v. 2).

Our elected officials need us to cover them in prayer regardless of whether we believe in everything they support. They need us and God is calling us to pray.

PRAYING FOR THE NEW PRESIDENT

In leading a nonpartisan ministry that encourages Christians to pray, vote, and engage, we send out prayer prompts each week, reminders to vote around every election, and educational and inspirational steps for Christians to engage. On Monday, January 25, 2021, our ministry sent out a prayer prompt just as we do every Monday. That day it read:

> Today, let's pray for the new President, Vice President, and their administration in accordance with 1 Timothy 2, that we may live peaceful and quiet lives in all godliness and holiness. Let's pray for our authorities to operate in righteousness, wisdom, and godliness. READ and PRAY 1 Timothy 2:1–2.

We had more people unsubscribe that day than I could fathom. I was shocked at the response of self-professed Christians who, on Inauguration Day, January 20, 2021, refused to pray for our new president, Joe Biden, and vice president, Kamala Harris.

We are failing as the body of Christ to truly engage in politics correctly if we do not remain kingdom people. We must obey the Word of God and follow the Spirit of Christ regardless of our political affiliations.

In politics we must choose sides when we vote and when we govern. But as Christians we must remember that we live in an upside-down kingdom. We move against the flow of the world and love and pray for people regardless of the label behind their names. God's love is deeper and wider than our prejudices if we will allow Him to work in our hearts.

A DREAM ABOUT BETO

> And it shall come to pass in the last days, says God, that I will pour out of My Spirit on all flesh; your sons and your daughters

shall prophesy, your young men shall see visions, your old men shall dream dreams.

—ACTS 2:17

In December 2021 I had a dream about someone I didn't expect: Beto O'Rourke. I very rarely have dreams that stick with me, but I woke up reliving this extremely vivid dream of me talking with Beto.

Robert Francis "Beto" O'Rourke is a former city councilman from El Paso who served in Congress from 2013 to 2019. Becoming famous after a nonpartisan road trip from South Texas to Washington, DC, with Republican congressman Will Hurd, Beto was seen for a while as a different breed of politician—one that pulled people together. This was until he ran for president and played to the hard left of the Democrat party. After leaving Congress, Beto founded Powered by People—a voter registration and mobilization engine in Texas to register Democrats and empower a movement in our state.

When this seasoned politician, who had a knack for raising money, ran against Sen. Ted Cruz in 2018, he came within 2 percentage points of winning. He ran for president in the 2020 Democratic primary and then for governor of Texas against Greg Abbott in 2022. Making headlines all along the way even as he lost, Beto was either loved or hated.

In my dream I was staring into Beto's eyes and spoke these words: "Congressman, God has a plan for your life, and it goes way beyond politics. He loves you and your family deeply, and He wants you to know Him more. He sees your heart to serve."

Yet the part of the dream that stuck with me deeply was when I said, "Congressman, I want to apologize to you on behalf of every Christian in your congressional district who didn't pray for you when you served in Congress."

It was a strong dream, and the impact of it stayed with me. I prayed many weeks and months about it, wondering why I had this visitation. I concluded there were some things that God wanted to do in my heart—and maybe in the body of Christ at large.

Weekly, I asked the body of Christ around America to pray for their elected officials regardless of their party. But deep inside I thought, "Do I really pray for elected officials regardless of their party? Am I letting my political party affiliation for years cloud my ability to see God's heart for these individual public servants and their families? What is God's heart for them?"

HEADING TO LAREDO

A few months after the dream I journeyed to Laredo, Texas, to minister with our evangelistic partners, Time to Revive.

In 2017, I had been deeply impacted by a move of God in Dallas-Fort Worth where the founder of Time to Revive, Kyle Lance Martin, and his associate, Wade Aaron, united three hundred churches in the DFW metroplex, taking to the streets for fifty days on a mission to share the gospel. Our house church got swept up in this miracle season. The Lord allowed me to be a part of leading twenty people to salvation in Jesus, and on the back end of the fifty days, I began leading Saturday outreaches as the Time to Revive chairman in East Dallas County. This continued until the day I ran for Congress.

One day a week Christians Engaged currently uses the Time to Revive boardroom in Richardson, Texas, allowing our small team to gather as we grow. Also, Jason Evans, the Texas director, comes on the road with us, teaching people how to share the gospel in our expanded On-Ramp to Civic Engagement seminar.

I don't want anyone to think that political activity in and of itself can save America; rather, I want Christians everywhere to be equipped to share their faith wherever they go, even as they engage with civic government. Therefore, our partnership with Time to Revive is critical for the spiritual health of our ministry.

In February 2022, Jason, Kyle, and the whole Time to Revive team gathered for a week in Laredo, Texas, a city right on the border of Mexico, to minister to the people. They gathered twenty churches, along with a whole crew of missionaries from around the nation. I felt strongly that I needed to get out on the streets and lead teams for a few days—even in the middle of the 2022 primary season.

Getting out of partisan politics as a career and running a Christian ministry full time, I could feel my heart shifting. I was spending more time thinking about the American people outside of a party affiliation. Over and over, I made it known that I believed if Christians would get involved in *all* political parties, they could make a huge difference wherever they went. I believe that with my whole heart.

At Christians Engaged we choose to not limit our discussions on prayer, voting, and engagement to only Christians who believe in a certain ideological grid. We talk to curious citizens across the ideological spectrum from all over America, connecting them to practical education and teaching them what the Bible says regarding the hot topics.

Driving myself down to Laredo, I prayed that God would help me minister to every person I met. Whether they were here legally or illegally, were of my race or not, or spoke Spanish or English, I wanted them to experience Jesus. I asked God to let me have His heart for all people and to minister to everyone the same, opening my eyes to see the harvest field where He led me.

I didn't have a clue what I was praying.

I HAVE TO GO MEET BETO

I have many stories from my three days in that border town, leading outreach teams and having divine encounters with people. But on the second night, while we were eating dinner outside the host church, Kyle sat next to me and shared with me about ministering to the county judge that day. He told me how receptive the man was and how he believed the judge was a real believer in Jesus. After knowing Kyle for four years, I trusted his discernment and his ability to minister to everyone wherever God would lead him. He had the same love and compassion for an international government leader as he did with a single mom on the streets. This man is humble, and he walks with God.

When Kyle finished telling me the story, I responded, "I am so glad you got to minister to the county judge! What an incredible testimony. I guess he is a Democrat." Catching myself, I said, "Of course he is a Democrat. We are in Laredo, Texas. There is no way a Republican gets elected countywide here."

Kyle reiterated the idea that the judge was a real believer in Jesus, that he had genuine faith. I told him that I was sure he was. But did I really believe that?

Kyle then told me how he had ministered to a man I'll call Steve at a market a few days before. He was impressed to share with him a word from God and prayed over him. Steve was so honored by the encounter that he invited Kyle to a special meeting. Kyle said, "Beto O'Rourke will be here tonight in Laredo as part of his race for governor, and Steve wants me to come pray over Beto at a private meeting he's hosting."

"Wow!" I exclaimed. "You absolutely have to go, Kyle. Please pray over Beto. What an incredible opportunity! Go!"

Then he stopped for a moment. "I don't think I have a release to go. I am supposed to minister here tonight at this church, and people are coming from all over the city."

"And why are you telling me this?" Suddenly I felt uncomfortable. The dream that I hadn't thought about in weeks came rushing back to me. I knew why Kyle was telling me this. I told Kyle about my dream and said, "I have to go meet Beto." It was one of the clearest directives I have ever had.

Kyle quickly connected me to Steve and registered me for the event, and off I went. My heart was pounding.

After parking and following the directions I'd been given, I realized that I was not at the private meeting venue Kyle had been promised but at a full-fledged Beto for Governor rally. It was an outside party with a bar at the back and picnic benches scattered around the yard. Surrounded by a black metal fence, it was a perfect concert venue. The local news media was there with lights positioned to where Beto would be speaking, and a crowd began to form. As upbeat rock music played, I took in the Beto banners, the black-and-white signs ready for people to grab as they left, the volunteers, and the diverse crowd gathering. About fifty people were there so far.

Meanwhile, a battle was going on in my mind. "What am I here for? What am I doing here?" I had to set my heart on why I had come to Laredo. I was on a ministry trip, period. I was called to minister and love people. "What has changed from what I was doing on the streets today?"

I asked myself. Wasn't I still a minister tonight walking into a venue with a whole bunch of Beto lovers?

Going up to a lady waiting by herself, I told her about the outreach we were doing there in Laredo. I explained that I was with a ministry called Time to Revive, pointing to the T-shirt I was wearing, and then asked the normal question that we used on the streets: "How can I pray for you?"

She asked me why I was there. I told her quickly about Kyle's encounter with Steve and asked if she knew him. She didn't. Then, surprisingly, she allowed me to pray with her for her grandkids.

I was settling in, trying to avoid any TV cameras. The idea that a TV camera might catch me at a Beto O'Rourke rally terrified me. I was there as an ambassador of the kingdom of God, but that didn't mean I wanted anyone to know about it.

"My political reputation will be destroyed if someone sees me here," I thought.

Beto finally arrived, and after another fifteen minutes of talking with several people, he made his way to the front of the crowd, which was now about one hundred people. He moved to where his staff directed him to stand in front of the TV cameras and lights.

I had asked around about Steve, but no one knew him. I knew I was in for a long night.

"What in the world am I doing here listening to Beto speak?" I thought. I instantly felt an urge that I knew was from the Lord. I opened the Notes app on my smartphone and decided to write down everything in Beto's speech that I agreed with. "The list is going to be *very* short," I muttered to myself.

If nothing else, Beto was a great public speaker. This Democrat politician drew large crowds all over our state repeatedly. He inspired young people, suburban moms, public educators, and diverse groups of people to come together to work for the common good.

As Congressman O'Rourke spoke that night, I wrote down three things that I agreed with him on. And I have to say, I was shocked.

He said that we needed to get all teachers back to the classrooms, that enough was enough. Online education alone was no longer serving the children of Texas well. *I agreed.*

He said that we needed to get rid of the STAAR test, that teachers were teaching only to the test, and that we needed to have a more holistic approach to education. *I agreed.*

He said that Governor Abbott had screwed up by not protecting our electric grid. *I partially agreed.*

During the horrible winter freeze of 2021, many Texans had been affected when the grid went down, and we all froze for days. Many people around the state had really suffered. Sen. Bob Hall, my former client, had been talking about the security of our grid for years. It was a problem, but it was not all the governor's fault.

Now, I vehemently disagreed with Beto when he started attacking the Texas Heartbeat Bill, which was saving unborn children's lives all over our state. And I didn't agree with his desire to legalize cannabis, but I listened and tried desperately to hear him out.

At the end of the twenty-minute speech, I finally found Steve, met a staffer for Rep. Henry Cuellar, prayed for her, and attempted to hang out with people. Steve told me what I already knew: Kyle was supposed to have come to another location before the rally—something that was not clear to him. Steve was still so pleased I was there. He told me again of his encounter with Kyle that week and then came up with a plan. Steve said, "Beto is going to hang out here and talk and take pictures with everyone who wants to meet him. Why don't you get in the very back of the line, and when you get to the top, I will introduce you and tell him I invited you here."

Sounded like a plan.

I got in the line and was still desperately trying to watch my heart. I started a conversation with a young Hispanic woman, a public-school educator who attended the First Baptist Church in the area. She was learning the Bible in a Sunday school class she was regularly attending. She was so blessed that I prayed with her in line that day and enthusiastically told me of her love for Jesus and her love for Beto.

When I finally made it to the front of the line, Beto's staffer asked if I wanted her to take my smartphone and shoot a few pictures of me with Beto.

"Sure," I said.

Inside I was freaking out. "I am already in way over my head," I thought. "I will delete them later."

Greeting Beto, I said, "Congressman, it is a pleasure to meet you. My name is Bunni."

He looked down at me with a smile on his face, probably happy to be at the end of the line and almost done. "Thanks for calling me Congressman. I haven't heard that in a while."

Returning the smile, I responded, "Well, it's your last official title; it is what people should call you."

Seeing that the line had now ended and that I was standing with Beto, Steve came over quickly. He officially introduced me to the former congressman and briefly told him the story about Kyle, the ministry going on in the city, and why I was there.

I said, "It has really been a blast to be here in Laredo, bringing churches together and praying for people all over this city. Steve thought it would be a good idea for Kyle, our founder, to come over and pray for you before the rally. He was unable to come, so he sent me. It is an honor to be here and meet you, sir."

"Great to meet you, Bunni," Beto said with a smile.

It was time for me to just go for it, so overcoming the fear in the pit of my stomach, I launched into why I was putting myself in this awkward position.

"Sir, what Kyle didn't know when he asked me to come meet you was that two months ago I had a dream about you. I had a dream that I was standing before you like this, and I was telling you how much God loves you and loves your family. I was telling you how He sees your heart to want to serve people and that He has a destiny for your life that goes way beyond politics."

As I was speaking, I could feel the Spirit of God coming on me. I had known that feeling all my life—whether at church, in our home, or on the job. It was not unlike my meeting with Vice President Pence. I was staring boldly into Beto's eyes, and he was looking right back at me.

Right there in that moment, I was living out the dream.

I went on, "God knows you and He sees you, and He wants you to know Him even more. I also saw in this dream where I was apologizing to you on behalf of Christians in your congressional district for not praying for you regularly." Then I said it: "On behalf of many in the body of Christ in your congressional district who have never prayed for you, sir, whether they are Protestant or Catholic, I am sorry, Congressman."

When I said that last line, I choked back the tears that were in my eyes. I couldn't help feeling the emotion of the moment.

Pausing, he said, "So you are telling me that God gave you a dream about me?"

"Yes, sir! I know it is wild," I said.

Beto replied, "I don't have any words for that. What do I say to that?"

Continuing, I said, "I am as surprised as you are, Congressman. I don't dream, but when I do, I take notice of it. And here I am standing in front of you far away from my home in Dallas in Laredo, Texas."

"Can I tell you one more thing?" I asked. He nodded. "The craziest thing is this: I am a Republican. I have been a political activist and consultant in the GOP for over sixteen years working for members of Congress. I ran for Congress myself in 2018 and ended up in a runoff in Dallas County and East Texas."

"What is your name again?" he asked quickly.

"Bunni Pounds."

"Bunni, I have heard about you." He looked a little shocked but still polite. "Wow! Nice to meet you."

To get through it, I didn't take a breath as I continued, "On top of that, Rafael Cruz is like a father to me. Senator Cruz's cousin, Bibi, is one of my dearest friends, and I pray regularly for Ted, Heidi, and their girls. I love the Cruz family."

He stood there, looking stunned yet completely in tune with me. His staff member was visibly shaking. I am sure she did not know what to think of this conversation.

"I walked into this night knowing God was sending me to pray for you, and while you were speaking, I wrote down some things that we agree on." From off the top of my head, I rattled off the three things I had written down in the notes on my phone. Then I added this: "Sir, at the end of the day, we are not Republicans and Democrats. We are Americans who all care for our nation. I believe with my whole heart that you are doing what you feel you are supposed to do. Though we may not agree on the path, we all want the best for America."

I was resting in the peace I felt, not even thinking about my next words. "Knowing all of this, would you still allow me to pray for you? Because I would be honored if you would."

Still looking me straight in the eyes, Beto O'Rourke said, "Absolutely, Bunni. I would be honored for you to pray for me." He proactively extended his forearm to me, and I grabbed it.

Praying a quick two-to-three-minute prayer, I asked God to reveal Himself to the congressman in new ways; to give him divine wisdom; to protect his family, his soul, and his emotions; and to surround his staff with peace and joy.

God was there. His presence was real in that quick prayer meeting with Beto. I was at complete peace as his staff member and Steve, who were listening in, were also impacted. At the end I thanked Congressman O'Rourke again for the honor of praying for him and his family.

I was about to move away when I heard Beto ask, "Bunni, can I have your cell phone number?" He continued, maybe seeing my hesitation, "Let me say, Bunni, this has been one of the most meaningful meetings I have ever had. I would like to get in touch with you in the future."

"Absolutely!" I said and rattled off my number to him.

He instantly sent me a text: "This is Beto."

"If God gives you anything else for me, please let me know," he said.

Trying to regain my composure, I made my way out past the venue's black gate. His staffer followed me out. "Here is my card. I wanted to give this to you. Reach out to me anytime. I really have no words for what just happened there. That was deeply impactful," she said.

I thanked her, and she continued, "I am on the road with Beto all the time planning events like this, and my husband is also involved in politics. We are doing what we feel we are supposed to do, but it is extremely hard. My kids are home with our nanny." She took a deep breath, then said, "Would you mind praying for my kids?"

That night as I sat in my car, I cried. It was deep. I couldn't stop. I couldn't drive for a while. God was breaking me of all my prejudices—ones I hadn't even realized I had.

LIVING IN THE KINGDOM

Being a part of the kingdom of God requires that we live opposite of the world's systems. As born-again believers, we are supposed to be different, going against the flow of the culture in our businesses, our careers, our schools, or wherever we find ourselves. In Christ we are new creations (2 Cor. 5:17). Operating in politics for all these years has forced me to look at the ways of our culture and consciously choose the narrow path versus the wide path (Matt. 7:13–14). Many times I don't get it right, but sometimes I do. Moving toward Christlikeness is always the journey that Jesus is taking us on. His greatest desire is to know us and to conform us into His image. He is the Potter, and we are the clay.

> Beloved, I beg you as sojourners and pilgrims, abstain from fleshly lusts which war against the soul, having your conduct honorable among the Gentiles, that when they speak against you as evildoers, they may, by your good works which they observe, glorify God in the day of visitation.
>
> —1 PETER 2:11–12

Being in the kingdom of God yet living in this fallen earth, we are sojourners. We are passing through. If we conform to the world, we will lose our spiritual identities and forget our destinies. That is not the heart of God for our lives.

The power that we should carry is found in Jesus' love that transcends the norms of our time. It goes beyond our own hearts and minds as we yield to Him.

Speaking to the Pharisees about the Sadducees, whom they competed against in their Hebrew culture, Jesus said:

> "You shall love the LORD your God with all your heart, with all your soul, and with all your mind." This is the first and great commandment. And the second is like it: "You shall love your neighbor as yourself." On these two commandments hang all the Law and the Prophets.
>
> —MATTHEW 22:37–40

When we engage in politics and government, the systems that we work in force us to choose sides. As we do so, we must still remember that we are a part of another kingdom—a heavenly kingdom.

If we are Christ followers, our prejudices ultimately will not win. We must lift our eyes and see something bigger than our own lives: we must see the harvest of people that Jesus loves.

Though I speak with the tongues of men and of angels, but have not love, I have become sounding brass or a clanging cymbal. And though I have the gift of prophecy, and understand all mysteries and all knowledge, and though I have all faith, so that I could remove mountains, but have not love, I am nothing. And though I bestow all my goods to feed the poor, and though I give my body to be burned, but have not love, it profits me nothing.

—1 CORINTHIANS 13:1–3

Loving with abandon can fill us to the fullest. Being created in the likeness of God, then being led by the movements of His love, brings out our true purpose and destiny. God is love. Love causes a reaction and a response; it is not dormant. Love is not complacent—love does.

Chapter 10

LOVE DOES

LOOKING AT ALL the adventures in my life inside and outside politics, I would have to say that the worthy ones have been motivated by one thing: love.

Love causes us to do things we would never have imagined we could do. It allows us to walk a little less selfishly, a little more sacrificially, and a lot more vulnerably before others and before God. It causes us to step out and give.

RUNNING AN AMAZING RACE

Tim and I love the show *The Amazing Race*, an adventure reality game show that usually takes contestants to ten to thirteen nations per season as the teams compete for a million dollars. We have watched every season, starting when the boys were young. Pairs from different walks of life and with different types of relationships (married couples, siblings, fathers and daughters, friends, and so on) go on a race around the world during which they must overcome physical, cultural, and memory challenges to make it to the mat at the end of each leg. The team that arrives last could be eliminated from the game.

Tim and I used the show as part of our homeschooling geography class, taping old seasons with our DVR from the Game Show Network. Then we would watch the new seasons as a family when they came out live. Considering that the show has aired for thirty-four seasons, let's just say we have spent a lot of time watching people run around the world competing for a million-dollar prize.

We love the show's travel aspect with participants journeying from nation to nation and encountering various cultures. Tim and I also like to shout at the TV, telling the teams what they should or shouldn't do. We are continually analyzing how we as a couple would take on the challenges we've seen on the show, thinking through the logistics of jumping off a cliff on a bungee cord, eating maggots in cheese, or doing the final quiz that checks the contestants' remembrance of the whole race.

How far would we push ourselves to win a million dollars? How far would we go to impress our adult children to prove that we are not old? Would our competitive natures push us toward the prize? Would we endure to say that we were the winners of *The Amazing Race*?

Though this race is not even real life, it serves as an example of something that could push us to be better people. What pain would we endure to win? How hard would we push?

Movies have been produced and books have been written about people who have gone to extreme measures to take care of the people they love. We love these adventure stories that show us how we as parents or grandparents would do anything to protect the children God has blessed us with.

What if our kids got sick and needed treatment that we couldn't afford? How would we respond? If our new grandbaby needed a healing treatment or a tool to make his life easier but it didn't exist, would we try to invent what he needed? What if we had to carry a pitcher on our heads and walk for miles a day to get water for our family like many mothers and fathers do around the world? What would we be willing to do for love? How sacrificially would we live for our loved one?

The question for us today is, How can we run an amazing race of love throughout our lives?

In the Bible we see examples of extravagant love that moved people to action. Mary of Bethany poured a pound of expensive ointment and anointed the feet of Jesus (John 12:3). One of the lepers Jesus healed came back to Him to say thank you. Esther boldly went before the king, risking her life out of love for her people. Most of the first-century apostles died as martyrs for the love of their Savior. The apostle John, who rested on the breast of Jesus, was sent into isolation on the island of Patmos for his love of the Lord. In his exile he was given the great Revelation of Jesus Christ.

Love motivated them and moved them to action.

My new season with Christians Engaged has been so fulfilling because I get to disciple people, teaching them the nuts and bolts of this political world while also teaching them the Bible. I have come to realize that if we don't mix faith, the Word of God, and passion for Jesus into this space, we will just have cold, hard government. Our ministry is a way for me to teach government and politics while I teach Jesus.

Most people don't become activists, teachers, campaign managers, or legislative assistants just to have a nine-to-five job. They do what they do to make a difference. And that is what I want to give people through my life and example: a vision for more.

My various jobs in politics and running campaigns have been fulfilling only because I have mixed my passion for making this a better world with my daily walk with Jesus. It is because of Him that I have been able to walk in peace, joy, and patience, as well as loyalty and forgiveness. Finding Him in mundane tasks, in simple friendships, and in the constant stressful situations has made my life rich and full. That is what I want for the next generation of Christians who will dip their toes into this sometimes-hard-to-navigate world. I want them to step into destiny out of a passion for our nation—but to do it with God.

To walk beside elected officials, treat them as real people, and minister to their souls is a great calling. Seeing a Christian activist go from a county party chairman to a congressional member (like Michael Cloud) and being able to help him on that journey is a powerful testimony. Shining amid our cities, counties, states, and nation with the love of God while speaking the truth of what we believe is a thankless job—but also a much needed one. It is time for the church to become activated in this political world and shine. If we don't, then who will?

YOU HAD ME AT "HELLO"

It was my first fundraiser in Van Zandt County. For years I had run other people's campaigns and raised money for everyone else, but now I had to stand up in front of the room and ask their help for myself as the candidate. This rural community event would be the practice round before my high-dollar donor event the following week.

The longtime Van Zandt County Republican chairman, Lance Lenz, and his wife, Sherrill, were going to introduce me at another supporter's home. I adored this couple who had served in this capacity for over twenty years while homeschooling their kids. No one wanted to run against this chairman because he was so even keeled and treated all parties with such respect. One of the longest-serving GOP chairmen in the Republican Party of Texas, Lance trained and inspired others. Sherrill was his equal part in all of it.

At the last minute I found out that Sherrill was going to introduce me, not Lance. I was totally taken aback by that, as she had been a hard one for me to win over. They were among the first ten of two hundred exploratory calls I had made to see whether I could potentially get support. Though Sherrill liked and respected me, she had not seemed too thrilled about supporting a woman as her congressional representative. For the same reasons that she took issue with women in the pulpit, she wasn't so sure about women in such levels of governmental leadership. I respected her beliefs, though it didn't help me with my ultimate goal of winning her endorsement.

That night Sherrill gave me one of the greatest introductions I have ever received. She told everyone why she believed in me for Congress, and it came down to her trust in me. She trusted my record in politics, my life, my heart, and the steadfastness of my convictions.

Looking very professional in my new business suit, I stood before a crowd of over fifty people from that East Texas county. Some of the folks already supported me, while others came to hear what I had to say, still trying to make up their minds. I had prepared a simple three-point message, emphasizing that I was an executive leader with small business know-how and the *real* conservative in the race whom they could trust. I was also the only candidate who had the endorsement of Texas Right to Life. It was a line I would repeat over and over during the primary.

It was the first time I stood before a crowd to sell my candidacy. And these are the words that came out:

First of all, thank you so much, Sherrill, for that incredible introduction and endorsement. I know how much you deliberated to make those statements. Thank you. Thank you and Lance for your friendships. It means the world to me.

Before I say anything else about why you should vote for me and why you should support me for Congress, I need to say this: I am running to be your member of Congress for the Fifth District of Texas because I love you. I love the people of the Fifth District of Texas.

I instantly stopped and panicked.

"What have I just said?" I thought. "What is all this lovey-dovey stuff coming out of my mouth?" This was not my professional, business-sounding speech. If I could have slapped the side of my head without anyone seeing, I would have. I needed to be tight and professional, and this was not it. I had to convince everyone to elect me as their member of Congress, so I pulled myself together and went on with my speech. I felt I did well.

At the end of the night as everyone was grabbing refreshments, a young man in his late thirties got my attention. He was stocky, with a bushy beard, dressed in jean overalls and a flannel shirt. He looked like a typical man from East Texas. I later found out that this young man and his dad owned and operated their own tow truck business. They were doing very well for themselves.

"Listen," he said, "I have never supported a politician ever before, outside of voting. And I have definitely never written a check to anyone running for office before. But I am giving you a $500 check tonight, and my dad is giving you a check as well."

He was excited and continued to share his heart: "When you opened your mouth and went into all that stuff about how much you love the district, you love the people of the district, and you love me—I was captivated. I could see the love in your eyes. What kind of politician says that? Let me answer that for you: no one! Listen, girl, you had me at hello."

I had thought my vulnerable, transparent heart would be my greatest liability in my race for Congress, but it became my greatest asset.

People—from students to veterans to donors to volunteers—wanted to know that I cared about them.

Before people care to listen to everything we know, they want to know how much we really care.

LOVE MOTIVATES US

At the end of my campaign for Congress, the day after my loss, I sent out the following note to all my supporters. The words encapsulated my heart during that season, though looking back, they actually summarized the reason I got into politics in the first place: my love for America, love for liberty, love for the unborn, and, most of all, love for God.

> Friends,
>
> I read a book many years ago by a man named Bob Goff called *Love Does: Discover a Secretly Incredible Life in an Ordinary World*. He told personal stories of adventure that he lived out of a heart of love for people, and I was inspired again to serve people and love with abandon.
>
> I love the people of the Fifth District of Texas. I have served them for ten years, and out of that love I jumped into a race for Congress to make sure they were represented well with a solid conservative.
>
> Along this journey I have discovered new friends and patriots that I never knew before. I am so thankful for you!
>
> Friends who I have worked with for years in the trenches of the Republican Party throughout our great state and the conservative movement believed in me and our cause.
>
> My former boss and mentor, Congressman Jeb Hensarling, walked beside me encouraging me in this journey.
>
> My family gave me up for almost six months and we sacrificed our livelihood to run this race. I'm blessed by Tim, Ben, Israel, Teo, and all our family and friends.
>
> It was a worthy cause and if I had to do it all over again, I would choose to run again.
>
> Fighting for liberty and our conservative values is never wasted.

We did it and we did it together. Nothing is wasted when we stand up for what we believe in with our whole hearts.

Though we came up short in the time frame we had to work with, we fought the good fight, and I am proud of our efforts together. I will never forget every dollar you spent, every call you made, every person that stood at the polls for me in the heat, and the passion that flowed out of your hearts for America and our district. We left it all on the field and I can rest knowing that we did everything we possibly could.

I called Rep. Gooden the night of the runoff, congratulated him, and pledged to help him unite our party so that we could make sure that we put a Republican in Washington come November.

I won't stop being an advocate for the unborn, a fighter for limited government, and a woman who loves her God, her family, her community, and our nation. Thank you again for your friendship, love, and support.

For Liberty,

Bunni Pounds

Being obedient to the call of God on our lives is a response to love. Walking with Him every day is a response to His love. Trying to save America must come out of love. If we do it for any other reason, it will be worthless.

I JUST WANT TO MARRY YOU

I was on my way to Latin America as a young twenty-one-year-old having just graduated from Bible school the year before. I had raised monthly missionary support and was being sent out from my local church, Calvary Cathedral, in downtown Fort Worth. Pastor Bob Nichols was going to license me into the ministry. Bible school had been an incredible season in my life, but I was now ready to get out on the road and do the stuff.

My plan was to join Youth With A Mission (YWAM) in Costa Rica for their six-month Discipleship Training School before going to the Guatemala YWAM base. On my first mission trip down south, after spending one month in Guatemala with a missionary named Nancy and my best friend, Nita, I called my mom and told her I wouldn't be coming back in the time frame I initially promised. I stayed for an additional two months before making my way home through Mexico. Then six months later I went back to Guatemala with Nita to check out the YWAM base in the capital city. That was where I planned to serve and minister to the Guatemalans long term.

When I got back to Texas, I found out I was accepted by YWAM, and while working at Calvary Cathedral, I quickly started to raise support. I planned to get my plane ticket the following week. While I was waiting, one of my best friends, Tim Pounds, had overheard me tell someone that I wanted to go to the State Fair of Texas before I left. At a Bible study we both attended, Tim asked if he could pick me up in his Bluebonnet Pest Control truck and take me.

Tim and I had been a part of each other's lives for a long time. We had met at a weekly home group hosted by Mark and Cherri McIlheran in Colleyville, Texas, which was connected to the Fort Worth church pastored by Jim Borchert and David Halvorson. At that point Tim had experienced a miraculous deliverance from seven years of drug addiction, and I was a Bible school student whom God was desperately trying to humble. Let's just say that when we met, we were not a match made in heaven. Tim was twenty-five years old, and I was eighteen.

At no time in the first three years of our friendship was either of us interested in the other. If I had to describe our relationship, I would say we were only friends—like a brother and a younger sister. The leader of the home group, Danny Norris, took us both under his wings and taught us how to pray, how to meditate on the Word of God, and how to work. He also taught us how to save money and how to patiently wait for the return of Jesus in joy. We loved him and everyone in that group.

Over the years, Tim and I were in each other's lives a lot. Tim would come bowling with me and my dad; we watched movies with friends at my mom's house, where I lived; and he would call me late at night when I was working at LIFE Outreach International. I even went to a barbeque at his nana's house, where I met all his family. It was before cell phones and email were common, and we had to use old-school telephones to communicate. We never thought much about the time we spent together. We didn't overanalyze it because our group of friends were all involved in each other's lives. We were all so on fire for God that we couldn't think of anything else but being in the Word of God together and fellowshipping with like-minded people.

Tim's inviting me to the state fair was a breach from the norm in our relationship, as we had always hung out in a group with other friends. As we wandered around the fair that night, something was changing and different. I couldn't stop thinking about Tim.

To be honest, I'd had lingering romantic thoughts about Tim for three weeks prior to that evening. One reason for this was that my dad had made a backhanded comment, saying, "Bunni, I really like Tim. Don't you like Tim?"

I batted away my dad's silliness with "Dad! Tim is like my brother. Stop!"

But the seeds had been planted. In those weeks I noticed that Tim kept looking at me differently at the Bible studies we attended together. He suddenly started ignoring me. At IHOP after the meetings, instead of sitting with me like he always did, he started sitting on the other side of the room with someone else. That was not his normal mode of operation. "What is going on?" I wondered.

I kept thinking that the enemy was attacking my mind with these random thoughts of Tim because I was heading to the mission field to serve God. I tried to ignore them.

But it was harder to shove these feelings and thoughts aside at the state fair. We got on the huge, iconic Ferris wheel, the Texas Star, and I kept thinking that Tim was going to grab my hand. He didn't, though I wished he had.

All night as we walked around—and I cracked up at his jokes—there was electricity in the air. "Is there any way he doesn't feel this?" I asked myself.

We ended up at IHOP, one of our favorite places to sit, drink coffee, and talk. About two hours into the conversation we realized that we had never spent time alone before. In all those years of hanging out, getting to know each other and our families and friends, and walking together in our relationships with God, we had always been with other people. We were alone together for the first time.

I will never forget that chilly October night. When we got into his white pest control truck, Tim didn't start the truck.

I waited. "What's happening?" I wondered.

Then he turned to me, and with a quivering voice, he simply said, "Bunni, I don't want to hold your hand. I don't want to kiss you. I just want to marry you."

My instant response was tears—as always.

This had been my dream since I was a thirteen-year-old girl getting on fire for Jesus. Later at Bible college I had read Elisabeth Elliot's book *Passion and Purity* and been mesmerized by the love story between her and Jim. They had sought God for His will in every step of their young lives. As a young woman seeking God with my whole heart, I hadn't wanted to get distracted with boys. Though I'd had moments of my heart wandering, my dream had always been that Jesus would give me a husband when I least expected it, maybe in a best friend. Here God was fulfilling my dream right in front of me, handing me Tim—not on a silver platter but in a pest control truck.

Three days after seeking God and getting more clarity, it was decided: I was going to marry Tim Pounds. I was not going on the mission field but marrying a pest control man. My lifelong adventure would be in America unless God called us together somewhere else.

God gave me Ecclesiastes 4:9–10 to hold on to:

> Two are better than one, because they have a good reward for their labor. For if they fall, one will lift up his companion. But woe to him who is alone when he falls, for he has no one to help him up.

I responded with a commitment to love Tim forever, *till death do us part*. Love does.

THE VICE PRESIDENT AT DALLAS LOVE FIELD

The knot in my stomach that wouldn't quite go away during the campaign was a lingering fear I couldn't shake. "What if I can't reach the expectations of my former boss, and what if I fail the vice president?" I worried.

Mike Pence had put his name on me in front of the world by endorsing me for Congress. Normally a vice president endorsed only someone whom the president endorsed. Going against this political norm made national news; the *New York Times* wrote that Mr. Pence backed me "in a tweet that blindsided key White House aides."[1] Rumors were flying about Pence and Trump's relationship and speculation on how they navigated the leadership of the Republican Party together. The fact was that President Trump didn't know who I was, but the vice president had endorsed me anyway—and that put even more pressure on me in my mind. It was a big deal! *What if I failed?*

After the race ended and our Disney World trip was over, I sat on my couch for another week. My doctor had prescribed that I remain silent for a while to rest my vocal cords. Instead of speaking, I read my Bible and a book from my unread pile called *The Evangelicals: The Struggle to Shape America* by historian Frances FitzGerald. This strategic book that I just happened to pick up was the beginning of my cry for God to show me my next steps. I wanted Him to specifically show me a relevant church that could impact politics and our nation. I knew the next Christian movement to impact America would have to look and operate differently than movements that had come before like the Christian Coalition.

During this season I was worried about rebuilding my own life, what I had taken my husband through, and the toll on my staff's careers and my former boss's legacy. But I also hated the idea that I had failed Vice President Pence. In my mind, by losing, I had undermined the reputation of his endorsement. I had never failed before in my entire life, and here I had done it on the national stage.

The next week, the chairwoman of the Dallas County Republican Party and a political ally of mine, Missy Shorey, called around ten o'clock at night. She excitedly told me that Vice President Pence was coming to speak to the Southern Baptist Convention in Dallas and would be landing on a private airstrip at Dallas Love Field the next day. She was gathering a crowd to meet him at the airport at six in the morning to have a good showing for the news media that would be covering his arrival in town.

"You have to be there, Bunni. You have to see him," Missy pleaded. Then she demanded, "I am putting you on the list. Don't fight me on this."

I had barely gone back to my office since the race, so there was nothing in me that wanted to show up at the airport early in the morning, especially to stand in a big cattle call of well-wishers. She explained that the Republican nominees who had won their runoffs—Ron Wright, Van Taylor, and Lance Gooden—were invited to be at the bottom of the plane's stairs when the vice president arrived. Lance was out of town, so he wouldn't be there. But Missy kept pushing, "I need you to be there. You need to see Vice President Pence."

I was sick to my stomach thinking about it.

I had gone from being someone important—getting VIP treatment at political events as a front-runner for Congress—to being no one, relegated to a group of around two hundred people whom Missy was desperately trying to gather. (Tragically Missy passed away suddenly the next year at a young age, shocking the national political community. But she left a lasting legacy as she inspired everyone around her every day—including me—to go beyond our comfort zones for the sake of America.)

"OK, I will be there," I replied reluctantly. I didn't want to go, but something in my heart told me to do it.

Showing up at the airport early the next morning, I went through security and then stood around the airport hangar with GOP leaders and activists from the surrounding counties. I was surprised to see people from Tarrant County, Collin County, and even Kaufman County joining the Dallas County GOP folks whom Missy had so successfully recruited. Keith Bell, who had secured the nomination for state representative in Kaufman and Henderson Counties, was there. Some of the key volunteers from my race had come. Even Jake Ellzey, who had lost his congressional runoff to Ron Wright, was there.

"I guess if Jake is here, I am not the only loser on-site," I thought. (After Rep. Ron Wright's death, Jake ran again and beat out an incredible challenger in Susan Wright, Ron's wife, for that congressional seat. He currently serves in Congress.)

Hours into this adventure, we finally went out to the tarmac to greet the vice president's plane. I was way in the back behind hundreds of people while the GOP nominees for Congress, Van Taylor and Ron Wright, and the mayor of Fort Worth, Betsy Price, stood out away from the people waiting for the plane to land. Then I got a text from Sarah Makin, former conference staffer under Congressman Hensarling and now employed with the vice president's office. "Hey, Bunni, it's Sarah Makin. I am on the plane with the vice president, and he saw your name on the manifest of those meeting him at the airport. He wants to see you," she texted.

I had been feeling like old news and washed-up political garbage. I was stunned that he would want to see me.

Sarah said that she would disembark from the plane, come over to the crowd behind the metal security fence, and call to me to get me to the front. She did just that. When she called my name and I made my way through the crowd, people sneered at me, wondering why I was being asked to push myself to the front of the group.

As I waited for Vice President Pence, I felt sick.

The vice president came down the plane stairs and greeted all the VIPs gathered at the bottom, who then talked with him for a few minutes. He then walked over to the crowd waiting to greet him. Shaking hands while the news media got their pictures, Pence worked his way down the line. Surrounded by Secret Service members, he got to me and stopped.

I nervously put out my hand. "Sir, it is Bunni Pounds."

"I know it's you, Bunni." he said, keeping my hand in a firm handshake and looking straight into my eyes. "I just wanted to come over personally to tell you how proud I am of you. You made me so proud with the race you ran."

Feeling sorry for myself, I responded, "I totally failed you, Mr. Vice President. You went out on a limb for me, and I didn't win."

Then he quickly said, "Bunni, I would do it all over again. I believe in you. I just wanted to tell you this is not the end of your story, and I am with you again whenever you need me."

I had no words; all I could say was a deep, heartfelt "Thank you, sir."

Forever the staffer I asked the vice president if I could take a picture of him with a little boy who had been waiting patiently beside me to meet him. I grabbed the picture on my phone for the young man's family. Mike Pence thanked me for making the little boy happy. Then he was gone.

It was another day of breaking down. As soon as I got to my car and away from the crowd, I wept.

JEB'S PORTRAIT UNVEILING

Months later, on my way to Romania to teach the Word of God, I stopped in Washington, DC. Van Taylor, Ron Wright, and Lance Gooden were all soon to be sworn into Congress, and Congressman Jeb Hensarling's retirement party was finally here.

Jeb was leaving office after sixteen years in Washington, DC—eleven of which I had walked with him through all the ups and downs, either as a staffer, a consultant, or a friend running for his seat.

Having served as chairman of the Financial Services Committee for six years—managing his own "field," with Maxine Waters as the ranking Democrat on the committee—he was to be honored with a painted portrait that would stay in the committee room forever. It was a deep honor for Chairman Hensarling and his whole family.

The beautiful, commissioned portrait shows Jeb standing in front of his desk in a navy suit with his Member's pin on his lapel. On the desk are a gavel and a picture of his family. I had arranged for a photographer to take that family photo for our annual Christmas card project, and it was one of my favorites. In front of the picture of his family are four books: his Bible, of course, and his three other favorite books—*The Road to Serfdom* by F. A. Hayek, *Capitalism and Freedom* by Milton Friedman, and *Atlas Shrugged* by Ayn Rand. All these works had shaped his political philosophy and motivated Jeb to come to Congress in the first place. Yet throughout his years in the House, it was the Bible that became the one he clung to the most.

Because of the size of the room, the portrait unveiling was limited to only three hundred invites. Many of the congressman's favorite political friends gathered—HUD secretary Ben Carson; Rep. Kevin Brady; his former boss, Sen. Phil Gramm; Speaker Paul Ryan; United Methodist pastor and Democrat congressman Emanuel Cleaver; and over one hundred staff members who had served with him throughout the years, including county judge Richard Sanders and me.

I sat on the third row on the right, facing the podium in front of the portrait, as Jeb; his wife, Melissa; and his children, Claire and Travis, were all being honored for their faithfulness and service to our nation.

Then in walked Vice President Pence to give his remarks.

Later I found out from Jeb that the moment the vice president came in and sat down, he asked Congressman Hensarling, "Where is Bunni?"

Surprised, Jeb answered, "I don't know where Bunni is—somewhere over there," pointing to the far-right side.

It was an incredible ceremony. Sincere and worthy accolades were heaped on Jeb, to his chagrin. We took a picture together in front of the portrait. Always the staffer I took pictures of the Hensarling family, shook hands with other former staffers, and interacted with other members of Congress I hadn't seen in a long time.

I wasn't planning to say anything to Mike Pence, but Jeb turned to me at some point and said, "Are you going to greet the vice president? He was asking about you earlier."

"What? Really?" I was still shocked at the favor these two great men gave me. Just the idea that they thought about me from time to time was mind blowing.

"Go say hi," Jeb pushed.

Right when I had made my mind up to do it, the vice president's staff started working to get him out of the room. They were grabbing his arm and trying to whisk him out the door. I moved behind him, and Jeb shouted, "Mr. Vice President, Bunni would like to say hi before you leave."

"Bunni?" Mr. Pence stopped and quickly turned around. "Bunni, it is so good to see you. I was asking Jeb about you. I was hoping I would see you."

I sheepishly replied, "It is an honor to see you, sir."

Knowing his staff was getting impatient, he quickly went on. "I wanted to tell you again that I am so proud of you. You are not done. God has more for you in the future." Then came the statement I thought may have been an afterthought on his part but obviously wasn't: "I want you to know that I would help you again. I am with you forever."

There it was. Now over six months after my loss, the vice president of the United States was confirming to me, *again,* the call of God on my life. As much as I wanted to lament the past, that day I knew that I had not disappointed Jeb or the vice president and that I had to stop being disappointed in myself. As I have thought about the race in the years following, regret has never filled my heart, because I know I was motivated by love for people.

AWAKENING THE CHURCH FOR THE WELL-BEING OF AMERICA

Love is what motivated me to start Christians Engaged. I love America and want to see liberty protected in our nation. I am also passionately in love with the body of Christ, and I believe the church is the only answer for our flailing country.

Seeing how the church was weak in prayer, voting, and engagement, Christians Engaged started reaching Christians across denominational lines, nationwide, to empower them for the well-being of America—one heart at a time. We built the first 501(c)3 voter mobilization communication for the church in all fifty states and built an incredible on-demand video library to educate the body of Christ with in-depth courses on civics and biblical worldview on the hot topics of our day.

My belief is that the church of Jesus Christ is the only answer for an America that needs reformation and revival in all areas of our culture.

The two greatest deceptions in modern America are thinking we can live without the presence of God and thinking we can live without the Word of God. This is what makes Christians Engaged different from a political movement: we understand that we need Jesus and His Word in our personal lives, families, churches, and nation. We must lead by engaging in politics and government as the people of God, but we must do it while walking in intimacy with Jesus.

We are a civic engagement discipleship ministry with an activation component. We instruct people about getting involved with government and learning the hot topics of our day. But know this: we understand that if we do not lead in these areas with humility and truth, then we as Christians have nothing to give. We believe now is the time to invest more in the discipleship of the church than ever before.

Within this ministry I have gathered many of my favorite government and ministry friends who all have expertise that I don't have—including my staff, board, and advisory board. Together we build curriculum and create products for the church.

I continue to pray for my brothers and sisters serving in Congress. They are doing a tough job within a broken system that has to be reformed. I don't envy them, but I work diligently to encourage them and to motivate other Christians to pray for and build relationships with them.

BOB GOFF

A few years ago I wrote a draft outline for this book and sent it to Bob Goff. The man has written four *New York Times* bestsellers, but he still puts his personal cell phone and email at the back of his books. He lives intentionally and has been an inspiration to me to pursue love in all places, even in this political world.

I didn't have the guts to call Bob a few years ago—I didn't want to be *that person* who really took him up on a phone call—but I did send him a longer-than-he-probably-wanted-to-read email with my story and the outline for this book. I told him my purpose in writing these stories was to inspire someone else to get involved with this grand nation and to, even in the slightest way, walk with Jesus while they do it. My hope is to inspire every Christian, in every part of this nation, to walk with Jesus in whatever he or she is called to do.

While on a plane going home from a speaking engagement, Bob wrote me a response. He thanked me for reading his books and encouraged me to inspire others through my story. He took time out of his busy schedule to encourage me. I recently learned from his book *Undistracted* that Bob answers every email and picks up his cell phone for everyone who calls. He does this because of the influence of another man—Christian musician and missionary Keith Green. In the early 1980s when Bob was just a young college student, he wrote Keith a letter. Keith replied with a note to encourage Bob.

This lifestyle of extravagant love is something I want. I want to give sacrificially. I want to move toward impacting others one day at a time. I want the love that does.

POLITICS AND RELIGION

I am sure we have all heard the saying that there are two things we are not supposed to talk about: politics and religion. Supposedly, these two topics stir the pot and make people uncomfortable and edgy.

I have broken that unspoken rule over and over in the adventure that has become my life. My two favorite topics on earth are Jesus and politics. I preach Jesus because He is my Savior, my Lord, the One that captured my heart as a young thirteen-year-old girl in a dark convention center, and He is the only hope for humankind.

Since I lead a civic engagement discipleship ministry whose main goal is to educate Christians on the issues, encourage them to pray for their elected officials, and energize them to vote in every election, we open ourselves up to misunderstandings. Many within the body of Christ do not think the church should be mobilizing politically. The church, they say, is supposed to be preaching the gospel only.

The word *gospel* literally means "good news." It is the sharing of the story of Jesus and the plan of salvation. This *is* the good news of our faith, and there is nothing more important than the power of the gospel. Giving Americans the gospel is the only way to change worldviews and mindsets. Nothing we do within politics or government is more important than giving people Jesus, but we have to talk about important issues—both political and theological.

Once we gain some wisdom from the Word of God and are discipled, we must get outside the four walls of the church building. We are called to go into the world and make disciples of all nations. Teaching them might involve inspiring them to go into city, county, state, and federal governments to impact laws, hearts, and minds. We might be training people to get involved in the pro-life movements or partisan politics to promote a more biblical platform. We might be training people to engage in the pro-Israel movement or get involved in media and journalism. Yet if we send people into the world's systems but don't help them understand the preeminence of the gospel in our lives, then it is in many ways worthless.

Unlike a political movement we at Christians Engaged acknowledge the fact that the gospel is always number one. We must always remember who we are, even as we engage in politics and government. We are Christians first.

As the body of Christ we need to run for office, campaign for people, and get involved in our city councils and commissions. But in everything we do in this hour, we cannot forget who we are while we do this important work. Political activity, in and of itself, will not save America. We must be Christians who share the gospel. We are people of the *light*. We are supposed to be the influencers and ones who carry wisdom and discernment, knowing how to navigate issues and problems with truth and integrity. But as we do, we cannot stop sharing the good news—the gospel. We must be missionaries to America in every sense of the word.

If we leave Jesus completely out of our work, what do we have to give?

We can't push the gospel on people to the point where we are unable to do our work in government or our careers with excellence. We must be strategic about when and where we share our faith, but the gospel should also not be ignored.

Texas state senator Bryan Hughes, who I had hoped would run for Congress, rarely makes a speech without mixing in the story of the gospel and the hope that he has in his life. He does it with tact and compassion, but he wants people to know why he has hope for our state and our nation. It is priceless every time I hear him.

We open our mouths and share why we have peace during storms, why we have joy in a troubled world, why we are free from shame and fear, and why we can love people even though they don't deserve love.

We Christians who navigate the political realm are called to a higher standard than those who don't profess the name of Christ. We should be able to operate within it yet show the mudslinging world that we are different.

We are different because the gospel has changed our lives. This is our mandate as new creations in Christ:

> If anyone is in Christ, he is a new creation; old things have passed away; behold, all things have become new. Now all things are of God, who has reconciled us to Himself through Jesus Christ, and has given us the ministry of reconciliation, that is, that God was in Christ reconciling the world to Himself, not imputing their trespasses to them, and has committed to us the word of reconciliation.
>
> Now then, we are ambassadors for Christ, as though God were pleading through us: we implore you on Christ's behalf, be reconciled to God. For He made Him who knew no sin to be sin for us, that we might become the righteousness of God in Him.
>
> —2 Corinthians 5:17–21

How can God use a simple woman who loves politics and government? How can God use me to bring someone to Jesus or show someone that God sees him or her? How can God use any of us?

God does it through the Bible—the Word of God—which is the power available for us all. We can all be ambassadors for Christ everywhere we go, every day of our lives. This is the great adventure. I have been so touched over the last few years as we, through Christians Engaged, have been teaching people to interact with government. At the same time, God has been reaching people when we least expected it.

In 2021 Sidney, a young engineer, came to Jesus at one of our On-Ramp to Civic Engagement seminars. He was baptized at the cowboy church that hosted us. His pastor continues to let me know that he is growing in the Lord.

That same year a GOP candidate who came to one of our events just to network gave his heart to Jesus. He was a Mormon.

A young Catholic woman started crying when listening to the words from Jeremiah 1, Psalm 139, and Luke 1 at one of our seminars. I was sharing what the Bible had to say on the issue of life in the womb. She had mobilized voters around women's rights but was convicted in her heart at these words and left the pro-abortion movement.

This is how God works: one heart at a time, one life at a time—even through a civic engagement ministry. Jesus said:

> You are the salt of the earth; but if the salt loses its flavor, how shall it be seasoned? It is then good for nothing but to be thrown out and trampled underfoot by men. You are the light of the world. A city that is set on a hill cannot be hidden. Nor do they light a lamp and put it under a basket, but on a lampstand, and it gives light to all who are in the house.
>
> —MATTHEW 5:13–15

How has the gospel been funded to the ends of the earth, for the most part? Answer: the people of the United States of America.

Gordon-Conwell Theological Seminary's World Christian Database put out a "Status of Global Christianity" table in 2020 showing that in 2000, Christians worldwide gave $320 billion to Christian causes. They predicted that by mid-2021, the amount would be $848 billion.[2] God is not dependent on the US to reach the world, but He has mightily used America, and I believe He wants to continue to use us for the purpose of world evangelization.

Why do Christians need to get involved in civic engagement and politics? Because America must continue to be free and prosperous.

I believe the Founding Fathers of this nation have given us a gift that we must cherish and work to preserve. Serving as a member of the Second Continental Congress, which was meeting in Philadelphia to draft the Articles of Confederation at the time, John Adams wrote a letter to his wife, Abigail, in April 1777. He was suffering for America, hundreds of miles away from his wife and children in Massachusetts, when he wrote:

> Posterity! You will never know, how much it cost the present Generation, to preserve your Freedom! I hope you will make a good Use of it. If you do not, I shall repent in Heaven, that I ever took half the Pains to preserve it.[3]

God has set us in this nation, in this generation, for such a time as this.

How will we respond? What will we do to preserve this nation for the next generation?

Every day, I jump out of bed so excited to do this work. I get to take my theological background, missionary heart, and years of Bible study and combine them with my political experiences and knowledge to empower the body of Christ in this key moment in history.

I love to talk first about Jesus, then about this thing called politics as I encourage other believers to not be afraid to do the same.

Why?

Because love does.

My daily prayer has become "Jesus, please use this girl with a political résumé for Your glory. That is all I want."

EPILOGUE

AS THE CORONAVIRUS raged around the world in the spring of 2020, our nation was going through a challenging time. Our start-up ministry, Christians Engaged, was trying to adapt and bring hope to fearful hearts by leading prayer calls, doing small inspirational videos, and figuring out how we could be helpful in the national conversation. It was the beginning of a global pandemic, and people were terrified of doing anything—even going to the grocery store.

I woke up one morning feeling extremely burdened for the rural mayors, specifically around Texas. These men and women had signed up for a volunteer job they thought would be a service to their community. Instead, they got hit with some of the biggest decisions of their lives. Our county judge in Dallas County, Clay Jenkins, was already making headlines as he started enforcing strict rules that limited freedoms for our urban area. I tuned in daily to the press conferences that Vice President Pence and the Coronavirus Task Force were holding—praying for the man who had believed in me.

It was a challenging time for all of us at Christians Engaged, but we were not drawing back from our call as a ministry to awaken people to the need to interact with their government.

I had a thought that morning: "What if we inspired people to pray and minister to their elected officials by asking them to look up the names of their mayors and county judges and pray for them?" Most people don't even know what a county judge does. We could inspire them to learn something during this tough time.

Then I thought about the vice president. I had been praying for Mike, Karen, and their family while he was in the White House, considering myself to be one of his chief intercessors. I thought, "What if we had people around Texas also write letters of encouragement to the vice president and the Coronavirus Task Force?"

I felt the Lord's direction on this plan, so I worked with Ian to build out a web page and a communication plan to get it out to people. We called this simple initiative Letters of Hope.

My desire was to communicate to these elected officials that they had not been forgotten by the citizens who were depending on them to stand strong. Jesus knew them, Jesus saw them, and Jesus wanted to walk with them each day through their trials of governing—especially during this trying time for our nation and the world.

Ian asked me to do a quick video explaining the program and showing people three letters I had written personally. With Ian recording, I sat at my kitchen table with my hair in pigtails and wrote three letters of encouragement on the only cards I could find: ugly 1970s-style, brown-and-orange thank-you cards I had lying around. After Ian wrapped up the recording, I finished writing out the addresses, put stamps on the cards, and ran them to the mailbox. I went back to work and focused on my full-time job for Congressman Cloud, as I was still working for him at the time.

Less than two weeks later a Washington, DC, number ending in 0000 flashed on my phone screen. Thinking it was the Republican National Committee or the National Republican Congressional Committee asking for money again, I let it go to voice mail.

A couple of hours later I listened to my messages. "Hi, Bunni Pounds. This is Vice President Mike Pence calling. I just got your wonderful note. Thank you for your prayers. Your words of encouragement mean a great deal to me and my family and our team here. So appreciate you so very much. God bless you, Bunni." After a slight pause he continued, "And if you see our friend Jeb Hensarling soon, please give him my very best. Thanks again."

Freaking out, I called Jeb instantly. "Jeb, my ugly card I wrote for Christians Engaged got to the vice president. If I had known he would see it, I would have written him a longer, more personal note and not used an ugly card." Then it hit me, and I gasped. "Jeb, I must be on a special list at the White House for this letter to get through."

In a matter-of-fact response Jeb replied, "It looks like you are, Bunni."

Through that simple phone call from the vice president on April 15, at 12:26 p.m. EST, right before he went to do a daily Coronavirus Task Force press conference, Jesus wanted me to know that He knew where I lived. God let me know, again, that I was not forgotten.

Jesus didn't need to use the vice president. He could have simply reached me in the woods with my Bible open, but that is what He chose to use that day. God wanted me to know that He hadn't forgotten me in that little cabin in Victoria or in this new season of pioneering a non-profit. Jesus was not done walking with me on adventures.

I was seen and I was known—not just by people but by Jesus.

My Hope for You

By the way, wherever you are right now, whether in your highest of highs or your lowest of lows, Jesus sees you and knows you. He has a way of reaching us in ways we don't expect.

My prayer throughout the planning, writing, and editing of my simple story in politics is that He would surprise you with His presence, touch your heart so deeply that you know He is near, and capture your heart completely with His love. He died for you so that you could live and walk with Him every day.

Simply let Him in by picking up His Word.

Why don't you start with this prayer He prayed for you right before He went to the cross?

> *Father, I desire* that they also whom You gave Me *may be with Me where I am*, that they may behold My glory which You have given Me; for You loved Me before the foundation of the world.
> —John 17:24, emphasis added

Now, pick up a Bible and read John chapter 17. Then, after that whole chapter touches your heart, read the whole Book of John. After that incredible book, fall in love with the rest of God's love letter to you.

With the ultimate manual for wisdom and purpose, go out and impact your nation. He promised He would be with you.

AFTERWORD

BY THE HONORABLE MICHELE BACHMANN

WHEN I FIRST went to Congress, I was assigned a congressional mentor, Congressman Jeb Hensarling. I later went on to serve with him on the Financial Services Committee for many years.

When I met Bunni Pounds, I was instantly connected with her by our shared friendships and our history in government, but I was also instantly connected to her heart for intercession and her love for the church and Israel.

Though she came up slightly short in her race for the seat Congressman Jeb Hensarling previously held, I knew this young woman was going to make a positive impact one way or another. Her passion and concern for America were evident. Ultimately, she landed where she was supposed to be, in a role that allows her to awaken and educate the body of Christ in this critical moment in time.

I am so proud to walk beside Bunni as she educates Christians on how to pray for America, the importance of voting in every election, and how they can practically engage in their civic duties and with government from a biblical viewpoint.

After serving for more than sixteen years as an activist and political consultant and over twenty years as a Bible teacher and church planter, she is uniquely qualified to speak into the lives of pastors, national ministry leaders, and Christians across America who want to impact the nation.

She stepped out humbly after a time of brokenness and said, "Jesus, use me!" As a result, Christians Engaged is filling a huge hole in the body of Christ. Her story should inspire us all to walk daily with Jesus and disciple the nation one elected official or neighbor at a time.

With its voter mobilization communication system for Christians in all fifty states and a growing library of on-demand video courses to educate Christians on the issues and how to become civic leaders in their cities, states, and nation, Christians Engaged is on the cutting edge. I encourage you to connect with this dynamic ministry today! Take the pledge to pray, vote, and engage. Now is our time to protect liberty in America and to go deeper in Jesus.

—THE HONORABLE MICHELE BACHMANN
DEAN, ROBERTSON SCHOOL OF GOVERNMENT AT REGENT
UNIVERSITY
MEMBER OF CONGRESS FROM 2007 TO 2015
2012 US PRESIDENTIAL CANDIDATE

Standing in the rain greeting voters during the 2018 primary

This great group of volunteers gathered to knock on doors the last Saturday before the primary in 2018.

> **Mike Pence** ✓ @mike_pence
> Proud to stand with Bunni Pounds for Congress in TX-5! Bunni is a strong conservative & will be a great supporter of the #MAGA agenda! Vote @bunnipounds on May 22

Getting a private meeting with Vice President Mike Pence was one of the proudest moments of my life. My campaign created this graphic from a picture we took at that meeting and his tweet endorsing me during the primary runoff.

Graduating from Christ For The Nations Institute in Dallas, 1994

With Dr. Stuart Spitzer in East Texas during our political races.
We became good friends during this intense season.

Texas senator Bryan Hughes showing his support during my primary runoff election
in 2018

Rep. Jeb Hensarling (R-TX) and me at the Reagan Day Dinner after my private meeting with Vice President Pence

Sen. Bob Hall; his wife, Kay; and Rafael Cruz in 2018 at a Dallas fundraiser that Rafael headlined for me. Rafael Cruz and I really connected during my 2018 campaign, and he became a big encourager to me.

I posed with Lance Lenz, GOP chairman of Van Zandt County, and his wife, Sherrill (center), after speaking at the first fundraiser for my campaign.

Tim and me in 1995 telling everyone at our home group that we had gotten engaged in the parking lot of IHOP

Tim and I had a Jewish roots wedding, though we are Gentiles.
We were married under a chuppah and even broke the glass,
wanting to experience all the symbolism in this beautiful
ceremony.

Taken in 2000, this is one of the final advertising pictures of our family before
we sold Bluebonnet Pest Control.

After a great debate during my 2018 campaign, I celebrated with our son Ben and my then future daughter-in-law Giulia in Van Zandt County, Texas.

After having to miss my 2018 campaign, Israel came home from three years in Romania with a beautiful worship leader, my daughter-in-law Teodora.

In front of the US Capitol, where in 2019 I lobbied members of Congress to maintain a strong relationship with Israel

Rep. Sean Duffy (R-WI) posed for a picture with me, his Texas-based political consultant, after a 2015 lunch fundraiser in San Antonio for his campaign.

Rep. Lance Gooden (R-TX) and I came together in Dallas in 2019 to lay down our offenses as I helped pay off the remaining debt his campaign carried from the 2018 campaign.

Many of my previous supporters and staff members joined me in supporting Rep. Lance Gooden (R-TX) in Dallas.

Looking back at the sea of people gathered for TheCall: Rise Up on the National Mall in Washington, DC, in 2017. Just a few weeks later, I was running for Congress out of nowhere.

In a matter of a few years, Bunni Pounds & Associates had become one of the best political consulting firms in Texas. Here the team is posing for our Christmas card in 2017, right before I launched my campaign for Congress.

On *Life Today* with James and Betty Robison in 2022 along with Dave Kubal, president of Intercessors for America, to discuss how to integrate praying for the nation into our lives

For over fourteen years I led worship at local churches, conferences, and our house churches, even cutting two full-length worship albums of my own songs.

Ron and I spent Election Day 2018 at the polls in Arlington, Texas, talking to voters and believing for the best. We had done everything we could; now it was up to God.

During the 2012 midterms, I had been keeping track of all the election results and just told Rep. Jeb Hensarling (R-TX) that he officially won.

With Rep. Van Taylor (R-TX) at the polls talking to voters on
Election Day 2018

With Rep. Michael Cloud (R-TX) and my husband, Tim, on Election Day 2020. I ran
his campaign that election cycle, and even though the final vote wasn't in, we were
confident he would win a huge victory—and he did.

Holding up our first pledge card at Joy Church in Mesquite, Texas, to get commitments from believers to pray, vote, and engage regularly

For the first national Wake UP! Conference of Christians Engaged in 2021, I invited a man I had learned so much from through the years—James Robison.

In the first year after I launched Christians Engaged, while running a campaign for Rep. Michael Cloud (R-TX), I spoke more than one hundred times at in-person and virtual events throughout Texas about our vision and mission.

At one of our first Christians Engaged panels held at Grace Community Fellowship in Wharton, Texas, with (from left) Scott Bauer, Trayce Bradford, and Rep. Michael Cloud (R-TX)

First Liberty Institute attorney Lea Patterson and I appeared on Fox News amid the media firestorm created by the letter from the IRS. Before we went on, we asked God for favor—and He definitely answered.

Rep. Lee Zeldin (R-NY), a former client, and Rep. Claudia Tenney (R-NY) came to one of my DC fundraisers to support me in my race for Congress.

I flew into Houston to solidify Sen. Ted Cruz's (R-TX) endorsement and spent an hour with him face to face, but for some reason I didn't get the endorsement until the night before the runoff.

TED CRUZ VS. BETO O'ROURKE

BUNNIPOUNDS

I used this graphic by Bethany Stephens with my blog post "Ted vs. Beto: 10 Reasons Why Every Christian Should Vote Ted," which got twenty-three thousand hits in forty-eight hours.

When I met Rep. Beto O'Rourke (D-TX) in 2022, I used the opportunity to tell him my dream and speak God's heart for him.

Me with our young campaign assistant James Cardenas on Election Day 2020. James came to faith in Jesus with his girlfriend, Kobi. It was our favorite part of that campaign.

NOTES

FOREWORD

1. James Robison and Jay W. Richards, *Indivisible: Restoring Faith, Family, and Freedom Before It's Too Late* (New York: FaithWords, 2012), xix.

CHAPTER 1

1. Michael Bie, "Hayward Family Values," Classic Wisconsin, accessed July 2, 2023, https://archive.ph/20120728231509/http:/www.classicwisconsin.com/features/famval.html.

CHAPTER 2

1. Mike Pence (@Mike_Pence), Twitter, April 10, 2018, 4:01 p.m., https://twitter.com/Mike_Pence/status/983797156971778048.
2. "Keith Bell," Ballotpedia, accessed July 3, 2023, https://ballotpedia.org/Keith_Bell.
3. Mark P. Jones, "The 2017 Texas House and Senate, from Left to Right: Post Special-Session Edition," *TribTalk*, November 20, 2017, https://www.tribtalk.org/2017/11/20/the-2017-texas-house-senate-from-left-to-right-post-special-session-edition/.

CHAPTER 3

1. *Merriam-Webster*, s.v. "politics," accessed July 3, 2023, https://www.merriam-webster.com/dictionary/politics.

CHAPTER 4

1. Rich Flowers and Jayson Larson, "Henderson County Responds to Nativity Complaint," *Athens Review*, December 8, 2011, https://www.corsicanadailysun.com/news/local_news/

update-henderson-county-responds-to-nativity-complaint/
article_caae2cb9-efbe-5a2c-ae2b-fcc41cc0a80a.html.

2. Flowers and Larson, "Henderson County Responds."

3. Rich Flowers, "Thousands Attend 'Rally for the Nativity'
Saturday," *Athens Review*, December 17, 2011, https://
www.athensreview.com/news/thousands-attend-rally-for-
the-nativity-saturday/article_8568aa0b-dfb0-564c-8e66-
7a3d44408dea.html.

CHAPTER 6

1. Bernadette Hogan, Nolan Hicks, and Emily Crane, "Lee
Zeldin on Why He Has 'Zero Regret' After Losing to Gov.
Kathy Hochul," *New York Post*, November 9, 2022, https://
nypost.com/2022/11/09/lee-zeldin-has-zero-regret-after-
losing-to-gov-kathy-hochul/.

2. Kerry Picket, "New York Republicans Flip House Seats
Amid Gubernatorial Loss," *Washington Times*, November
9, 2022, https://www.washingtontimes.com/news/2022/
nov/9/new-york-republicans-flip-house-seats-amid-
guberna/.

3. Ray Bogan, "Constituent Who Outed Rep. Joe Barton's
Lewd Facebook Messages Speaks Out," Fox News,
December 1, 2017, https://www.foxnews.com/politics/
constituent-who-outed-rep-joe-bartons-lewd-facebook-
messages-speaks-out.

4. Anna M. Tinsley, "Cancer Strikes a North Texas
Congressman, but He Says He Will Stay in DC and Fight,"
Fort Worth Star-Telegram, July 29, 2019, https://www.star-
telegram.com/news/local/arlington/article233254201.html.

5. Paul Cobler, "Texas Rep. Ron Wright Still Running
for Reelection Despite Lung Cancer Diagnosis," *Dallas
Morning News*, July 29, 2019, https://www.dallasnews.
com/news/politics/2019/07/29/texas-rep-ron-wright-still-
running-for-reelection-despite-lung-cancer-diagnosis/.

Chapter 7

1. Joseph Guinto, "Jeb Hensarling: The GOP's Most Powerful Nobody," *D Magazine*, October 21, 2009, https://www.dmagazine.com/publications/d-magazine/2009/november/jeb-hensarling-the-gops-most-powerful-nobody/.
2. Patrick Svitek, "U.S. Rep. Van Taylor Ends Reelection Campaign After He Admits to Affair," *Texas Tribune*, March 2, 2022, https://www.texastribune.org/2022/03/02/van-taylor-reelection/.
3. Congressman Van Taylor, email sent to author from Van Taylor Campaign, January 2, 2023.

Chapter 8

1. "Open Your Eyes! Charlie Kirk, Dutch Sheets, Mario Murillo (June 17, 2021)," *Flashpoint*, June 18, 2021, 17:16, https://flashpoint.govictory.com/episode/open-your-eyes-charlie-kirk-dutch-sheets-mario-murillo-june-17-2021-%e2%80%8b/.
2. First Baptist Dallas, "The Church in the Kettle | November 7, 2021 11:00am Teaching," Vimeo, November 7, 2021, https://vimeo.com/643277527.
3. *Encyclopedia Britannica*, s.v. "St. Joan of Arc," July 7, 2023, https://www.britannica.com/biography/Saint-Joan-of-Arc.
4. Rachael Bade, "Lawmaker Behind Secret $84K Sexual Harassment Settlement Unmasked," Politico, December 1, 2017, https://www.politico.com/story/2017/12/01/blake-farenthold-taxpayer-funds-sexual-harassment-274458.
5. "Freedom Starts Here," First Liberty Institute, accessed July 10, 2023, https://firstliberty.org/about-us/.

Chapter 9

1. Abby Livingston and Patrick Svitek, "Ted Cruz Defeats Beto O'Rourke in Difficult Re-election Fight," *Texas Tribune*, November 6, 2018, https://www.texastribune.

org/2018/11/06/ted-cruz-beto-orourke-texas-midterm-election-results/.

CHAPTER 10

1. Alexander Burns, Jonathan Martin, and Maggie Haberman, "Pence Is Trying to Control Republican Politics. Trump Aides Aren't Happy," *New York Times*, May 14, 2018, https://www.nytimes.com/2018/05/14/us/politics/pence-trump-midterms.html.

2. M. Johnson and Gina A. Zurlo, eds. "Status of Global Christianity, 2021, in the Context of 1900–2050," *World Christian Database* (Leiden/Boston: Brill, accessed July 12, 2023), https://www.gordonconwell.edu/center-for-global-christianity/wp-content/uploads/sites/13/2020/12/Status-of-Global-Christianity-2021.pdf.

3. Letter from John Adams to Abigail Adams, 26 April 1777 (electronic edition), Adams Family Papers: An Electronic Archive, Massachusetts Historical Society, Boston, https://www.masshist.org/digitaladams/archive/doc?id=L17770426ja.

ABOUT THE AUTHOR

Bunni Pounds is the president and founder of Christians Engaged. She was a political consultant for sixteen years, once leading a firm with thirty-two clients and nine people in her office. For years she worked with members of Congress running their campaigns.

She then ran for Congress herself in 2018, becoming the only woman to make the Republican runoff in Texas out of six open seats and the only person in the US endorsed by Vice President Pence during the 2018 primary season. Though she came up slightly short, God has been using her over twenty years of Christian ministry experience and longtime political experience to lead what is now a nationwide ministry.

A graduate of Christ For The Nations Institute and Dallas Baptist University, Bunni loves Jesus above all and loves sharing the gospel with anyone who will listen—from the halls of Congress to her own hometown.

Bunni has been married to her husband, Tim, for twenty-seven years. They have two grown sons, who are both married, and two precious grandchildren.

CONNECT WITH US

Connect with us at ChristiansEngaged.org. Let's wake up the body of Christ together.

TAKE THE PLEDGE

The first connection place with Christians Engaged is to take our pledge to *pray, vote,* and *engage.* We send out weekly prayer alerts, voting reminders to vote in *every* election, and information on how you can get engaged for the well-being of our nation. Take the pledge at ChristiansEngaged.org.

CIVICS AND "HOT TOPICS" CLASSES

Our On-Ramp to Civic Engagement class is your beginning point into civic education and involvement. In the over-six-hour class, you will learn about party politics from a nonpartisan perspective, ways to get to know your elected officials, issues from a biblical perspective, truths about religious liberty, the roles of the courts in a free society, ways to share the gospel and make an impact in your communities, and insights on operating with integrity as a Christian while engaging in politics. Other classes offered include Salt & Light: How to Impact Our Local Communities; Austin 101 (Texas Legislature); Nehemiah: How to Rebuild the Walls of a Nation; Biblical Justice; and Biblical Economics.

WEEKLY SHOW AND MORE

Join Bunni and friends every week for our *Conversations with Christians Engaged* podcast. Listen on our YouTube channel, Facebook page, or wherever you get your audio pods. Check out all our additional free content—our articles, prayer calls, and more.

SPEAKING

Bunni loves to speak to any-size group, whether it be a Sunday morning church service, a conference, or a special event for a club or community group. Invite her or other Christians Engaged leaders to your area. We love to encourage churches to pray, vote, and engage regularly.

SUPPORT THE MINISTRY

Christians Engaged is here to awaken, educate, and empower the body of Christ in all fifty states to pray, vote, and engage regularly. We work across denominational lines as a Christian ministry with a doctrinal statement and code of conduct for our team. We are funded by individual people like you. God is so faithful. Thank you!